# Gun Violence and Public Life

# Gun Violence and Public Life

*Edited by*
*Ben Agger*
*and*
*Timothy W. Luke*

*Paradigm Publishers*
Boulder • London

Copyright © 2014 Paradigm Publishers

Published in the United States by Paradigm Publishers, 5589 Arapahoe Avenue, Boulder, CO 80303 USA.

Paradigm Publishers is the trade name of Birkenkamp & Company, LLC, Dean Birkenkamp, President and Publisher.

Library of Congress Cataloging-in-Publication Data
Gun violence and public life / edited by Ben Agger and Timothy W. Luke.
    pages cm
 Includes bibliographical references and index.
 ISBN 978-1-61205-666-1 (pbk.: alk. paper)
 1. Gun control—United States. 2. Violent crimes—United States—Prevention.
 3. Firearms—United States. I. Agger, Ben, editor of compilation.
 HV7436.G8765 2014
 364.150973—dc23

                                                                    2013035490

Printed and bound in the United States of America on acid-free paper that meets the standards of the American National Standard for Permanence of Paper for Printed Library Materials.

18 17 16 15 14   1 2 3 4 5

# Contents

# Preface

THE PAST SEVERAL YEARS IN THE UNITED STATES HAVE BEEN MARKED BOTH by astounding violence and strong resilience. First, after surviving gunshots to her head and body in a January 2011 assassination attempt, US Rep. Gabrielle Giffords (D-AZ) announced her retirement from the House on January 22, 2012, so that she could concentrate on her long recovery from the wounds inflicted on her by Jared Lee Loughner, who killed six others in this rampage shooting. In a separate event, James Holmes opened fire in a crowded theater during a July 20, 2012, movie premiere in suburban Denver, killing twelve and wounding many others. On the morning of December 14, 2012, twenty-year-old Adam Lanza gunned down twenty first graders and six teachers at a Connecticut elementary school and then turned his gun on himself after murdering his mother in her bed at home. More recently, the world watched the trial of George Zimmerman, who was acquitted on July 15, 2013, by a jury of a murder charge for his role in the February 2012 killing of Trayvon Martin, an unarmed Florida teenager. In the wake of these high-profile incidents, the issue of guns in American public and private life has been pushed to the forefront. After the Newtown shootings, President Obama appeared to redouble his political efforts to push for new legislation requiring gun registration and limiting gun-magazine capacity. Meanwhile, gun-ownership pressure and interest groups have pushed back, insisting that the US Constitution's Second Amendment, which protects the right to keep and bear arms, is, and must remain at, the center of American liberty. An acrimonious national conversation over gun rights and gun control is ongoing, but it has so far only generated some heat, not much light, and no new legislation at the national level.

New restrictions were put into place in a few localities and states, like the enactment of limits on gun magazine capacities to fifteen rounds and the requirement of new background checks in private gun sales in Colorado. Passed by the Democratic Party–controlled legislature during spring 2013, this success stirred an intense backlash by Colorado voters who have the power of recall under the state's constitution. In a special recall election on September 10, 2013, the Democratic President of the Colorado Senate, John Morse (Colorado Springs), and a Democratic Senate colleague from Pueblo, Colorado, Angela Giron, were both recalled and replaced by Republican legislators. Their recall did not affect the overall balance of power in the state's legislature, but it sent a very strong signal to other pro-gun legislators across the nation. If voters in the state where both the Columbine High School and Aurora movie theater gun rampages occurred were willing to oust lawmakers who worked hard to pass more restrictive new gun laws, then pro-gun interest groups made it clear that they would oppose all other legislators, judges, or officials who supported comparable moves anywhere else in the United States.

In this timely book, a group of US and international authors reexamine the complex and conflicted issues of gun violence in public life. Of particular interest will be comparative gun-homicide rates, the instructive case of Canada, the efficacy of existing gun controls, risks associated with gun ownership, concealed-carry gun-permit data and policies, the role of the mass media and computer game violence, masculinity/femininity and guns, school shootings, and the growing militarization of US police forces. While neither demonizing nor mythologizing guns, the assembled authors provide rigorous evidence-based analyses that work to shed light on possible policy directions. As social scientists, we are open to the counterintuitive and unanticipated dimensions of these topics, as deeper recurrent patterns emerge and what seems obvious often turns out to be false.

This book picks up where other earlier books on gun violence and school shootings leave off, including Katherine Katherine Newman et al.'s *Rampage: The Social Roots of School Shootings* (2004), Dave Cullen's *Columbine* (2009), and Doug Kellner's *Guys and Guns Amok* (2008). Our book is distinctive because we examine sociological correlates and civic consequences of gun violence in the culture and society at large instead of dwelling on single horrific incidents such as Columbine. We do not rehash prior debates over the Second Amendment, but instead focus empirically on national and international (especially Canadian) gun-homicide rates and the effectiveness of gun controls. We also look at the incidence of violent gun crimes conceptualized (via the concept of risk) as a growing public-health problem, particularly for many municipalities where shootings are a leading cause of death for many young, male, minority, and urban populations, as well as a health hazard for women, children, and other family members. Finally, we introduce various alternative frameworks for thinking differently about gun violence, gun control, and gun use, each of which has strengths and weaknesses. From this evidence about the benefits and risks of guns in matters of human security, we tease out some policy implications, which include possibilities for pursuing both aggregate-level and individual-level reforms.

Given our academic backgrounds, it might be tempting for some readers to view this project as another simplistic jeremiad in favor of greater gun control, but we are not comfortable with that framing. One of our empirical conclusions is that many legislative efforts often are temporary remedies that are at best merely cosmetic measures or symbolic politics. There are deeper issues involved in the role of violence in public life, which resonate with the reasoned insights of the Founding Fathers, including Benjamin Franklin, who maintained that those who readily give up essential liberties to gain temporary security deserve neither liberty nor security. We are also not taking anti–Second Amendment stands in these analyses. We view the right to bear arms both historically and sociologically. This right is obviously not uncontested, and we recognize that the people who debate the appropriate capacity of gun magazines and the legitimacy of owning assault-style rifles cannot find much detailed guidance in the documents written by James Madison and Thomas Jefferson in the early days of the Republic. In response to a number of rampage shootings in the early 1990s, divisive and restrictive new gun laws were implemented in 1994 that built upon prior laws passed from the 1930s through the 1980s. Even with these stricter laws, however, limiting magazines, banning assault rifles, or establishing new background registries did not prevent mass shootings at Columbine, Virginia Tech, Aurora, or Newtown.

If some legislative efforts do not solve major social problems, like armed violence in our public life, then why are they accepted as workable policy solutions? Since these steps continue to come up short, what more substantive policy changes—as well as alterations in our individual and collective behavior—might be tried along with the passage of new laws to attain greater effectiveness? We grapple with such questions in the critical studies that unfold here. In large measure, we return to the 1960s ideal that fundamental societal change cannot bypass the self, but must be enacted by each person in his and her everyday life. We can neither preach peace without practicing it nor avoid armed violence without preparing for it. Here, the personal is political, and the political personal. Although legislation has moved the nation forward somewhat for minorities and women—think of the Civil Rights Act of 1964 or Title IX in 1972—we cautiously conclude that greater gun controls as a legislative agenda cannot really address the sources of young men's rage and alienation or prevent them from rampaging in theaters, schools, parades, malls, or fast-food outlets. As we learned during the sixties, we have to change "everything" radically in order for particular things to change. In addition, it is difficult to imagine a less violent public life on our own shores when we as a country seem eternally embroiled in a state of permanent war in foreign conflicts that waste lives and wealth without attaining their stated strategic goals or political aspirations.

In any case, we wish to contribute here to a broad substantive national conversation about men who open fire, politicians who demonize or deify weapons, the rise of a culture of greater incivility, a public who understands little about its obligation as citizens, and a perpetual politics of division. We will not shy away from inconvenient truths, but hope instead to begin to learn from them.

## Chapter 1

# Gunplay and Governmentality

## Sovereignty, Subjectivity, and Shootings in the United States

**Timothy W. Luke**

THIS CHAPTER PROVISIONALLY MAPS UNEXPECTED LINKAGES BETWEEN sovereignty and subjectivity through a critical analysis of mass shootings in the United States of America. These connections appear to be unavoidable, if not foundational, ties that must be untangled to gain critical insight into the deeper significance of gun violence in America and the seemingly impossible challenge of addressing more thorough and effective firearms regulation in the United States. Ironically, the Bill of Rights—or the first ten amendments to the US Constitution—plays a crucial role inasmuch as such legal principles, along with their supporting judicial enforcement, enable this imbrication of sovereignty, subjectivity, and shooting as normalizing and normative programs; as written, the Bill of Rights expresses America's uniquely liberal order of governmentality.

The Second Amendment provides for a well-regulated militia as well as the right of citizens to keep and bear arms. The implements of war known as "arms" and the relation between those things and the men allowed to wield them are, first, essentially enshrined by this liberal republic as a foundational principle, and, second, substantially justified as individual and collective property rights to own, keep, and use a vast array of lethal things. As a quintessential question for governmentality, the role of weapons as "things," which also serve as key implements for the male citizens most typically involved in questions of sovereignty, subjectivity, and shooting, remains one of tremendous conflict and complexity. Firearms, in relation to the men and women who keep and bear them as political subjects, cannot be untangled from the US regime's mesh of power relations, especially given how firmly male subjectivity is anchored to personal and group rights to keep guns to inflict violence on others. Moreover, as Foucault hints, government emerges with its own finality in becoming able to manage in "a right manner of disposing things so as to lead . . . to an end which is convenient for each or things to be governed" (Foucault 1991, 95). Arguably, the prevailing system of juridical rights, like the US Bill of Rights, is egalitarian in principle; yet, it has supported "the development and generalization of disciplinary mechanisms," like the keeping and bearing of firearms, which can erupt in violent rampages as "the other, darker side of these processes" (Foucault 1979, 222). This chapter traces out a few of these conflicted complexities to explore the challenges of gun ownership and regulation in the United States.

## I. Sandy Hook and the Spectacle of Gun Violence

Gun control in the United States once again became a front-burner policy issue after the December 14, 2012, shootings at Sandy Hook Elementary School in Newtown, Connecticut. That morning, using firearms purchased legally by his mother for target shooting, Adam Lanza shot his mother to death while she slept. He then drove a short distance to the elementary school where he shot and killed twenty children and six adult school staff members before turning his weapon on himself. The mass-media coverage of the incident turned up reports that Lanza's mother, who grew up around guns with her family in rural New England, had pursued target shooting with her son in order to build a closer relationship with him as her family was disintegrating.

Although the 2007 mass shooting at Virginia Tech had more victims (thirty-three dead and seventeen wounded), the Sandy Hook attack is the worst-ever mass shooting at a public K-12 school in the country (Agger and Luke, 2008; Kellner 2008). Moreover, the Sandy Hook shooting was particularly traumatic, as it came only five months after the bizarre shooting at a showing of *The Dark Knight Rises* movie in an Aurora, Colorado, multiplex, during which James Holmes allegedly killed twelve people and left fifty-eight wounded. The very young age of all the Sandy Hook student victims and the valiant yet failed efforts by six of the school's administrators and teachers to protect them, the high number of their bullet wounds (three to eleven shots in each victim), and its tragic occurrence during the ordinarily cheerful holiday season combined to be a shocking circumstance. To have two such horrific incidents at two unlikely sites and times in a single year proved to be a catalyzing moment for many in both the general public and government who had been deeply opposed to the country's existing gun laws. Coming only five years after the Virginia Tech massacre—thirty-three people shot and killed, seventeen others wounded—the Newtown school shooting left the impression from its many televisual mourning rituals (Kellner; Kimmel and Leek; Worrell, this volume) that no educational institution at any level in the United States would ever be safe from deranged gunmen. This crime immediately ignited a fresh nationwide debate over guns and their governance, and also about how to prevent such deranged subjects from mounting similar attacks in the future.

Yet, within months, if not weeks, the media's initially favorable narrative in support of gun control—during which reporters, news anchors, or writers depicted how anomalous this shooting incident was in historical terms—gradually fell by the wayside. In turn the media's daily coverage returned to stale mass-media scripts about legislative gridlock stalling efforts to broaden gun controls (Luke 2008, 1–28). As Schildkraut and Muschert (this volume) recount, those narratives adeptly began rehearsing old rhetorical routines on the already well-worn stages devoted to these policies all across the mediascape. These routinized scripts stretch back at least to the August 1966 shootings at the University of Texas at Austin, perpetrated by Charles Whitman: tremendous shock over its actual occurrence, heartfelt declarations about its sensational exceptionality, near-universal denials about its normality, ardent calls to immediate corrective actions, growing equivocation over which specific public-policy action to take, and then fading to more general inattention punctuated by intermittent brief moments of notice here and there. Soon, the tragedy largely fades from public notice as fresher news stories with "larger bleeds for bigger leads" capture the attention of editors, reporters, and audiences. Subsequent frantic efforts by survivors are then launched to form organized action groups to combat the building lassitude, but finally a gradual normalization of the event occurs to the point of most people not remembering what happened, even as the organized interest groups struggle to keep the issue alive.

Plainly, the violent deaths of so many small children during the holidays accentuated this tragedy; this horror kept more awareness of the event lingering longer than in other cases. In general, however, it could be said that holiday cheer more or less dampened the attention that had been given to this violent criminal news story. Interest in the Sandy Hook shooting spiked again about a month later, around the second anniversary of the attempted assassination of Rep. Gabrielle Giffords (D-AZ), as Congress reconvened in January 2013. Renewed interest led to some committed legislators feverishly working the halls of government in Washington, DC, to leverage support for new gun-control bills. Much more intensive lobbying by the National Rifle Association (NRA), local sportsmen's groups, firearms-industry political action committees, and other citizens' networks, however, led to the bills' growing obstruction, irrelevance, and finally defeat on the Senate floor on April 17, 2013.

Despite all the death-centered drama surrounding the Sandy Hook shooting, and President Obama's strong vocal support in favor of the new gun-control bill's passage—which he made in good faith during many trips around the country in 2012 and 2013—it appears in too many ways that the prevailing wisdom of the NRA has gradually come to define the lessons of the Newtown shooting for many Americans: Resonating through decades of TV crime dramas, epic Western films, and international cinema conventions, this simple interpretation of reality was articulated by the NRA's executive vice-president, Wayne LaPierre, when he said, "The only thing that stops a bad guy with a gun is a good guy with a gun" (*Washington Post*, December 21, 2012). The unspoken, but openly signaled, subtext of this message is that "the good guy" also must have a really good gun, which could include a no-nonsense paramilitary home-defense shotgun or an assault-style semi-automatic rifle that would stop the bad guy dead in his tracks. In its coverage of Rep. Giffords's 2011 shooting, even the esteemed *Wall Street Journal* pumped up the mystique of "rampage guns," like the Glock 19, as "the weapon of choice for good and bad guys" (Fields 2011, A5). Such sloganeering is regrettable, but its common circulation is open recognition that there are deeply rooted rhetorical traditions rooted in, as Welch (this volume) argues, Americans' basic "right to rebel," which underpins the United States' deeply normalized acceptance of deadly gun violence.

## II. Governmentality and Guns

A critical discussion of gun violence and its place in the public sphere of the United States of America, especially in the wake of so many high-profile mass criminal shootings since 2007, would seem to raise few doubts about the necessity of more stringent gun controls. Yet as the fast and furious reaction by the shooting public in the aftermath of the Newtown shooting—which helped the bipartisan defeat of tougher new laws in April 2013—reveals, this assumption has proven to be mistaken. Much of the public's reaction has unfolded in far more complex ways, which illustrates how the previous foregone conclusion of the need for more gun regulation is quite misplaced.

Foucault argues that government "has a finality of its own," and therefore "it can be clearly distinguished from sovereignty" (1991, 94). Sovereignty should direct the rulers—aristocratic or democratic—toward realizing some common good, collective welfare, and lawful order. Consequently, "what characterizes the end of sovereignty, this common and general good, is in sum nothing other than the submission to sovereignty. This means that the end of sovereignty is circular: the end of sovereignty is the exercise of sovereignty" (Foucault 1991, 95). Curiously, in a constitutional republic like the United States, the sovereign, however, is "the people," and their moral agency as political subjects is rooted in always remaining armed and ready to be dangerous. Their "common good" is to ensure obedience to the law for themselves and their officials, thus the circularity in their sovereignty claim underscores that the primary aim of a sovereign people must be, as Machiavelli would say, retaining their popular sovereignty. Indeed, to keep and bear arms, if the citizens are well informed and fully trained, is regarded in the republican tradition as an integral part of the citizenry's retainer for service in pursuit of security and sovereignty.

Governmentality, therefore, entails a considerable measure of "implementality" to the extent that finding the right disposition between people and things requires finding some practicable mix of specific multiform tactics to train people and order things—albeit in particular age, class, ethnic, gender, and racial orderings—that will, in effect, secure the peace of well-governed states. Given that the material things in question here are guns, military units, and armed services, most of "the people" (whose right disposition as moral subjects, or ethico-political actors, is becoming accustomed to, produced by, and/or put into effect here) are young men.

In this regard, the Second Amendment is, on the one hand, a multifaceted writ of implementality inasmuch as it is conceptualized abstractly to provide individuals and groups with lethal implements of war. Those provisions are put into effect with definitive planned procedures, which can carry out the self-defense of the sovereign to assure its own security, label the specific articles of lethal equipment to be mobilized in pursuit of these goals, and protect those same deadly instruments needed as tools or utensils of power to accomplish the work of being empowered by becoming armed. When operationalized concretely, however, guns are closely linked by military training, paramilitary organization, and collective policing to disciplinary practices, or "systems of micro-power that are essentially non-egalitarian and asymmetrical" (Foucault

1979, 222) directed at identifying and training warriors, who are still mostly male subjects. As material markers of actual current, or future potential, mobilization for armed struggle, guns then have brought their own gendered "infra-law" into "the infinitesimal level of individual lives" as they also operate "as methods of training that enable individuals to become integrated into these general demands" (Foucault 1979, 222). Nonetheless, as Agger, Kellner, Kimmel, and Leek (this volume) assert, there are, historically and institutionally, major age, class, gender, racial, and regional biases in which specific subjects, like young males, are mostly engaged as subjects with these tactical preparations, either to follow scrupulously the "infra-laws" of organized disciplinary practices or to succumb savagely to disorganized and spontaneous "infra-lawlessness"; both states are made possible by being armed.

The origins of "implement" as a concept come into English from Medieval Latin's *implèmentum*, or an item of stock, which follows from the Late Latin *implère*, meaning to fill, fill up, or bring to fullness. These semantic streams are rich, because they signal how weapons might reveal the individual yearning and collective need to satisfy an enduring existential lack as effective agents (Glynos 2001, 197–198). Indeed, the insecure feelings and non-sovereign anxieties of "being unarmed" that follow from a lack of the necessary equipment, tools, or utensils to put into action some definite plan or procedure are centrally in question here. Remarkably, to maintain "a Free State" in the United States, the Constitution names "arms" as the instruments, tools, or devices most suited to serve this purpose for its loyal sovereign citizens. General implementations of legal guarantees, or formal liberties to outfit or equip citizens with such specific deadly implements, are arrayed at the same time with multiple structures of rigid disciplinary practices to ensure the orderly observance of various laws and rules in the full layeredness of this peculiar implementality. Indeed, the "technologies of the self" and "technologies of society" (Foucault 1988) immediately complement each other. The Second Amendment is an exemplary case of how "the representative regime makes it possible, directly or indirectly, with or without relays, for the will of all to form the fundamental authority of sovereignty," while the disciplinary practices of militia organizing, collective drilling, and gun bearing "provide, at the base, a guarantee of submission of forces and bodies" (Foucault 1979, 222). The liberal art of government thus constantly seeks to assure freedom by identifying the open dangers that "risk producing the opposite" (Foucault 2010, 69).

Freedom is constantly being fabricated, and it can get out of control. A provision for well-regulated militias, juridical rights to keep and bear arms, and at times specific requirements for citizens (who are young, male, and often rural in their distribution) to procure the arms, ammunition, and other accoutrements needed for collective defense, paradoxically must mobilize certain disciplines to enforce many greater controls. Even though the murder rate in the United States has declined from 10.2 per 100,000 people in 1980 to 4.7 in 2011 (see Young, this volume), the perception that property crimes, violent assaults, and rampage murders are frequent events helps anchor these anxious neoliberal directives about individuals' maintaining their armed sovereignty and security. It is a difficult balancing act, but the American population at large remains very well armed and quite docile. Even though criminal elements and disturbed individuals occasionally abuse how firearms are kept and borne by committing unlawful armed acts, the infra-laws of disciplined gun ownership "are a set of physico-political techniques" (Foucault 1979, 223) put to use for the common regulation, procedural ordering, and disciplined conduct of modern political subjectivity in the United States. Moreover, the violent violations of these disciplinary practices always serve the larger logic of strong social control. New, atrocious incidents of violence or looming zones of threat only deepen the legitimacy of "the people" still keeping and bearing arms under these fluidly organized conditions of state recognition and regulation.[1]

There are many unexpected, occluded, or inarticulate questions about guns and their owners that are left unspoken whenever this debate begins. Yet these questions must be studied openly no matter how contradictory they remain or how hard they are to answer, because these silences and shadows are full of critical issues tied to the implementality of firearms in the United States. Many liberals scoff at gun owners who hold tightly to their assault-style weapons, asserting that today's civilian populations are powerless against the latest high-tech military forces. At the same time, even the United States, with all of its military might, has not decisively prevailed in a total victory against such irregular forces equipped with such small arms in any war it has fought since Vietnam. Sometimes these contradictions are collective anxieties or individual fears about some existential void of personal security, but at other moments they are brimming with the fears swirling around in the communal politics of the moment. Firearms and their implementalities can be pitched into these voids, and they become potently productive power points, anchoring the subjectivity of citizen shooters—both good and bad.

Stokely Carmichael of the Black Panther movement from the 1960s once noted during the 1960s, "violence is as American as apple pie," and the very existence of an American public sphere ironically began with, directly rests upon, and cannot be easily disconnected from the readiness of Americans to willingly bear arms or engage in gun violence. In many ways, the Panthers' brazen but lawful measures to arm themselves during the 1960s in Oakland and other big California cities ignited the initial contemporary efforts to introduce gun controls in the United States. These first forays, ironically, were backed by right-wing Republicans during California governor Ronald Reagan's first term in office. While the laws were hotly debated, and then passed only in part, they failed to limit the Panthers or other Californians from gaining legal access to guns. From 1521 as Spanish settlers organized in New Spain in the Southwest, to 1607 at the English settlement in Jamestown, Virginia, to 1614 at the Dutch Fort Nassau on the Hudson, and the founding of New France and Quebec City in 1608, European settlers came to current territories of the United States as invading colonists. The invaders used violence and guile to dispossess Native Americans of their lands to make them European colonies, kill or maim those who resisted, and then reduce the surviving Native American residents to become their docile subjects. Likewise, these colonial regimes promulgated decrees to regulate gun ownership and bar groups of surviving Native Americans, slaves, black freedmen, and indentured servants from bearing arms. The most ruthless and relentless devotees of this gunplay-driven model of governance—after global wars from 1618 to 1763 left most of North America under English dominion—were the citizens of original thirteen American colonies, and the republic that they founded in 1787.

Next, American sovereignty, subjectivity, and shooting actually mutually reinforce each other, once one looks at the foundational practices and principles of the United States from its violent beginnings in the Seven Years' War (1756–1763) and the American Revolution (1775–1781). Apart from recent sensationalized high-profile criminal shootings, American identity as a nation-state constitutionally and culturally rests, to a considerable degree, upon maintaining an armed citizenry and state, though it is comparatively quite disciplined. Many of the nation's Founding Fathers fought in the ferocious French and Indian Wars, which were the campaigns of the Seven Years' War fought in North America between England and France over which one of their kingdoms would hold full dominion over North America. The British Crown asked its Anglophone colonists to defend its rule; colonial British forces and leaders, including George Washington, were essential in winning this fight, which they regarded as civic and military efforts worthy of earning them special consideration as more sovereign political subjects under the Crown's rule.

When this consideration was not granted, the initial overtures in the dramatic struggle for American independence were isolated incidents of gunplay as male citizens in somewhat disorganized and ineffective local militias began shooting at British forces seeking to take away their arms (Cornell 2006). The

Crown's interest in controlling weapons was quite complex. It often was pitched as much against frequently unauthorized game poaching on common land as it was against the possible threat of sedition, but those legitimate royal regulatory prerogatives were quickly consumed by the fires of revolutionary zeal in the United States. The battles of Lexington and Concord on April 19, 1775, have become, for example, vivid chapters in the lore of the American nation's founding. These bloody hours of armed struggle between the local Massachusetts militia and royal regulars over the control of arms and munitions stored by that commonwealth's citizens for their own protection are celebrated every April in Massachusetts (along with Wisconsin and Maine) as Patriots' Day, a state holiday.

As the first stanza of Ralph Waldo Emerson's "Concord Hymn" details, the birth of the United States arguably began at the North Bridge over the Concord River in the skirmishes of that day between British redcoats and local militia volunteers: "Here once the embattled farmers stood, and fired the shot heard round the world." Even though Thomas Jefferson of Virginia wrote the colonies' "Declaration of Independence," such armed clashes between American settlers and British military forces in Massachusetts and other colonies over who should control the arms within their colonial governments and civil societies helped ignite the Revolutionary War. Few recall these struggles today, but the United States was born, in part, from acts of gun violence to protect and preserve the right of American settlers to keep and bear arms against the whims of that time's highest duly empowered state authorities, as this "Minute Man" mythos reiterates rhetorically for every new generation of Americans (Cornell 2006). While the mythos of the militia is one of rebellion, the keeping and bearing of arms has a "political anatomy" and "mechanics of power" whose discipline also "produces subjected and practiced bodies, 'docile' bodies" (Foucault 1979, 138).

Lastly, the public sphere of debate over gun violence, gun ownership, and gun control—at least since the assassination of President Garfield in 1881—mostly highlights certain types of overly sensationalized gun crimes after their commission by disturbed individuals. Those public self-examinations also have raised other associated worries about gun crimes that involve mental illness, violence against women and children, anarchist dispositions, communist subversion, and/or senseless rages. These messy realities are all duly noted, but citizens do not always register their disappointments or displeasures over such deviant, insurgent, or petulant acts when gunplay is involved.

Instead, public discussions tend to religiously reserve the rights of sovereign citizens, law-abiding political subjects, and officially recognized shooters to retain their weapons. Behind the curtain of the republic's deliberate embrace of individual and group diversity, the fluid collective subjectivities of the gun-bearing, gun-owning, and gun-shooting public in the pursuits of gun sporting are regarded as very normal, particularly for men. Indeed, they are such respectable paths for affirming strong civil identity that the rigors of gun sports commonly have been cultivated among grade-school students, Boy and Girl Scout troops, civic groups, and the citizenry at large. As part of these various social organizations for shooting, the implements of deadly force are spread among "the people" to enforce definite disciplinary demands on subjects to obey the infra-laws of gun safety, gun care, gun shooting, gun storage, or gun handling. When properly trained in these settings, the political subject should become fully integrated into another modern techno-culture of cautious, conscious care not unlike those associated with owning and driving automobiles. Firearms as "things" do have very specific rites and routines for "men" to relate by, for, and of their governance. Body and mind must be drilled to always accept a weapon in ways that ensure it is unloaded, on safety, and unready to kill, rather than the opposite. Properly trained, the subject can readily reverse or redirect these rituals to kill with the weapon, but "disciplinary coercion establishes in the body the constricting link between an increased aptitude and an increased domination" (Foucault 1979, 138). Given these techno-culture connections, some gun-control advocates have called for licensing gun owners and insuring guns, like automobiles, but the foundational role of firearms in securing sovereignty have largely squelched these efforts.

Like it or not, firearms, revolution, and war are keystones in the overarching structures of American political culture, and the normative forces of popular bellicosity are willingly accorded considerable reverence. At the dawn of America's superpower, General George S. Patton allegedly opined that "compared to war all other forms of human endeavor shrink to insignificance" (cited in Farago 1964). Particularly after the terror attacks of 9/11, neoconservative intellectuals relentlessly celebrated how war and military prowess have been the formative influences in "the world America made" (Kagan 2012), while more critical observers agonized over the extent to which "war is a force that gives us meaning" (Hedges 2002) in the twenty-first century.

These beliefs still guide many citizens and their leaders. The direct and indirect effects of such values in America's political imagination are deeply rooted in the nation's founding and survival, and the United States has spent much of the past century engaged in military hostilities during imperial forays, world wars, and anticommunist interventions. Long after the end of the Cold War, it remains formally at war with the Democratic People's Republic of Korea (better known as North Korea) after drawing up an uneasy armistice with that nation in 1953, American troops are still battling insurgents in Afghanistan, and American military units are training Syrian rebels in Jordan as well as preparing to funnel more arms and equipment to the uprising against President Assad's Ba'athist regime. Although many American leaders have claimed that the long twilight struggle of free democracies against unfree tyrannies is the war to end all wars, it never seems to end.

The White House and Congress also have appealed to the populace for decades to "wage war" at home against poverty, illegal drugs, cancer, urban decay, crime, industrial pollution, obesity, global terror, inflation, and everyday racism. Because war culture holds such significance, launching such public policy initiatives with a tone of belligerence is believed to make them more worthy of concentration, effort, or sacrifice. Yet, such rhetorical commonplaces powerfully punctuate how much something could be fundamentally addled in this nation. Many communities across the United States tolerate obesity, drugs, cancer, pollution, and racism—yet usually fail to invest monies in decent housing, better schools or good jobs—but they appear more than ready to find the wherewithal to equip their police forces with military-grade SWAT units, armored cars, surveillance cameras, or other expensive high-technology gear in municipal-level arms races to gain some modicum of greater security with more weapons. Such spending is meant to deter new "9/11s" or "Sandy Hooks" from happening, but to what extent do these developments also disclose a social contract that is corroded, cracked, and crumbling?

Amid these ideological and material forces of sovereignty, the allure of assuming, if only for minutes, the power of raw brutality exercised by the sovereign can be fatally intoxicating for many desperate male citizens. He (or she) who would exercise the exception (Agamben 1998; Schmitt 2006) can be overwhelmingly seductive. With more and more families living paycheck to paycheck, an aura of utter hopelessness and total lack clings to many in the "99 percent" who may have little sense of their human significance. With so much respect accorded daily to those serving in society's armed forces—military, paramilitary, and police—all over the world, it is not shocking that at some random moment anyone with a semiautomatic firearm might overstep their personal ambit as a sovereign agent to become a rogue subject who creates his or her own mad acts of exception, determining who lives and who dies in senseless seconds of mass shootings. This possibility is now a global legend. It perversely invests the shooter with might as well as mystery. One wonders if wanton violence is an essential element in today's cultural disorder. In turn, to what extent are the militarized efforts from the White House to city hall to deter and/or destroy those who would become—or already are—violent, now one more strained emergency writ that helps maintain much of what is believed to be the nation's "social order?"

## III. Gunplay as Sovereignty and Subjectivity

The root consensus in the American civil religion about guns is divided, but its support also runs deep into the times before the Republic's creation. Of course, armed criminal deviants should be sanctioned, and most are, before much violence occurs. When some, however, are shot down in epic moments of gunplay, it only reinforces the importance of having "a good guy with a gun" always ready to take down "a bad guy with a gun." Once again, it demonstrates how American democracy historically is largely a gun-toting exercise. A nation rooted in colonial conquest, born from armed insurrection, reaffirmed in a bloody civil war, and surviving today as the world's sole remaining superpower, the United States cannot easily control guns because its very existence began and continues with what it is: a militant nation-state that keeps and bears arms in its households and civil society as well as in its official state military units. All of these violent provisions, however, coexist with extensive disciplinary controls over such armed individuals forged as "a 'mechanics of power'" for the democratic sovereign and its political subjects in which firearms have defined "how one may have a hold over others' bodies, not only so that they may do what one wishes, but so they may operate as one wishes, with the techniques, the speed, and efficiency that one determines" (Foucault 1979, 138).

Whether as an example of a revolutionary democracy, a country at civil war, a global superpower, or a declining rogue hegemon, the United States in each instance fits into the category by virtue of its enthrallment with gun violence. Moreover, heavy elements of racial bias, class privilege, and group identity (Agger; Kimmel and Leek, this volume) underpin horrendous crimes, like Sandy Hook or Aurora, because these extraordinarily violent mass shootings involved mainly young white males claiming white, middle- or upper-middle-class victims during various very bad days in suburbia. For nonwhite, disadvantaged, and inner-city populations, incidents of gun violence with high levels of killing and maiming are everyday commonplaces. Overall, American society virtually ignores or suppresses any awareness of the ongoing daily levels of gang violence in poor and minority neighborhoods. These areas at times produce a Newtown-style level of violence every day. In many rural areas, inner-city zones, and impoverished inner suburbs, gun violence is so ordinary it is simply beyond reporting or sensationalizing. Nonetheless, as O'Grady (this volume) claims, homicide rates in the United States have been declining for fifty years, while the American gun-murder rate is not in the top twenty-five countries in the world in the twenty-first century, even though it still has the highest rate per 100,000 in the world's developed countries (3.2 versus .8 for number-two Switzerland).

The linkages through guns to the right of keeping and bearing arms are what still tightly bind sovereignty and subjectivity for male citizens in the United States. Overall, the incidence of all crime has been declining in the United States for quite a few years, but the daily police ledger in most cities is filled with ordinary individual shootings as well as the more intermittent, but still frequent, mass-shooting incidents. These crimes do appear to have become more common since the 1980s, so, too, have the heavy-hitting interest-group lobbying campaigns, like those led by New York Mayor Michael Bloomberg, to change gun laws that might prevent such crimes (Kellner 2008). This connection is perplexing given that something like twenty to thirty equivalents of the Sandy Hook shootings happen every year in the big, old industrial cities like St. Louis, Detroit, Newark, and Chicago. During 2012 and 2013, a visitor to President Obama's home city of Chicago, Illinois, watching the local TV news often could see ten, twenty, thirty, or more photos of gun-crime victims on any weekend. Yet these deadly statistics rarely hit the national news, because these gun crimes happen as hundreds of daily one-off events mostly among the underclass, the rural working class, or racial-minority populations. As Agger (this volume) notes, the gender/class/race nexus is crucial for assessing the risks of gun violence. Of course, some gun-control activists push for much greater gun regulation constantly, but major recent efforts to advance such legal changes usually happen after major political assassinations, as they did in the 1960s, or following some mass-shooting incidents where mainstream suburbanites are targeted, as seen in the 2000s and 2010s. These inconsistencies are worth exploring, particularly given the reactions to changing gun laws.

The Second Amendment to the US Constitution is one short sentence: "A well-regulated Militia, being necessary to the security of a Free State, the right of the people to keep and bear arms, shall not be infringed." At one level, this constitutional amendment is highly contestable, but it is often cited as the central proposition of a federalism that fit both the world of the 1770s and 1780s as well as the context of this decade, the 2010s. Not long after the nation's inception, every state was empowered in the Bill of Rights as a legitimate government jurisdiction to raise and regulate militia forces to resist potential tyrannical acts by higher government authority, not unlike those that the British forces commanded to quell the colonists' rebellion in 1776–1781.

Conceived in insurrection against English royal power, the United States was fitfully and slowly founded upon a hard-fought victory in war waged by armed citizens after a rebellious unilateral declaration of independence on July 4, 1776. The material realities of its still-volatile origins are usually downplayed ideologically much of the time, but, as a "democratic experiment" or "national idea," the United States is—in many respects—what thinkers as different as Thomas Jefferson or Leon Trotsky would identify as a "permanent revolution." Morever, US political culture basically endorses the use of lethal weapons by citizens to rebel. Despite other popular uprisings in early US history—such as Shay's Rebellion in 1786–1787, the Whiskey Rebellion of 1791, or Fries' Rebellion in 1799–1800—this right was maintained as armed force by the central authorities reestablished civic order. Even after extremely bloody skirmishes along slave/free-state borders in the 1850s and 1860s, and the brutal War Between the States in 1861–1865, the Constitution's blessing to keep and bear arms remarkably has remained firmly in place as the second most foundational "right of the people" in the United States.[2] Following their surrenders, many defeated Confederate soldiers were allowed to retain their personal firearms, horses, and mules upon acknowledgment of their personal parole in the Confederacy's surrender. In turn, many of these arms and mounts were used to protect the bases of white power and privilege during and after the South's Reconstruction.

On another level, in what manner the right to keep, and who may bear, arms is typically constructed as a question of popular versus state sovereignty within every level of organized governmental jurisdiction versus those jurisdictions' citizens. The Second Amendment's wording is key: "the people," no matter how few or how many, are assumed already to have arms at their homes and/or local arsenals, and it is their right to keep those arms. The United States of America is a liberal society rooted in personal economic competition rather than the collective socialization of material wealth. The Constitution also foundationally appears to guarantee these property rights of its citizens to keep and use firearms. Indeed, this right to keep and use implements for deadly force is recognized as what ultimately also ensures citizens' personal security and political freedom within the states in which they enjoy these benefits. In this context, arms are understood, as they were in the eighteenth century, as personal firearms and individual bladed cutting weapons suitable for household use in hunting, home defense, or target practice, rather than as heavy armament like cannon, mortars, or bombs. After the surrender of Confederate Army units at Appomattox, for example, such Confederate arms and artillery were declared public property to be conveyed to the United States government. Today, such heavy weapons of war are also in civic and state arsenals, so few individuals have tanks, rocket launchers, or artillery pieces parked next to their RVs in the garage.

Regulatory practices on firearms vary widely today from very restrictive gun laws in Chicago or New York to quite lax gun laws in Arizona or Texas, but American governments at all levels, with federal guidance, do regulate how and which arms can be owned by individuals. Fully automatic weapons were largely banned in all states in the 1930s, and many more restrictions on buying certain weapons were deployed during the 1960s after JFK's assassination. These gun regulations often have been pitched as protecting the home market for domestic gun manufacturers that want to prevent the importation of cheap foreign weapons as much as they have been meant to stop gun crimes. Yet, as Young (this volume) indicates, household gun acquisition and ownership rates did not slow or peak until the 1970s, during that decade's economic stagflation.

A true military assault rifle is an instrument of war (being a weapon with a selective automatic-fire option and high-capacity magazine), and it is illegal to own one without a federal firearms license due to these machine gun-like attributes. Workable hand grenades, rocket-propelled grenades with launchers, live bombs, modern cannons, and both light and heavy machine guns are banned for individual ownership at home, but are stored in arsenals at the city and county level for use by states' police forces and militias. So-called assault-style rifles, which are military-derived designs manufactured for only semiautomatic fire can be sold to civilians. They are identified as being extremely dangerous, but only a fraction of gun crimes are committed with these weapons. As Qvortrup (this volume) demonstrates, murders with "knives" and "other methods" equal or exceed those with rifles, shotguns, or other long guns over the past two decades in advanced OECD nations, because handguns are still the most used murder weapon by a large margin.

Day in and day out, pistols are by far the more common choice of criminals, but many law-abiding citizens also choose to keep and bear handguns for themselves. Consequently, most gun murders and suicides are committed at very close range indoors, and pistols are the most commonly employed weapons in these crimes. While it is not often recalled today, gun-control campaigns during the 1890s and 1900s as well as during the 1960s and 1970s, which had the strong support of the NRA and many conservative politicians, focused in the 1970s on so-called Saturday Night Specials. These are easily concealed, cheaply made, usually small-caliber handguns that were inexpensive purchases by consumers in the lower socioeconomic classes. In the United States, this nexus meant African American inner-city youths, who often used these weapons in gang fights, robberies, or murders that were associated with street crime and general social disorder.

Gun controls on these small handguns at that time clearly were targeted efforts to reduce gun crime and police the behavior of African Americans in ways that implicitly enhanced the personal security of wealthier, suburban, white, and middle-class citizens that feared—as a group and alone—becoming the targets of such violence. Historically, the NRA has been very much in favor of these "gun controls," because they clearly did entail "people control" over the poor, outsider, nonwhite, and immigrant populations that could threaten the stability of ordinary middle-class American life on the street, at home, or in the workplace. Even though the NRA has willingly wrapped itself up in the Second Amendment, the vision of guns in the hands of foreign-immigrant anarchists, Native Americans, poor inner-city blacks, exploited Hispanics, or militant blue-collar workers did not exemplify the NRA's ideals of keeping and bearing arms in a "Free State." Indeed, 1960s gun-control regulations were meant as much to arm solid citizens to defend themselves against such threats in civil society as they were to prevent overweening state power from threatening the liberties of middle-class suburbanites.

At the same time, instances of gun violence, gun murder, and gun wounding all displace the role of human agents with worries about this "thing" called a gun, and occlude thinking about people performing certain violent, murderous, or criminal acts. People are violent; some will murder others, many become criminals, and guns can enable these behaviors. Other instruments can be involved, but the mass media rarely focus on claw hammer violence, pipe wrench murder, and baseball bat crime. Consequently, the implements of violence that count most decisively in the United States are guns, and the actual population of firearms is made subject to a continuous census—internationally, nationally, and locally—for the detailed workings of the disciplinary practices entailed by gun bearing.

Material realities here are quite obdurate. There are nearly a billion firearms in the world today, with 75 percent of these in civilian hands. Every year about 8 million new small arms are manufactured, along with 10 to 15 billion rounds of ammunition. While complete data is unobtainable, the legal international trade in these goods is over $7.1 billion per year. Despite the NRA's hysterical claims in automated phone calls to people's homes that the United Nations is coming to confiscate each American's guns unless gun owners join the NRA's defense of their gun rights, gun manufacturing actually remains quite strong in the United States. In fact, it is a very profitable business, because firearms are a common consumer purchase. Not everyone owns a gun, but the public culture behind American subjectivity has been shaped strongly by guns, and guns anchor American sovereignty. Owning a few guns in many households is not atypical, and buying one or more is a commonplace event in many suburban big-box sporting-goods stores on any given weekend. In this respect, the complex connections of this technological assemblage to a certain type of heinous crime, like mass shootings in schools, malls, or churches, are intriguing and apparently unbreakable.

## IV. Implementality and Insecurity

Gun control, firearms registration, or gun regulation are divisive policy solutions, because different social interests see their legal and political implications almost antithetically. Those wishing to end all gun violence, crime, and accidents believe that heavy legal restrictions on weapons will lessen their deadly and injurious effects. Those who want to retain gun rights see these criminal incidents as the moral fault of certain people who would still be violent, criminal, and hapless with or without guns. This group regards efforts to control guns as campaigns to control people, register their property, and regulate their behavior, all in contravention to constitutionally guaranteed property and personal rights. Seeking greater civil concord through "gun control" is still widely regarded as a displaced discourse about new destabilizing schemes for "people control," along with a possible abridgment of their popular sovereignty. Six months after Sandy Hook, and with the push to regulate guns more stringently, the NRA's membership expanded to 5 million on the eve of its 2013 annual meeting (Korte 2013, 1A).

This semantic turn also is evident in TV coverage of mass shootings. As part of their mobilization in the "war on crime" and "war on drugs" since the 1970s, many municipal, county, and state police units have been funded and trained for special weapons and tactics (SWAT) operations. Carlson (this volume) details this shift, in part, toward more militarized, state-centric policing. To justify these arms buildups at the local level, one sees over the past generation "the police and other segments of the criminal justice system" coming to embrace "the military/war model for formulating crime/drug/terrorism control rationale and operations" (Kraska 2007, 502). These units, in turn, are often called upon in many cities to respond to a variety of crimes that once would have been met with a squad car or two of regular uniformed officers. Shows of force by a SWAT unit can change the dynamics of many crime scenes—sometimes positively, sometimes negatively. At the same time, their existence provides an essentially light infantry-level of lethal force that is raised and deployed locally to face citizens and/or criminals that may well be using the same class of weapons and equipment in many confrontations. For some, SWAT units are overkill, but others see them as guarantees for good public order.

Gun training for use in shooting sports, hunting, and personal protection clearly carries many cultural norms, practices, and values that relate specifically to guns as technology, equipment, and weaponry. To live with guns may perhaps express the ethos of a cultural community that is often more rural, blue-collar, white, and male in its membership, but these generalizations do not always hold. Suburbia can be well-armed, while some cities' urban neighborhoods have plenty of firepower. Nonetheless, "a 'new micro-physics' of power" (Foucault 1979, 139) exerts its influence in all of these contexts in the disciplinary details of enhanced gun-handling aptitudes that come along with increased domination over those keeping and bearing arms.

The culture of insecurity fostered by the general rhetoric and local realities of wars on crime, drugs, and terror over the past generation appear to have motivated many citizens to acquire firearms for "home defense," "personal protection," or "neighborhood policing." The often drastic layoffs of uniformed police officers in many jurisdictions over the past decade, as neoliberal government cost-cutting policies have been implemented in many locales, leave more citizens sporting bumper stickers that show Model 1911 Colt .45 pistols or AR-15 rifles with captions like "Don't call 911" or "There is no 911 here." Where there is not enough money for SWAT teams, many Americans feel they must improvise along these same lines when they feel threatened; and, as Carlson (this volume) suggests many police officers in numerous jurisdictions support this "shared" or "responsibilized" approach to community policing.

Foucault's clear distinctions between governmentality and sovereignty in much of his writing can become blurred within a republic whose Bill of Rights guarantees first the freedoms of speech and assembly, and second, the right to bear and carry arms. Whether a skirmish occurred in 1607, 1619, 1620, 1776, or 1787, it has been evident to many sovereign people in the United States that objects such as firearms and ammunition are crucial implements for the production of wealth, procurement of the means of subsistence, and cultivation of a robust population. The mechanisms of implementality suggest that guns do fill the capacity or equip the performance needed by citizens to satisfy these tasks, while also filling up the void of powerlessness, identity, or hope that too many male citizens in the United States bear.

As one nation united "with liberty and justice for all," guns have been, are, and will continue to be essential means for attaining "the right disposition of things" in complexes composed of men and things in conditions of peace and war. Stated most baldly, firearms have been critical in the tactics of America's government "to arrange things in such a way that, through a certain number of means, such and such ends may be achieved" (Foucault 1991, 95). From colonial times through the American Revolution, firearms were essential implements for political subjects carrying out campaigns of conquest and domination. Firearms were used to seize lands in America, maintain order over slaves, establish new models of commonwealth, and stage a general insurrection against a foreign royal power. The desultory uprisings seen in 1787 and 1791 against the new federal republic rest, in part, on the prerogatives of armed citizens, public militias, and gun-holding voters founding a republic; these armed citizens were ambiguously asserting their authority to possess weapons as part of their civic duty, identity, and purpose in ways that put them in opposition with the new regime in New York. Quite clearly, the implementalities of things like firearms and munitions are integral to the acceptance by men of the finality of a government that "resides in the things it manages and in the pursuit of the perfection and intensification of the processes it directs; and the instruments of government, instead of being laws, now come to be a range of multiform tactics" (Foucault 1991, 95).

Contesting the conditions of gun ownership and use is another facet to "the governmentalization of the state" that paradoxically may express how "the problems of governmentality and the techniques of the state have become the only political issue, the only real space for political struggle and contestation" (Foucault 1991, 103). As the putatively sole possessor of a monopoly on the use of legitimate force within its territory and over its population, the state's disposition toward guns, gun owners, and gun use must address questions—external and internal to the provenance of states—about such devices for effectuating lethal violence. The answers are vital for state sovereignty and political subjectivity, "since it is the tactics of government which make possible the continual definition and redefinition of what is within the competence of the state and what is not, the public versus the private, and so on; thus the state can only be understood in its survival and its limits on the basis of the general tactics of governmentality" (Foucault 1991, 103). Despite their ties to crime and mass shootings, the implementalities of guns and their use are intertwined with citizenship, subjectivity, and security in the United States. To pretend otherwise will only further mystify the fetishized relations of gun production, consumption, accumulation, and circulation as tools of power for citizens and their magistrates alike.

Security must, as Foucault asserts, "rely on a number of material givens" as well as accept that it is "a matter of maximizing the positive elements, for which one provides the best possible circulation, and of minimizing what is risky and inconvenient, like theft and disease, knowing that they will never be completely suppressed" (2007, 19). Security aims at generating spatialities, interactions, and fields for agency and structure. The apparatuses of security are pragmatic anticipations of, and adaptations to, material serialities of circulation and accumulation that constitute the concreteness of everyday milieux. Indeed, "the apparatuses of security work, fabricate, organize, and plan a milieu even before the notion was formed and isolated" (Foucault 2007, 21). A milieu has the properties of being emergent, fluid, and mutable, namely, "that in which circulation is carried out ... the milieu is a certain number of combined, overall effects bearing on all who live in it. It is an element in which a circular link is produced between effects and cause, since an effect from one point of view will be a cause from another ... so it is this phenomenon of the circulation of causes and effects that is targeted through the milieu" (Foucault 2007, 21) as populations shaped and steered to occupy these settings.

Instead of policing territory around juridical notions of sovereignty, then, the concept of the milieu encompasses population, space, and materiel arrayed as eventuations of logistical flows of people, things, and events, all framed by artifice. As regimen, routine or regulation, the apparatus of security is pitched at "arranging things so that, by connecting up with the very reality of the fluctuations, and by establishing a series of connections with other elements of reality, the phenomenon is gradually compensated for, checked, finally limited, and, in the final degree, cancelled out, without it being prevented or losing any of its reality" (Foucault 2007, 37). Mass shootings are clearly violations of orderly milieux, and, viewed in the harsh light of mass media, mostly focus on the disruptive, transgressive, and unsettled effect on the populace.

As continuing threats to life and limb, guns could be regarded as endangering the state's population. Government's purpose is not government itself as much as "the welfare of the population, the improvement of its condition, the increase of its wealth, longevity, health, etc." (Foucault 1991, 100). Gun violence is increasingly seen as a collective welfare issue, a threat to personal longevity, and an endangerment of public health. Global, national, and municipal-level surveys frequently correlate gun ownership levels with homicide and suicide rates; yet, it is also clear that wealth and relative crime levels also can be correlated both apart from weapons and with gun ownership (see Qvortrup, Carlson, Young, this volume). More discretionary income permits individuals to slip into many relations of implementality as they acquire property and weapons; in certain places and with hard times, however, the latter can be, and is, used to defend the former.

The ongoing debates over gun ownership and its legal conditionality, there-fore, can be seen as a convenient discourse for articulating new technologies for the self as well as for society as population proves to be "the object in the hands of the government, aware vis-à-vis the government, of what it wants, but ignorant of what is being done to it" (Foucault 1991, 100). Developing new systems for understanding the self and society is an essential piece of governance over the body politic, which the fruits of modernity—guns, cars, housing, tele-phones, plumbing, appliances, etc.—both enable and track. Nonetheless, gun consciousness, culture, or community is a perfect foil to highlight what is being done. As Foucault suggests, "interest at the level of the consciousness of the individual who makes up the population, and interest considered as the interest of the population regardless of what particular interests and aspirations may be of the individuals who compose it, this is the new target and fundamental interest of the government of the population: the birth of a new art, or at any rate a range of absolutely new tactics and techniques" (1991, 100). At the nexus of gun ownership and gun control, guns as implements are now a tool to tap individual attitudes as well as public opinion.

Governmentality is a complex ensemble of relations between people, space, objects, and ultimately physical territory (as a complex, sophisticated, and mutable assemblage of activities rather than mere real estate). As Foucault maintains, "one governs things," which happen to be located within and in use territorially, but "what government has to do with is not territory but rather a sort of complex composed of men and things" (1991, 93). To the degree that "government is defined as a right manner of disposing things so as to not the form of the common good, as the jurists' text would have said, but to an end which is 'convenient' for each of the things to be governed" (Foucault 1991, 95).

At these multiple of conjunctures of people and things, the complexity of guns and governance gains more clarity. Arms are the single implement called out in the Bill of Rights by the federal government as a personal utility and common property named as "the things it manages and in the pursuit of the perfect and intensification of the processes it directs," that also "come to be a range of multiform tactics" (Foucault 1991, 95). One of those "multiform tactics" in relation to gun regulation continues to be an evasion of measures that might have been taken as "the form of the common good, as the jurists' texts would have said" (Foucault 1991, 95). The state's provision for arms as implements to be stockpiled, used, and owned by the citizens of the United States is one of its many "explicit *programmes*; we are dealing with sets of calculated, reasoned prescriptions in terms of which institutions are meant to be organized, spaces arranged, behaviors regulated," even though in turn most programmes do not "take event in the institutions in an integral manner; they are simplified or some are chosen and not others; and things never work out as planned" (Foucault 1991, 80). As an implement for shooting, a gun also must be handled programmatically to assure "the elaboration of the act itself; it controls its development and its stages from the inside" (Foucault 1979, 152).

With regard to arms, or more concretely, firearms, their status as implements of power, violence, and warfare make them ready to use as instruments of war, the means of violence, or tools of power that can put into practical effect the capacity of individuals and groups to carry out their common defense.[3] Neoliberalism's tendency to render individuals responsible for themselves, then, can explain, in part, why the states increasingly allow individuals, on the one hand, to get concealed carry gun permits and enjoy "Stand Your Ground" self-defense rights, while, on the other hand, allowing police departments to call for bans on assault-style semiautomatic rifles. If the latter cannot be enacted for all, individuals are urged to accept the former as their "backup" (often, as Carlson notes, with police support). The ownership, keeping, and bearing of such arms completes, fulfills, or satisfies the programs of discipline as the *dispositifs* of government and directives of discourse. With the Second Amendment, the juridical control of weapons is enhanced inasmuch as "we have passed from a form of injunction that measured or punctuated gestures to a web that constrains or sustains them throughout their entire succession … and with it all the meticulous controls of power" (Foucault 1979, 152).

While contradictory and contested, this multiform logic of implementality rests at the core of self-rule. There are no guarantees of complete safety; but, in the void of isolation, insecurity, and incapacity, arms can fill—if only notionally—the completion of governmentality. The Constitution slowly came to guarantee citizens equality under the law, but firearms in the hands of citizens can achieve, if only in part, that purpose as needed. As many have said of the United States since the 1850s, "God made men, but Samuel Colt (the maker of the world-famous Colt .45 revolver) made them equal." After the closing of the American West, the technical evolution of guns with high-powered cartridges, semi-automatic actions, and large-capacity magazines means that John Browning, Mikhail Kalashnikov, and John Garand, in turn, only have continued Samuel Colt's work to make men equal with new implementalities of modernity amid the accelerating spin of globalization.

The American public sphere, with all of its political freedoms, to some degree always relies upon armed violence, but the level of the state's disavowal of violence has been a seductive script for its leadership over the decades. Public life across the United States is an existence that unfolds in secured, guarded, and watched space, which the state's force of arms has created in hard-fought wars since 1776 and now sustains by projecting power all over the world. Heavily armed police forces now try to maintain this order at home, but they usually arrive after the fact at most crime scenes after "bad guys with guns" have committed horrific crimes. The loss of individual civic virtues unfortunately makes such circumstances far more frequent today. Despite such shootings, the role of firearms in the larger social contract makes it unlikely that gun control will ever be much more than the implementality of incumbent authority in a regimen for governing men and deadly things in American civil society and the state.

# Notes

1. Even looking back to the changes in gun-ownership controls after the shocking assassinations of President John F. Kennedy, his brother Robert F. Kennedy, and Martin Luther King Jr. in the 1960s, the scope of gun regulation following their deaths did not increase dramatically. After much debate, the Omnibus Crime Control and Safe Streets Act of 1968 and then, following that, the Gun Control Act of 1968 were both pushed through Congress and signed by President Johnson. Yet these laws mostly were aimed at restricting gun purchases by young people, the mentally ill, and illegal drug users. These pieces of legislation also sought to restrict the import and sale of certain very inexpensive foreign handguns, some military surplus weapons, and other actual assault rifles that did not meet a complicated "sporting purposes" scoring system that was written to favor domestic gun manufacturers. Nonetheless, after three high-profile political assassinations, including one with a foreign military surplus rifle and one with a cheap handgun, the NRA basically supported both acts of legislation, while having reservations about particular fine points of implementation in each one.

2. In these articulations, then, the Second Amendment gains a unique expression in writing of its status as American *nomos*, which has "the meaning of nature, or conduct in conformity with nature, or in any case with what is proper: a custom bordering on conformity with nature" (Foucault 2013, 152). For the United States, keeping and bearing arms is a written and unwritten law, whose qualities in official writ and popular practice echo what Theseus says about Athens in Euripides' *The Suppliant Women*:

> There are written laws;
> Thanks to these, it is the people who govern;
> The wealthy and the weak enjoy equal rights.
> And this is in contrast with the tyrant (cited in Foucault 2013, 152).

Like all well-governed societies, the *nomos* of America is woven into the fabric of civil society and the state, producing subjects suited to flourishing within them. That is, "education and writing function conjointly or alternatively to ensure, protect, and maintain *nomos* whose specific nature is not exhausted in either one or the other" (Foucault 2013, 152).

3. While many citizens continue to construct gun regulation juridically to serve some imagined common good of individual disarmament or collective gunlessness to attain peace, the regulation of arms remains a program of security and sovereignty whose calculations and reasoned prescriptions about violence organize institutions, arrange spaces, and regulate behaviors to arm individuals and communities. All implements can be abused, misused, or unused, so things connected to class will never always work out as played, as gun crimes illustrate. Despite their popularity, few people understand how guns actually work. A graphic depicting how a Glock 19 semiautomatic pistol operates, for example, in the *Wall Street Journal* story on the Giffords shooting shows the cartridge loading from the magazine into the firing chamber in one image. The next panel shows it all going down the barrel when fired rather than, in fact, the bullet alone going down the chamber with the casing being ejected for the next loading-firing cycle (Fields 2011, A5). This level of ignorance should frame the extremely high accidental rate of gun woundings and killings in the United States. Yet, options are chosen and policies simplified in the implementalities of firearms relating people and things that also allow for the fundamental right to keep and bear arms. Sovereign authority in the United States rests with the people, and they have chosen to confer their magistrates only certain powers as they retain specific rights themselves. Inasmuch as "the common good" implies obeying the laws, including gun laws, the vast majority of the people are willing to submit to their own directives of the obedience to the law. The relative balance of America's very high gun homicide and suicide rates against the infrequency of gun crimes given the number of guns in society underscores how most citizens constantly tend to obey the laws. Plainly, this exercise of sovereignty rests upon specific programs of discipline that guarantee "as La Perrière says: 'government is the right disposition of things, arranged so as to lead to a convenient end'" (Foucault 1991, 94). Of course, some will violate the programs of power, but their threat to civic order only justifies the need of others to be armed against such renegade acts.

# Chapter 2

# Guns, Crime, and Political Institutions

## A Comparative Perspective

### Matt Qvortrup

Guns are ubiquitous. There are more than 875 million firearms in the world, 75 percent of them in the hands of civilians. Indeed, there are 253 million more guns than there are cars. Each year, about 8 million new small arms, plus 10 to 15 billion rounds of ammunition, are manufactured (Alpers and Wilson 2012). This statistic means that there are enough bullets to shoot every person on the planet twice. This prompts the question: Are we less or more safe because of these guns? Are they a deterrent or are they too easy to use?

This chapter seeks to present a statistical overview of the facts regarding gun crime around the world and to test the claims made by proponents and opponents of gun control. Proponents of gun control often argue that there is a correlation between guns and homicides caused by firearms. Conversely, opponents of gun control argue that there is a negative correlation between the number of guns and the overall levels of crime (such as assaults and robberies). Using data from the United Nations Office on Drugs and Crime and the UN Small Arms Survey, this chapter tests both these hypotheses. The results are—as the reader will see shortly—startling. Neither view is supported statistically. First of all, we find no evidence that the number of guns in itself increases the number of gun homicides. However, contrary to the claim of the so-called gun-lobby, having more guns is associated with higher assault rates. Interestingly, the number of homicides can be explained statistically in terms of what political institution a nation has. Presidential systems have statistically higher levels of gun homicides, possibly because presidents have to cajole lawmakers into making unpopular decisions. That parliamentary systems have been found to have lower levels of gun crime may be a result of stronger party cohesion and party discipline, which anecdotal evidence suggests has made it easier for governments in parliamentary systems to introduce measures such as bans on assault weapons.

## Weberian Introduction

Max Weber famously argued that social scientists—while they could objectively study phenomena—were always biased in the subjects they chose to investigate (Weber 1949, 52). Hence, they should lay open their values and convictions before analyzing the data. This author was in an earlier incarnation Head of the Gun Crime Section in the British Home Office (the Ministry of the Interior). In that role, I was instrumental in introducing and drafting some of the world's most draconic gun-control legislation, namely the Criminal Justice Act 2003. As an official I was broadly sympathetic to the policy. However, I did not—in those days, at any rate—consider the conflicting empirical claims proposed by opponents and proponents of gun control. Subsequently, as a social scientist, I have taken the opportunity to consider the empirical evidence, even at the cost of revising my own convictions. The aim of this study is to objectively study the existing hypotheses and to come up with outlines of possible alternative explanations.

## Background and Previous Research

Debates about gun control often follow a familiar pattern. Proponents of gun control claim that there is a correlation between the availability of firearms and the number of homicides committed by such weapons, arguing that countries with tight restrictions on gun ownership such as Britain and Australia (Chapman et al. 2006, 365–372) have very low levels of gun crime—even though the findings are often based on a relatively small number of countries (Killias 1993a, 186–188). As a corollary, they also propose that countries with relaxed firearms legislation such as the United States have higher levels of homicides caused by guns (Cook and Ludwig 2006, 691–735; Ludwig 1998, 239–254).

Opponents of gun control argue that the availability of firearms reduces the risk of crime overall and leads to lower levels of burglary and assaults (Lott 2010).[1] The availability of guns, so the argument runs, deters would-be muggers and other violent criminals from committing crimes for fear that they might get shot.

## Data

The first question to answer in any dispassionate research is whether these hypotheses can be substantiated. This is a difficult task, as the figures are disputed. Still, some figures from generally trusted sources exist. This research is based on United Nations Statistics (for general crime figures) and the UN Small Arms Survey (for gun-ownership data). Both data sets have previously been used by both proponents and opponents of gun restrictions, and while the data sets may—in certain cases—be criticized for low reporting, the figures are generally perceived to be reliable (Hepbum et al. 2007, 15–19). The figures are included in Appendix A at the end of this chapter.

## Methodology: Comparative Method

This chapter is based on the method of comparative social inquiry.[2] This method has been summed up by John Stuart Mill in his classic work *A System of Logic*:

> The simplest and most obvious modes of singling out from among the circumstances which precede or follow a phenomenon ... is ... comparing instances in which the phenomenon does occur, with instances in other respects similar, in which it does not. (Mill 1888, 278)

In this study, we will first be comparing countries in which "the phenomenon" gun crime (and other crimes) "does occur," with "instances in which it does not." (We will subsequently do the same comparison as regards assault and robbery.)

Needless to say, the comparative method is not foolproof, as it may exclude individual and idiosyncratic factors that can only be obtained through "thick description."[3] These possible shortcomings notwithstanding,[4] the comparative method provides an overview and a perspective that we ignore at our peril. If we find a general pattern, this deserves at the very least to be subjected to further empirical analysis.

## Do More Weapons Lead to More Homicides?
## A Comparative Study

This chapter is based on the assumption that similar factors lead to similar results. Does the presence of guns lead to higher levels of homicides caused by firearms? Such a correlation was reported in the 1990s (Killias 1993a, 186–188). The question remains if this correlation still holds true, and if a reduction in the number of firearms in a society actually leads to lower levels of deaths caused by guns. Some data suggest that the correlation is not as strong as previously believed. For example, a single-country case study from Australia (where tight regulations were introduced after the 1996 Port Arthur mass shooting, which left thirty-five dead and twenty-three wounded) suggests that gun crime did not fall as much as expected (McPhedran and Baker 2008, 297–299). Using data from the United Nations Office on Drugs and Crime (UNODC) (Harrendorf et al. 2010) and data from the UNODC and the Small Arms Survey (www. smallarmssurvey.org), it is possible to test this hypothesis. Social background variables (Human Development Index, GENI-index, and GDP per capita) are taken from UNDP figures (http://hdr.undp.org/en/statistics/data) and political figures from Persson and Tabellin's (2003) data.

Statistical data can often seem daunting to the uninitiated, and quantitative figures must be analyzed with caution. But—basically—the interpretation of the data reported in Table 2.1 is simple: The higher the upper figure, the higher the correlation. For example, the figure 12.449 for presidentialism is a high figure and the standard error below (2.093) is low. This indicates that there is a high probability that countries that have presidential systems have a high level of gun crime. That this figure is statistically significant at the 0.01 level means that there is a 99 percent chance that this figure is statistically correct.

However, if the lower figure (the Standard Error) is large and the statistical significance (p) is high, the relationship is spurious and without much force. As Model One in Table 2.1 shows, there is little support for the hypothesis that more guns lead to more gun crime if we compare all UN countries from which we have data.

The figures throw up some interesting findings, some of which should not surprise social scientists. For example, there is no statistically significant

**Table 2.1 Regression Analysis: Determinants of Homicides by Firearms
(Standard Errors in Parentheses)**

| Variable | Model 1 | Model 2 |
|---|---|---|
| Constant | 6.5 | 4.13 |
|  | (5.6) | (2.8) |
| Guns per 100.000 | −.059 | .012 |
|  | (.065) | (.19) |
| Incarcerations per 100.000 | −.003 | 0.01 |
|  | (0.09) | (0.03) |
| GENI inequality | 14.08 | |
|  | (16.9) | |
| Presidentialism | 12.449*** | |
|  | (2.093) | |
| GDP | −8.02 | |
|  | (3.1) | |
| HDI | −4.45 | 3.30** |
|  | (6.7) | (1.9) |
| Assault Weapons Ban | | 3.148** |
|  | | (.88) |
|  | $R^2 = 0.48$ | $R^2 = .0.51$ |
|  | N: 194 | N: 34 |

\***: Significant at p< 0.01, \*\*: Significant at p< 0.05, \*: Significant at p< 0.1

correlation between homicides and incarcerations; jailing more people is not correlated with more or fewer homicides (B: −.003, and not statistically significant).[5] Similarly, the data suggests that higher levels of socioeconomic development are negatively correlated with the number of homicides caused by guns. However, none of these variables are statistically significant. The same, interestingly, is true for gun ownership.

The number of guns per 100,000 inhabitants is slightly negatively correlated with the number of homicides. The evidence suggests, if anything, that more guns lead to fewer murders, but the level of statistical significance is low (p< .36). Further, if we calculate the Pearsons Correlation Coefficient, we find that this is merely R= −0.10 (Significant at p=.16).[6] It goes without saying that a score of −0.10 is very low indeed.

Interestingly, the only statistically significant variable in Model 1 is the presidential one. Countries that have presidential systems as opposed to parliamentary systems are found to have higher levels of gun crime, and this correlation is statistically significant at the 0.01 level. (R=.43, p<.001). We shall return to this surprising finding below.

It could perhaps be argued that it is methodologically illegitimate to compare countries like the United States, Canada, and Britain with countries like Syria,

Venezuela, and Saudi Arabia. Mill, after all, argued that we should compare "instances *in other respects similar*" (Mill 1888, 278). Would the results be the same if we excluded nondemocratic countries, in countries in "other respects dissimilar"?

Instead of using all the countries in the world, Model 2 uses data only from OECD countries; that is, countries that are similar in terms of socioeconomic development and political institutions. In addition, we have added another variable, the availability of assault weapons.[7] The reason for this research design is as follows: One of the provisions of the Federal Assault Weapons Ban in the United States outlawed semiautomatic rifles, pistols, and shotguns that use a detachable magazine. After the law was introduced, there was a discernible drop in the number of homicides (see Figure 2.1). However, the ban lapsed in 2004 as part of its sunset provision. Since then, no replacement bill has made it out of congressional committee.

Based on the international evidence from the OECD countries, there is considerable statistical evidence that similar provisions have had a positive effect

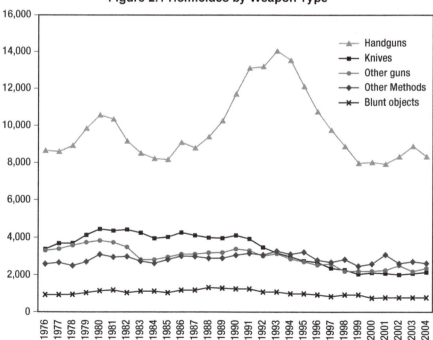

Figure 2.1 Homicides by Weapon Type

on the number of homicides. Indeed, the coefficient for the ban on assault weapons (1= if ban is in place and 0= if no ban is in place) is high (B:3.148) and is statistically significant at the 0.05 level.

## More Guns, Less Crime

The question remains whether the favorite hypothesis of the other camp—the more guns, the less violent crime (Plassmann and Whitley 2003, 1313–1369)—can be supported. This "gun behind the door" argument can be tested by correlating the number of robberies and assaults with the number of guns per 100 citizens. Why these variables? Robbery and assault are good proxies, as they are both crimes that involve the use of force.

### Robbery and Gun Ownership

Robbery—according to the common-law definition by Matthew Hale—is "the felonious and violent taking of any money or any goods from the person of another, putting him in fear" (Hale 1736, 532). Using data from the UNODC (Harrendorf et al. 2010) and data from the UNODC and the Small Arms Survey, it is possible to test this hypothesis.

Contrary to the expectations of Lott and others, the Pearsons Correlation Coefficient between robbery and number of guns per 100,000 inhabitans is a mere –.05. While the correlation is negative (more robberies, fewer guns), the figure is miniscule and the model is not statistically significant (p, one-tailed: .30). In short, the favorite argument by the NRA doesn't stand up to empirical scrutiny.

### Assault and Guns

In Britain, the United States, and other common-law jurisdictions, assault is "committed when a person intentionally or recklessly causes another to apprehend the immediate infliction of unlawful force" (UK Criminal Justice Act 1988, S.39).

An individual would, following Lott and others' hypotheses, be likely to be deterred from committing the crime of "assault" for fear that the victim might be armed. Using the same data as in the previous section, it is possible to test this argument. We could expect a negative value for the coefficient "gun ownership." In fact, we find the opposite. There is a relatively clear Pearsons

Correlation between *more* guns and a *higher* number of assaults: R=.23, significant at p< 0.05. This finding falsifies Lott's hypothesis at the international level. Overall, we thus find that the favorite arguments proposed by both the proponents and the opponents of gun control are falsified. At the international level—and things might be different in different countries—there is *no* correlation between the total number of guns and the number of homicides caused by firearms, though the availability of assault weapons in certain OECD countries is significantly correlated with higher death rates.The traditional arguments and hypotheses are no longer valid—if, indeed, they ever were. So what is the alternative?

## Institutional Factors and Gun Crime: The Failure of Presidential Government

As already observed, the only variable that was statistically significant in Table 2.1 was the variable for presidential systems. Basically, what the figure suggested was the perhaps surprising statistical fact that countries that have presidential systems (like the United States) are more likely to have high levels of gun homicides than countries with parliamentary systems (like in Britain, Australia, and Switzerland). Statistically speaking, the figures are impressive. But can they be explained?

It should be said at the outset that the explanation proposed here is a first pass and that it necessarily will have to be followed up by more detailed empirical investigations, which cannot be provided in a short book chapter such as this. Previous evidence by this author has found positive correlations between political institutions and domestic terrorism (Qvortrup 2011).

So what is it with presidential systems that make them more prone to gun crime? Is this finding credible or just a statistical coincidence?

While initially surprising, the figures are in line with recent evidence suggesting that institutions have a direct impact on policy outcomes. For example, Arend Lijphart has recently found evidence that institutions such as electoral systems, courts, and parliamentary institutions are correlated with policy outcomes such as higher economic growth, lower inequality, and lower levels of crime (Lijphart 2012).[8]

Further, research—especially in the United States—dating back to the 1990s has suggested that presidential systems are particularly prone to result in legislative gridlock (Weaver and Rockman 1995). This research, carried out primarily by scholars of American politics, has been accompanied by findings which independently have shown that presidential systems internationally have been less effective in dealing with reform (Linz 1994, 6). The hypothesis behind this work is that governments in parliamentary systems are more efficient in dealing with reforms, as they are less likely to be obstructed by the legislature. The situation has been summed up by Weaver and Rockman:

> Political parties in parliamentary systems tend to be much more cohesive in the legislature than in a separation-of-power system. If they were not, the executive would be constantly threatened with ouster from office. In America, on the other hand, it is not necessary for the executive to win in the legislature on all important votes to stay in office. As a result, control over individual legislators is not as important, and legislators are much freer to vote their constituency interests or beliefs. (Weaver and Rockman 1995, 12–13)

The hypothesis that arises from this could be that gun homicides are less likely to occur in parliamentary systems as governments find it easier to enact legislation. For example, in Israel, Sweden, Finland, and Switzerland—all countries with parliamentary systems—the governments did not find it difficult to introduce legislation requiring background checks before a firearm could be purchased, and all the parliamentary systems in OECD countries have bans on assault weapons, whereas the presidential systems (apart from Korea) have not. Needless to say, more research is needed to discern the finer points between gun homicides and political institutions, but given the rather unsatisfactory results of statistical analyses of pure criminological figures, this area of research seems to be a fertile field for further study.

## Conclusion

Earlier studies have suggested that the "availability of guns increases the likelihood of homicides … with guns" (Killias 1993b, 1722). The data analyzed here does not support this hypothesis. There is no statistical correlation between guns and the homicides caused by them if we compare all countries around the world, nor is there a correlation if we restrict our analysis solely to OECD countries. However, there is a very strong correlation between the ban on assault weapons and a low number of homicides if we look at comparable countries, such as the OECD member states. This suggests that bans on assault weapons are effective. The analysis found no evidence to suggest that the availability of guns is a deterrent to other violent crimes.

The analysis found strong evidence to suggest that the number of murders caused by guns is positively correlated with presidential systems. More research is needed to determine if this is due to causal factors, but anecdotal evidence suggests that parliamentary systems—which do not suffer from the gridlock that characterizes the US and other presidential systems—has enabled governments in parliamentary systems such as Britain, Japan, and Australia to pass legislation banning assault weapons and to react more quickly to popular pressures. Whether this is a "good thing," of course, is a political question.

# Chapter 2 Appendix Crime Figures and Gun Ownership

| Country | Number of People Incarcerated per 100,000 Inhabitants | Homicides Caused by Firearms per 100,000 Inhabitants | Assaults per 100,000 Inhabitants | Number of Firearms per 100,000 Inhabitants | Number of Robberies per 100,000 Inhabitants |
|---|---|---|---|---|---|
| Afghanistan | | | | | |
| Albania | 47 | | 18 | | 7.2 |
| Algeria | | | 108.6 | | 72.4 |
| Andorra | | | | | |
| Angola | | | | | |
| Antigua and Barbuda | | 7.14 | | | |
| Argentina | 52 | 3.02 | 366.4 | 10.2 | 905 |
| Armenia | 73 | 0.29 | | 12.5 | 5.6 |
| Australia | 95 | 0.14 | 797 | 15 | 81.8 |
| Austria | 73 | 0.22 | 440.3 | 30.4 | 61.6 |
| Azerbaijan | 192 | 0.12 | 1.9 | 3.5 | 2.8 |
| Bahamas | | 15.37 | | 5.3 | |
| Bahrain | 70 | | 464 | 24.8 | 31.3 |
| Bangladesh | | 1.12 | 0.4 | 0.5 | 0.6 |
| Barbados | | 2.99 | 611 | 7.8 | 170.1 |
| Belarus | 382 | 0.12 | 46.3 | 7.3 | 100.2 |
| Belgium | 43 | 0.68 | 627.2 | 17.2 | 211.4 |
| Belize | | 21.82 | | 10 | 182.4 |
| Benin | | | | 1.4 | |
| Bhutan | | | | 3.5 | |
| Bolivia (Plurinational State of) | 19.8 | | 54.2 | 2.8 | 110.9 |
| Bosnia and Herzegovina | 34 | 0.48 | | 17.3 | 20.4 |
| Botswana | | | 39.6 | 4.9 | |
| Brazil | | 18.1 | | 8 | |
| Brunei Darussalam | | | 119.5 | 1.4 | 0.5 |

| Country | Number of People Incarcerated per 100,000 Inhabitants | Homicides Caused by Firearms per 100,000 Inhabitants | Assaults per 100,000 Inhabitants | Number of Firearms per 100,000 Inhabitants | Number of Robberies per 100,000 Inhabitants |
|---|---|---|---|---|---|
| Bulgaria | 114 | 0.67 | 47.6 | 6.2 | 53 |
| Burkina Faso | | | | 1.1 | |
| Burundi | | | | 1.2 | |
| Cambodia | | 1.44 | | 4.3 | |
| Cameroon | | | | 2.8 | |
| Canada | 72 | 0.51 | 737.5 | 30.2 | 94.2 |
| Cape Verde | | | | 5.4 | |
| Central African Republic | | | | 1 | |
| Chad | | | | 1.1 | |
| Chile | 138 | 2.16 | 531.3 | 10.7 | 1275.6 |
| China | | | 9.5 | 4.9 | 24.5 |
| Colombia | | 27.09 | 63.4 | 5.9 | 61.7 |
| Comoros | | | | 1.8 | |
| Congo | | | | 2.7 | |
| Congo (Democratic Republic of the) | | 1.56 | | | |
| Costa Rica | 147 | 4.59 | 19.7 | 1.4 | 527.3 |
| Côte d'Ivoire | | | 66.1 | 9.9 | |
| Croatia | 54 | 0.39 | 27 | 2.4 | 32.6 |
| Cuba | | 0.24 | | 21.7 | |
| Cyprus | 58 | 0.46 | 15.9 | 4.8 | 9.5 |
| Czech Republic | 158 | 0.19 | 78.1 | 36.4 | 46.8 |
| Denmark | 51 | 0.27 | 214.1 | 16.3 | 48.8 |
| Djibouti | | | | 12 | |
| Dominica | | | | 2.8 | |
| Dominican Republic | 31 | 16.3 | 155.1 | 5.1 | 556.4 |
| Ecuador | 35.4 | 12.73 | 49.8 | 1.3 | 398.8 |

| Country | Number of People Incarcerated per 100,000 Inhabitants | Homicides Caused by Firearms per 100,000 Inhabitants | Assaults per 100,000 Inhabitants | Number of Firearms per 100,000 Inhabitants | Number of Robberies per 100,000 Inhabitants |
|---|---|---|---|---|---|
| Egypt | 70 | 0.57 | 0.3 | 3.5 | |
| El Salvador | 162 | 39.9 | 75.9 | 5.8 | 92 |
| Equatorial Guinea | | | | 19.9 | |
| Eritrea | | | | 0.5 | |
| Estonia | 242 | 0.24 | 291.5 | 9.2 | 74.7 |
| Ethiopia | | | | 0.4 | |
| Fiji | | | | 0.5 | |
| Finland | 60 | 0.45 | 586.9 | 45.3 | 32.3 |
| France | 56 | 0.06 | 180 | 31.2 | 10.8 |
| Gabon | | | | 14 | |
| Gambia | | | | 0.8 | |
| Georgia | 228 | 0.55 | 49 | 7.3 | 62.4 |
| Germany | 74 | 0.19 | 619 | 30.3 | 65.2 |
| Ghana | | | | 0.4 | |
| Greece | | 0.26 | 66.7 | 22.5 | 23.4 |
| Grenada | | | | | |
| Guatemala | 27.5 | 34.81 | 48.1 | 13.1 | 102.8 |
| Guinea | | | | 1.2 | |
| Guinea-Bissau | | | | 1.6 | |
| Guyana | | 11.46 | | 14.6 | |
| Haiti | | | | 0.6 | |
| Honduras | 148.2 | 68.43 | | 6.2 | |
| Hong Kong, China (SAR) | | | | | |
| Hungary | 120 | 0.07 | 127 | 5.5 | 31.9 |
| Iceland | 30 | 0 | 394 | 30.3 | 12 |
| India | | 0.26 | 23.1 | 4.2 | 1.6 |
| Indonesia | | | 9 | 0.5 | 29.8 |

| Country | Number of People Incarcerated per 100,000 Inhabitants | Homicides Caused by Firearms per 100,000 Inhabitants | Assaults per 100,000 Inhabitants | Number of Firearms per 100,000 Inhabitants | Number of Robberies per 100,000 Inhabitants |
|---|---|---|---|---|---|
| Iran (Islamic Republic of) | | | 114.4 | | |
| Iraq | | | | | |
| Ireland | 219.3 | 0.48 | 93 | 8.6 | 55 |
| Israel | 64.8 | 0.09 | 763 | 7.3 | 36.3 |
| Italy | | 0.71 | 123.7 | 11.9 | 121.7 |
| Jamaica | | 39.4 | 421 | 8.1 | 90 |
| Japan | 55.4 | 0.01 | 51 | 0.6 | 4 |
| Jordan | | 0.49 | | 11.5 | 14 |
| Kazakhstan | 282 | 1.34 | | 1.3 | |
| Kenya | | | 35.9 | 6.4 | 88.9 |
| Kiribati | | | | 0.6 | 14.2 |
| Korea (Democratic People's Rep. of) | | | | | |
| Korea (Republic of) | 63 | 0.03 | 34.3 | 1.1 | 10.4 |
| Kuwait | | | 86 | 24.8 | 11.2 |
| Kyrgyzstan | 235 | 0.54 | 3.9 | 0.9 | 45.5 |
| Lao People's Democratic Republic | | | | 1.2 | |
| Latvia | 212 | 0.22 | 67.9 | 19 | 98.6 |
| Lebanon | | 0.76 | 10 | 21 | 3.5 |
| Lesotho | | | | 2.7 | |
| Liberia | | 0.43 | | 1.6 | |
| Libyan Arab Jamahiriya | | | | | |
| Liechtenstein | | 2.82 | | | |
| Lithuania | 198 | 0.18 | 131.2 | 0.7 | 128.2 |
| Luxembourg | 37 | 0.62 | 296.5 | 15.3 | 95.8 |

| Country | Number of People Incarcerated per 100,000 Inhabitants | Homicides Caused by Firearms per 100,000 Inhabitants | Assaults per 100,000 Inhabitants | Number of Firearms per 100,000 Inhabitants | Number of Robberies per 100,000 Inhabitants |
|---|---|---|---|---|---|
| The former Yugoslav Republic of Macedonia | 86 | 1.21 | 21.6 | 24.1 | 24.7 |
| Madagascar | | | | 0.8 | |
| Malawi | | | | 0.7 | |
| Malaysia | 166 | 0.24 | 21.9 | 1.5 | 82.1 |
| Maldives | | 1.63 | 212.6 | 6.5 | 161.9 |
| Mali | | | | 1.1 | |
| Malta | | | 272.9 | 11.9 | 54.9 |
| Marshall Islands | | | | | |
| Mauritania | | | | 1.6 | |
| Mauritius | 132 | 0.1 | 1044 | 14.7 | 88.3 |
| Mexico | 97 | 9.97 | 223.5 | 15 | 504 |
| Micronesia (Federated States of) | | | | | |
| Moldova (Republic of) | 202 | 0.22 | 32.1 | 7.1 | 23.3 |
| Monaco | | | | | |
| Mongolia | 200 | 0.11 | 144 | 1.9 | 33.8 |
| Montenegro | | | 26.4 | 23.1 | 12.9 |
| Morocco | | | 186 | 5 | 83.4 |
| Mozambique | | | | 5.1 | |
| Myanmar | 2.5 | | | 4 | |
| Namibia | | | | 12.6 | 0.01 |
| Nauru | | | | | |
| Nepal | 11.2 | 0.3 | | 0.8 | 0.5 |
| Netherlands | 40.1 | 0.33 | 351 | 3.9 | 83.7 |
| New Zealand | | 0.16 | 839 | 22.6 | 59.7 |
| Nicaragua | 126 | 5.92 | 332.9 | 7.7 | 440.7 |

| Country | Number of People Incarcerated per 100,000 Inhabitants | Homicides Caused by Firearms per 100,000 Inhabitants | Assaults per 100,000 Inhabitants | Number of Firearms per 100,000 Inhabitants | Number of Robberies per 100,000 Inhabitants |
|---|---|---|---|---|---|
| Niger | | | | 0.7 | |
| Nigeria | | | | 1.5 | |
| Norway | 54 | | 346 | 31.3 | 29.7 |
| Occupied Palestinian Territory | | | 174.7 | | 5.4 |
| Oman | | | 28.9 | 25.4 | 6.7 |
| Pakistan | | | 0.1 | 11.6 | 0.1 |
| Palau | | | | | |
| Panama | 134 | 16.18 | 54.2 | 21.7 | 38.1 |
| Papua New Guinea | 38.8 | | 25.1 | 1.32 | 63 |
| Paraguay | | 7.35 | 36.3 | 17 | 31.5 |
| Peru | | 2.63 | 99.9 | 18 | 156.1 |
| Philippines | 38.6 | 8.93 | 0.1 | 4.7 | 8.4 |
| Poland | 197 | 0.09 | 76.3 | 1.3 | 92.2 |
| Portugal | 91 | 0.41 | 377.4 | 8.5 | 197.3 |
| Qatar | 57 | 0.14 | 37.4 | 19.2 | 8.4 |
| Romania | 138 | 0.02 | 43.9 | 0.7 | 18.9 |
| Russian Federation | 629 | | 26.9 | 8.9 | 90 |
| Rwanda | | | | 0.6 | |
| Saint Kitts and Nevis | | 32.44 | | | |
| Saint Lucia | | 5.49 | | | |
| Saint Vincent and the Grenadines | | | | | |
| Samoa | | | | | |
| San Marino | | | 0.7 | | |
| Sao Tome and Principe | | | | | |
| Saudi Arabia | 53 | | 63.2 | 35 | 2.9 |

| Country | Number of People Incarcerated per 100,000 Inhabitants | Homicides Caused by Firearms per 100,000 Inhabitants | Assaults per 100,000 Inhabitants | Number of Firearms per 100,000 Inhabitants | Number of Robberies per 100,000 Inhabitants |
|---|---|---|---|---|---|
| Senegal | | | | 2 | |
| Serbia | | 0.46 | 36.9 | 37.8 | 37.5 |
| Seychelles | | | | 5.4 | |
| Sierra Leone | | 2.28 | | 0.6 | |
| Singapore | 258 | 0.02 | 14.6 | 0.5 | 21.7 |
| Slovakia | 111 | 0.18 | 60.9 | 8.3 | 29.6 |
| Slovenia | 46 | 0.1 | 120.2 | 13.5 | 31.5 |
| Solomon Islands | | | | 0.4 | |
| Somalia | | | | 9.1 | |
| South Africa | | 17.03 | 1188 | 12.7 | 494.5 |
| Spain | | 0.2 | 414 | 10.4 | 201.2 |
| Sri Lanka | | 1.48 | 109 | 1.5 | 41 |
| Sudan* | | | | 5.5 | |
| Suriname | | | | 13.4 | |
| Swaziland | 156 | | 516 | 6.4 | 304 |
| Sweden | 63 | 0.41 | 845 | 31.6 | 94.2 |
| Switzerland | 43 | 0.77 | 108 | 45.7 | 54.6 |
| Syrian Arab Republic | 17 | | | 3.9 | 4.3 |
| Tajikistan | | 0.22 | | 1 | 2.7 |
| Tanzania (United Republic of) | | | | 1.4 | |
| Thailand | 163 | | 38.8 | 15.6 | 107.1 |
| Timor-Leste | | | | | |
| Togo | | | | 1 | |
| Tonga | | | | | |
| Trinidad and Tobago | | 27.31 | | 1.6 | |
| Tunisia | | | 371 | 0.1 | 11.5 |
| Turkey | 36.5 | 0.77 | 192 | 12.5 | 28.5 |

| Country | Number of People Incarcerated per 100,000 Inhabitants | Homicides Caused by Firearms per 100,000 Inhabitants | Assaults per 100,000 Inhabitants | Number of Firearms per 100,000 Inhabitants | Number of Robberies per 100,000 Inhabitants |
|---|---|---|---|---|---|
| Turkmenistan | 195 | 0.1 | | 3.8 | |
| Tuvalu | | | | | |
| Uganda | 285 | 0.87 | 92.7 | 1.4 | 17.7 |
| Ukraine | | 0.22 | 13.9 | 6.6 | |
| United Arab Emirates | 143 | | 53.7 | 22.1 | 13.2 |
| United Kingdom | 106 | 0.07 | 1365 | 6.2 | 188.7 |
| United States | 743 | 2.97 | 786.7 | 88.8 | 146.4 |
| Uruguay | 146 | 2.8 | 336 | 31.8 | 277.5 |
| Uzbekistan | | | | 1.5 | |
| Vanuatu | | | | | |
| Venezuela (Bolivarian Republic of) | 85 | 38.97 | 104 | 10.7 | 143.3 |
| Vietnam | | 0.99 | | 1.7 | |
| Yemen | | | 5.6 | 54.8 | |
| Zambia | | 0.35 | 211 | 8.9 | 25.8 |
| Zimbabwe | 109 | 4.78 | 765 | 4.4 | 101.4 |

Sources: Harrendorf, S., Heiskanen, M., and Malby, S., (2010) International Statistics on Crime and Justice, Vienna, UNODC; and UN Small Arms Survey (www.smallarmssurvey.org).

# Notes

1. For a contrary view, see I. Ayres and J. J. Donohue III, *Shooting Down the More Guns, Less Crime Hypothesis* (No. w9336) (National Bureau of Economic Research, 2002).

2. The classical study in this literature is Henry Teune and Adam Przeworski, *The Logic of Comparative Social Inquiry* (New York, John Wiley & Sons, 1970). For an update of more recent work, see C. C. Ragin, "The Distinctiveness of Comparative Social Science," in *Comparing Nations and Cultures: Readings in a Cross-Disciplinary Perspective* (Englewood Cliffs, NJ: Pearson, 1995).

3. See generally C. Geertz, *The Interpretation of Cultures*, vol. 5019 (New York: Basic Books, 1973).

4. On these shortcomings, see A. MacIntyre, "Is a Science of Comparative Politics Possible?" in *Philosophy, Politics and Society*, edited by Peter Laslett, Walter G. Runciman, and Quentin Skinner (Oxford: Oxford University Press, 1972), 7.

5. This corroborates findings reported earlier in P. Mason, "Lies, Distortion and What Doesn't Work: Monitoring Prison Stories in the British Media," *Crime, Media, Culture* 2, no. 3 (2006), 251–267.

6. Pearson's correlation coefficient is a measure between 0 and 1 (for positive correlations) and between 0 and −1 for negative correlations. Figures below 0.20 are normally considered to indicate no correlation.

7. Data for this category are taken from Philip Alpers and Marcus Wilson, *Guns in the United Kingdom: Facts, Figures and Firearm Law. Sydney School of Public Health, University of Sydney*, www.GunPolicy.org February 13, 2013. Accessed February 14, 2013.

8. See also Rein Taagepera and Matt Qvortrup, "Who Gets What, When, How—Through Which Electoral System?" *European Political Science* 11 (2012), 244–258.

# Chapter 3

# Homicide in Canada and the United States

## Bill O'Grady

### Introduction

THIS CHAPTER WILL BEGIN BY COMPARING AGGREGATE LEVELS OF POLICE-reported homicide—including lethal gun violence—in Canada and the United States. A discussion will then ensue about why homicide rates in the United States have been consistently higher than the rates recorded in Canada. From here the analysis will shift to more recent thinking on the issue during a period when levels of police-recorded interpersonal violence have been receding in both Canada and the United States. The chapter will conclude with a discussion of an alternate route for homicide research.

The mass shooting carried out by Adam Lanza in Newtown, Connecticut, on December 14, 2012, which killed twenty children and six adult staff, garnered the attention of news outlets from around the world. As a Canadian sociologist who has had a long standing interest in crime and violence, I am always intrigued by the debate that resurfaces in the mass media, seemingly like clockwork, when a mass shooting takes place in the United States: gun control. The Sandy Hook shooting was no exception. Soon after learning about the tragedy, President Obama assigned Vice President Biden, an outspoken proponent of stricter gun laws, to lead a White House Gun Control Task Force. Then the

National Rifle Association (NRA) chimed in. As a way to stem such violence in the future, the NRA's Wayne LaPierre called upon Congress to pass a law that would put armed police officers in every school in the country. Rather than limiting access to firearms for Americans, the NRA proposed to arm an even greater number of Americans. The debate about gun control in America was reignited once again.

While it is well-known that mass shootings are more common in the United States than in Canada, several incidents have taken place in Canada (for example, in 1989 Marc Lepine's assault-rifle shooting spree killed fourteen female students at Ecole Polytechnique in Montreal). Unlike in the United States, however, the fallout in the mass media after Canadian shootings normally does not revolve around debates between the pro- and anti-gun lobbyists and proponents. Even though the NRA has been actively involved in trying to abolish Canada's long-gun registry for more than a decade (arguably with some success, as the federal government abolished the registry in 2012), the US gun lobby has a lower profile in Canada than it does in the United States, and has not been as vocal after mass shootings that have taken place in Canada. What normally does emerge in the media following these kinds of shootings are questions about why such tragedies occur and the motives behind them. Was the perpetrator disturbed or mentally ill? How was the assailant able to get a high-powered assault rifle in a country where levels of gun control are much stricter that they are in the United States? Shootings such as these also raise questions about whether or not Canada is becoming more "American" in terms of its values and culture. Even Michael Moore, in his film *Bowling for Columbine*, weighed in on why gun violence is a greater social problem in the United States than it is in Canada. Informed by the work of Glassner (1999), the film suggested that, compared to Canada, Americans are much more besieged by a "culture of fear" (due to racist views that are promulgated by a corporate hegemonic media agenda) and that this fear fuels American gun culture and therefore gun violence.

Scholarly analyses of the differing levels of Canadian and American inter-personal lethal violence date back to at least the late 1970s, and have generally focused on aggregate levels of homicide, not only mass murders. While the two nations do differ in some key respects, according to Ouimet "Canada is the country which most resembles the USA" (2002, 34). Therefore, the two nations have been a natural point of comparison for researchers interested in under-standing why the two countries have substantially different levels of homicide.

This chapter will begin by comparing homicide rates in Canada and the United States from 1961–2011. Attention will then shift from a statistical description of these differences to explanations regarding why rates of homicide in the United States have been consistently greater than rates recorded in Canada, and an explanation of the fact that, after years of growth, homicide rates in the two countries have generally been declining since the mid-1990s. Here a range of explanations will be grouped on the basis of *criminal justice system* views versus *non-criminal justice system* accounts. Informed by the new neighborhood effects literature, the paper will conclude with a brief analysis and discussion about where the homicide research agenda ought to proceed in the future.

## Homicide Trends: The United States and Canada

Most research that has compared interpersonal violence in the United States and Canada has relied upon police-reported homicide data.[1] While not without some limitations, police-generated homicide statistics are considered to be much more valid and reliable than other data used to measure interpersonal violence, such as robbery and sexual assault, as these data are prone to well-known reporting and definitional issues.

As noted in Figure 3.1, since the early 1960s, homicide levels in Canada have been consistently much lower than rates recorded in the United States.

**Figure 3.1  Homicide rates per 100,000 in Canada and the United States: 1961–2011 on a one-scale Y axis**

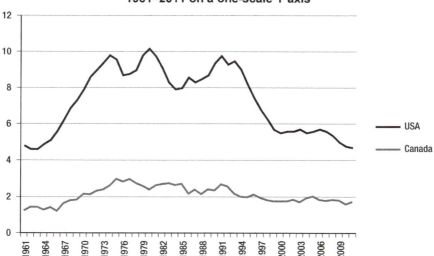

Between 1961 and 2011 homicide rates in the United States were consistently about three times higher than Canadian homicide rates. Not only are aggregate rates higher in the United States, so too are gun-murder rates. For example, data collected between 2004 and 2010 shows that the gun murder rate was over five times higher in the United States (3.2/100,000) than it was in Canada (.5/100,000) (BBC 2013). In fact, according to data in Figure 3.2, the United States leads developed countries in levels of lethal gun violence.

Drilling down deeper into differences between US and Canadian homicide rates reveals that not only is the rate of gun murder greater in the United States than it is in Canada, but there are also notable differences in victim-offender relationships. Homicides in the United States are more likely than homicides in Canada to involve acquaintances or strangers as opposed to family members (Sprott and Cesaroni 2002).

**Figure 3.2 Gun murder compared by country**

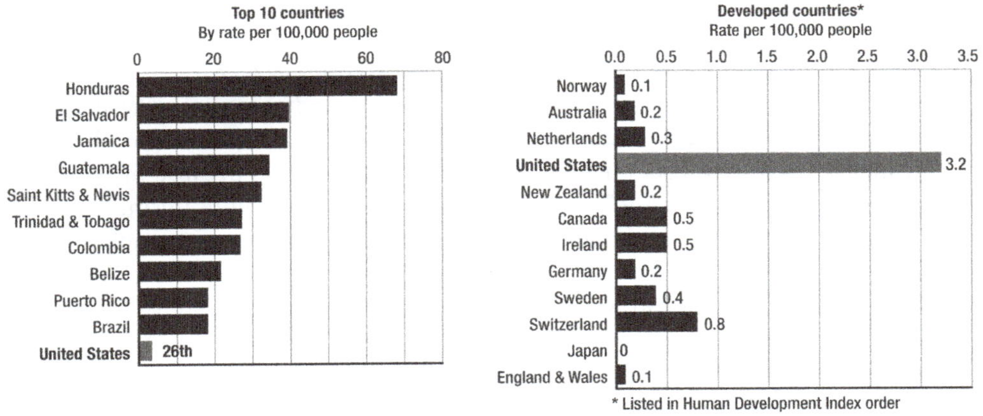

Source: UNODC. Latest data for each country (2004–2010)

## Explaining the Differences in US and Canadian Homicide Rates

Due to the ease of accessing good-quality data collected by the FBI and Statistics Canada, it is relatively simple to describe the various differences and changes that have taken place in homicide rates recorded in Canada and the United States. What presents a more daunting challenge is coming up with explanations to account for these differences in rates and trends over time. As the following review will demonstrate, there is no shortage of explanations for the differing American and Canadian homicide statistics. Unfortunately, there is not one, overarching, well endorsed "theory" that can account for the statistical differences and changes that have taken place.

As a starting point, let us begin by addressing the question of why homicide rates are greater in the United States than they are in Canada. Indeed, this issue has drawn the attention of the criminological community for some time. Almost forty years ago, research by Hagan and Leon (1977) and Hagan (1984) explored this query in some detail. Hagan's argument is essentially an analysis that draws on the work of Lipsit (1972), Porter (1979), and others during the 1960s and 1970s when sociologists were interested in exploring what were thought to be the different social systems of the two countries: one that was born with a revolution (United States), and the other (Canada), which was not.

To understand why homicide rates are higher in the United States than they are in Canada, Hagan argues that one must take into account that the United States and Canada have different value systems stemming from two sets of historical forces. One historical force that produced lower Canadian rates of violence had to do with Canada's ties to elitist, staid, and conservative Britain. Such ties were reinforced during and following the American Revolution when United Empire Loyalists migrated northward into Canada because of their rejection of the "mob rule" associated with American republicanism. This "Canadian Character" is thought to be characterized by deference to authority, supposedly derived from this British connection and loyalty to the Crown. In contrast, the American Revolution severed the American bond to Britain and institutionalized a deep and abiding antiauthoritarianism in the American psyche (Hagan 1984). Ostensibly, that attitude is reflected in a constitution that protects the right to bear arms.

A second noted consideration concerns a set of factors that are essentially geoeconomic in scope. The early years of economic development on the Canadian frontier made it more difficult for survival than was the case in United States. Due to its sheer size and geography, Canada was a vast and inhospitable country compared to the United States, and its natural resources were less accessible for extraction. While the economic development of the US frontier could be left to the initiative of the lone entrepreneur, the exploitation of the Canadian frontier required the assistance of state-supported armies, the police (RCMP), and other organizations such as the Roman Catholic and Anglican Churches. The "Wild West" shaped American attitudes toward authority, the state, and law and order quite differently from the way the relatively harmonious development of the Canadian frontier influenced Canadians' attitudes. Because of how the country began, Canadians became more respectful of authority and less inclined to break the law.

The argument that cultural variances account for differences in levels of lethal violence between the two countries has been subject to some criticism. In an analysis of homicide that favored structural explanations, Lenton (1989) suggested that differences in violence between Canada and the United States had more to do with social structural factors than cultural differences. For Lenton, factors such as differences in racial composition and economic inequality were argued as being more important for explaining the differences in the two countries' homicide rates. Yet, like Hagan, Lenton's analysis was undertaken during a period when rates of homicide were rising in both countries and little attention was directed at explaining why rates of homicide were rising in both countries.

Shortly after Lenton's article appeared in the *Canadian Journal of Criminology*, Kennedy, Forde, and Silverman (1989) provided a useful commentary in that same journal which noted that certain key points need to be considered in order to undertake a more theoretically informed comparative analysis of American and Canadian homicide. They noted that in both countries, homicide rates vary considerably by region. In the United States rates tend to be highest in the south, while in Canada rates generally increase traveling from east to west. Another critical factor is the nature of victim-offender relationships. To understand intimate-partner homicide, for example, may require a different conceptual framework than what would be needed to explain the phenomena of gang-related killings. The same logic also applies for multiple-victim shootings (like the 2012 Lanza shooting in Newtown, Connecticut) compared to those where there is a single victim. Finally, the issue of race clearly needs to be factored in as well. In the United States blacks are overrepresented in homicide rates, while in Canada Aboriginal people are killed and are charged in disproportionate numbers. Therefore, arguments focusing on cultural or structural explanations of overall homicide rates between the two countries should not neglect regional, situational, and circumstantial differences as they most definitely affect violence.

In more recent years, with the drops that have taken place in levels of homicide in both countries—even though the United States continues to have a homicide rate about three times greater than Canada's—rather than focusing on the differences between the two nations' homicide rates, comparative explanations have tried to come to terms with the similarity in homicide trends in the two countries. Consider the trend lines contained in Figure 3.3 where US and Canadian homicide rates are graphed on two independent Y axes. Here we make

**Figure 3.3 Homicide rates per 100,000 population for United States and Canada: 1961–2011 on two independent Y-axis scales**

two notable observations. The first is the drop that has taken place in both US and Canadian homicide rates that began in the early to mid-1990s. The second is the similarity in both lines throughout the entire fifty-year period. In fact, research by Ouimet (2002) has shown that these similar peaks and valleys in the two countries rates of homicide have existed since the early twentieth century.

Not long after homicide rates began to decline in both nations, analysts were confronted with trying to come to terms with explaining these shifts. As will be shown, while some explanations are amenable to empirical testing, others are less open to testing. And for the ones that are testable, no single explanation has been widely accepted or endorsed by academia or policymakers. For the most part, these accounts can be grouped into two categories: criminal-justice-system-related explanations and non-criminal-justice-system explanations. I shall begin with a review of a viewpoint from the former category: that of rising prison populations.

At first glance it may seem, certainly at least in the United States, that rising prison populations are the reason why homicide rates in America are at their lowest point since the early 1960s; more bad guys in jail equals fewer bad guys on the streets. In correlational terms, the number of inmates incarcerated between the early 1990s and 2011 has nearly doubled, while over that same time period the homicide rate has fallen by about half. So there is certainly a strong correlation at play here. The logic behind why increases in incarceration have led to a decline in homicide may also have to do with the fact that 20 percent of inmates in the United States are serving sentences of twenty years to life (Moore 2009). In addition, since criminological research shows that violent offending peaks for males when they are in their mid-twenties, many inmates are now being released from prison during a period in their lives when they are older and much less likely to be engaged in violent crime. Research in New York suggests that this may be happening (cf. Conklin 2003). However, when looking at the bigger picture, both in other US states and also in Canada in terms of incarceration rates, this argument loses strength. In Texas, for example, where rates of incarceration were also rising to levels which were considerably greater than the national average, the state experienced only a minor drop in homicide during the time period studied. In fact, the drop in Texas was far behind the drop that took place in homicide rates in California, where growth in levels of incarceration were more modest (Ouimet 2002). In Canada, where levels of incarceration have been relatively constant from 1993–2011 (Dauvergne 2012), homicide rates fell by over 20 percent.

A second criminal-justice-system explanation posits that changes in policing practices have caused a shift in homicide, particularly in the United States. The increased use of stop-and-search gun controls and the increased use of computer technology have been argued to have lowered crime, including murder (Eck and Maguire 2000, cited in Ouimet 2002). In fact, many in the law-enforcement community attribute New York's crime reduction in the 1990s (including homicide) to specific "get-tough" policies carried out by former mayor Rudolph Giuliani's administration.

> The most prominent of his policy changes was the aggressive policing of lower-level crimes, a policy which has been dubbed the "broken windows" approach to law enforcement. In this view, small disorders lead to larger ones and perhaps even to crime. As Mr. Giuliani told the press in 1998, "Obviously murder and graffiti are two vastly different crimes. But they are part of the same continuum, and a climate that tolerates one is more likely to tolerate the other." (www.nber.org/digest/jan03/w9061.html)

Despite the growth and popularity of broken-windows policing, research suggests that reductions in homicide have not been caused by more aggressive policing of "antisocial behavior." For example, rates of violent crime in New York City were already on their way down before broken-windows policing was adopted; other jurisdictions in the country (San Diego, for example) also experienced a drop in homicide during this period when a community-policing model was in effect—an approach basically antithetical to broken-windows policing (Weisburb et al. 2006). The same sort of trend is also evident in Toronto, Canada's largest city. In the late 1990s, the Toronto Police Service endorsed a style of policing that was in many ways informed by the broken-windows model, yet homicide rates were falling in Toronto before the change in policing practice (O'Grady et al. forthcoming).

Non-criminal-justice factors have also been offered to explain drops in homicide in both countries. Changes in the illegal-drug trade, legalized abortion, the "civilizing process," demographic explanations, and improvements in medical trauma technology have all been credited with the drops that have taken place in rates of homicide, particularly in the United States. Let us first consider the role played by changes that have apparently taken place in the illegal street-drug trade.

### Changes in the Crack Cocaine Drug Market

Over fifteen years ago a report from the National Institute of Justice (1997) suggested that drops in crack cocaine use explain why homicide rates began to decline in several US cities beginning in the mid-1990s. The study found a strong correlation between changes in crack use in the "criminal population" and homicide rates. The study tracked homicide rates and crack use in six cities in the United States from 1987 to 1993, using data on drug use obtained from the Justice Department's program to test newly arrested individuals for narcotics when they are taken into custody. In five of the six study cities, the report found that homicide rates followed closely with cocaine-use levels among the adult male arrestee population. The report noted that when homicide rates increased in the mid-1980s with the advent of the crack epidemic, rates of positive cocaine tests simultaneously increased. Similarly, when homicide rates declined, cocaine-test positive rates also generally declined. The report, however, did not specifically address the question of why crack use declined. Some suggest that crack cocaine lost its luster because the drug increasingly became associated with sensationalized media images of "crackheads" and "crack babies" and thus caused a decline in new users during this time (Bowling 1999).

Some criticized the study, claiming that its sample of cities was too small and did not include some large cities like New York. Fagan et al. (1998), for example, remarked that the study failed to account for rising unemployment, increasing income inequality, and growing racial segregation, all of which caused urban decay in cities, thereby making more marginalized people susceptible to crack use and the culture associated with drugs, guns, and gangs.

## Abortion and Homicide

The effect of legalized abortion on homicide (sometimes referred to as the Donohue-Levitt hypothesis) is the proposition that legalized abortion has reduced crime, including homicide. Because unwanted children grow up in less loving and more unstable environments, they are more likely to become criminals, even murderers, when they get older, runs the argument. The evidence to support this contention is, for the most part, based on the inverse correlation between the availability of legalized abortion and subsequent homicide. Donohue and Levitt (2001) assert that eighteen years after the landmark *Roe v. Wade* US Supreme Court decision, levels of homicide in the United States began to fall in the early 1990s. In other words, murder rates began to fall at a time when non-aborted, and therefore unwanted, young men would have been coming of age. There is of course no way of proving a causal relationship between legalized abortion and homicide, since there is no way of knowing whether if these abortions had not occurred that crime rates would have persisted or even increased. Moreover, abortion rates in the United States peaked in the mid-1980s, and since then have generally been on the decline (CDC 2010). Incidentally, before his death in May 2103, Henry Morgentaler, a well-known Canadian pro-choice advocate and abortion physician, also made similar claims and used comparable logic to explain declines in Canadian homicide (National Post 2001).

## The Civilizing Process

A "civilizing process," according to another group of analysts, is responsible for the decline in homicide. Research by Pinker (2011), for example, argues that the past—where revenge, sadism, and tribalism were the norm—was a much more violent period than the present. Due to the spread of government, literacy, trade, and cosmopolitanism, human beings increasingly control their impulses, empathize with others, bargain rather than plunder, and deploy powers of reason to reduce the temptations of engaging in violence. While arguments like this may explain the decline of violence over the centuries, it is difficult to fathom that such monumental changes in the human condition could have transformed so suddenly in the United States in the mid-1990s.

*Lethality*

The concept of lethality has also been used as an explanation to understand why the homicide rate has declined in both Canada and the United States in recent years. Unlike the previous explanations that have been reviewed in this chapter, this theory is more amenable to empirical testing. According to Harris, Thomas, Fisher, and Hirsch (2002), advances in medical science mean that some violent crimes that would have been homicides in the past are now aggravated assaults (to use US legal language). In other words, largely because of advances in technology (for example, air medevac services), medics are able to arrive at crime scenes more quickly today than in the past; when they do arrive, they are able to keep patients with stab or gunshot wounds alive while en route to hospital trauma units. Upon arrival at the hospital, sophisticated medical treatment means that fewer stab and gunshot victims succumb to their injuries. They argue that research on the causes and prevention of homicide would be better focused on serious assaults, of which only a small percentage today result in death.

Andresen (2007) was able to test this theory with data from Canada and the United States. However, after a rigorous statistical analysis, the medical-science hypothesis was shown not to be "robust." The analysis showed that there was no disparity in rates of aggravated assault and homicide, trends that would need to have occurred in order to support this theory. The main reason suggested about why advances in medical trauma have not had much of an impact on lowering homicide rates is because "victims of homicide have been, and continue to be, dead or almost dead before they receive any medical attention" (201–202).

*A Demographic Effect*

The final explanation, which is also relatively receptive to empirical testing, is what researchers refer to as the "demographic effect." The idea here is that as the proportion of people (particularly males) in the high-offending age groups (fifteen to thirty years) decreases, so does the homicide rate. However, according to a study by Sprott and Cesaroni (2002) that reviewed research testing this hypothesis in the United States and their own analysis using Canadian homicide data, there was little evidence from either country to support the idea that demographic changes were responsible for lower homicide rates. In fact, their analysis of Canada showed that only 14 percent of the decrease in rates of Canadian homicide that took place from 1995–1999 were due to changes in the age structure of the population. According to their review of research in the United States that explored the impact that demographic changes had on American homicide rates, not much was found to be related to demographic shifts in the population.

## Where Do We Go from Here?

As this review has shown, several explanations have purported to explain both why the rate of homicide is greater in the United States than it is in Canada and why rates of lethal violence have been falling in both countries in recent years. For the latter group of explanations, analysts normally look for one common factor (or interrelated sets of factors) that would explain these changes. However, there is currently no overwhelming proof that would support any one of these theories. It remains unclear why homicide rates are greater in the United States than they are in Canada, and there is no certainty about what has caused homicide rates to decline in both countries for almost the past twenty years. This impasse, I argue, puts the homicide-research community at a crossroad. On the one hand, analysts can continue to draw upon macro-level data and correlate/ regress structural factors (for example, abortion rates, incarceration rates, advances in trauma technology, policing styles, drug markets, demographics) or cultural factors (for example, culture of fear, gun culture, civilizing processes, national psyches) with rates of homicide, focusing on units of analysis such as nation-states, regions, provinces, or cities.

Another way of thinking about this is to change the unit of analysis altogether and focus our attention on homicides that take place in neighborhoods. We all know that cities such as New Orleans, Washington, DC, and Detroit have relatively high homicide rates compared to the national average. Yet there are some neighborhoods within these cities where homicides are rare. Focusing on what goes on in neighborhoods has been drawing greater attention in what has been described as the "new neighborhood effects" literature (Sampson et al. 2002). This line of thinking has been used to inform some recent homicide research in the United States. For example, Kubrin and Weitzer (2003) showed that in St. Louis, Missouri, the spatial distribution of retaliatory homicide is most likely to occur in the highest-disadvantaged neighborhoods. In another spatial analysis carried out in southeast Los Angeles, Griffith and Tita (2009) found that lethal violence was more likely to be concentrated in neighborhoods that were characterized by concentrations of public housing.

Perhaps one of the most strident calls for promoting a neighborhood agenda can be found in Robert Sampson's 2012 Presidential Address to the American Society of Criminology. In the address, Sampson made the case that place—as manifested in neighborhoods—has an important impact on crime and that researchers need to better understand how neighborhoods shape human behavior. Basing this argument largely on the results of his book *The Great American City: Chicago and the Enduring Neighborhood* (2012), Sampson argues that neighborhood context has a profound influence on the social well-being of its residents. Levels of crime and violence are seen to be closely linked to levels of collective efficacy (cohesion and trust among neighbors). Community-level variations in civic engagement, neighborhood change, residential moves and neighborhood migration, leadership networks, elites, and urban inequality all coalesce to influence levels of crime and violence (Sampson 2013).

Arguably, within the Canadian context, this way of thinking may also be relevant when it comes to understanding the distribution of homicide at the city level. Consider Toronto, where the homicide rate in 2011 was 1.6 per 100,000 people. On this basis, the city is often touted in the media as being one of Canada's safest cities, given that its homicide rate is below the national average (1.7 per 100,000 in 2011). In fact, Statistics Canada noted that in 2011 there were thirteen Census Metropolitan Areas (CMAs) in Canada that had higher homicide rates than Toronto (Winnipeg was the CMA with the highest rate, at 5.08 per 100,000 population) (Perreault 2012). However, if we drill down a bit deeper and explore rates of homicide at the neighborhood level in Toronto, a completely different picture emerges. There are some neighborhoods where there are few or no reported homicides, yet there are others where homicide rates are greater than the American national average. For example, using 2011 data, forty-five homicides were recorded by police in Toronto. This translates into an aggregate homicide rate of 1.6 per 100,000 population. However, when homicide rates are broken down according to Toronto's seventeen police divisions, arguably representing at least seventeen different neighborhoods, rates range from 0 per 100,000 in 52 Division to 5 per 100,000 in 31 Division. The overall rate of 1.6 per 100,000 is therefore simply an arithmetic mean derived from data taken from a city where homicide rates vary extensively according to neighborhood. Taking this fact into account, it may be more productive to understand why there are low levels of homicidal activity in downtown Toronto while there are alarmingly high rates in the northwestern, suburban region of the city. Indeed, there is some reason to believe that these differences are linked to the types of processes that Sampson has identified are also at work in Chicago. The area of the city, or neighborhood, that had the highest homicide rate, with an average rate homicide rate of 5.1 per 100,000 population from 2005 to 2011, is known as the Jane and Finch corridor, located in the northwest section of the city. According to research by Hulchanski (2010), Toronto is increasingly being divided into a city of wealthy neighborhoods and poor neighborhoods, with fewer middle-income neighborhoods. The Jane and Finch area of the city is increasingly losing ground, especially compared to more centrally located neighborhoods in the city which are in the process of or have already undergone gentrification and urban renewal. Compared to the rest of Toronto, the Jane and Finch area has a higher rate of new immigrants, a higher rate of youth and children, a higher rate of single parents, a higher rate of low-income families, a higher proportion of rental households, a higher rate of unemployment, a lower percentage of population with university education (despite being located next to York University), and a higher percentage of population with less than a high-school education (www.cbc.ca/fifth/lostinthestruggle/hood.html). It may not be a coincidence, then, that the area also has a homicide rate that surpasses the American average. It would also be interesting to know if illegal handgun ownership and possession is greater in this neighborhood than is the case in neighborhoods where homicide rates are lower. Also interesting would be the exploration of the victim-offender relationships of those involved in such lethal violence.

It is beyond the scope of this chapter to provide a more detailed analysis of homicide at the neighborhood level in Toronto, or in other Canadian neighborhoods for that matter. However, to understand the social dynamics of homicide, it may be wise for more research to use the neighborhood as the unit of analysis and pay more attention to the community context. Even though research has shown the complexities that are involved in properly measuring and defining neighborhoods (Hipp and Boessen 2013), if one is interested in understanding why homicide rates are changing (increasing or decreasing), or why some cities, provinces/states, or even countries have different levels of homicide, exploring neighborhood as the context may be a worthwhile direction to pursue—whether it be in urban, suburban, or even rural areas. Changes in homicide rates that are recorded in a city over time are really just a summation of aggregate changes that have taken place in homicides at the neighborhood level.

## Conclusion

There is no doubt that moving the unit of analysis down to the level of the neighborhood would pose significant challenges for comparative homicide research, particularly those that are tied to data-availability, definitional, and measurement issues. However, given the lack of explanatory power that currently exists in homicide research at the macro level,[2] criminologists may be wise to look more carefully at the role played by community-level influences for understanding lethal violence without losing sight of the broader political and economic context within which neighborhoods exist. Indeed, analysts of homicide cannot lose sight of the neoliberal shifts that are occurring in Canada and the United States, which have a direct bearing on why some neighborhoods maintain or enhance their vitality while others continue to struggle or even cease to exist altogether. This phenomenon can be seen in some neighborhoods in deindustrialized cities like Detroit. At the same time, however, we must be mindful that even in the most violent and crime-prone neighborhoods, the vast majority of citizens are not murderers. There is a fine line between taking crime seriously in historically troubled neighborhoods and stereotyping and typecasting all residents as members of a violent underclass (cf. O'Grady et al. 2010).

## Notes

Special thanks to Jessica Rumboldt, who provided assistance on an earlier draft of this chapter.

1. While there are some definitional differences between how homicides are defined in the developed countries (including Canada and the United States), this chapter follows the precedent of comparing homicide rates between developed countries which has been endorsed by the United Nations Office on Drugs and Crime (www.unodc .org).

2. This includes taking into account the well-known and influential study by Land, McCall, and Cohen (1990).

# Chapter 4

# *The Usual Suspects*

## *Violent Media, Guns, and Mental Illness*

### Jaclyn V. Schildkraut and Glenn W. Muschert

"WHEN SOMETHING LIKE THIS HAPPENS, EVERYBODY SAYS IT'S AN EPIDEMIC, and that's just not true" (Amanda Nickerson, in Glaberson 2012). While this reaction to the December 14, 2012, shooting at Sandy Hook Elementary School[1] is one of the more realistic responses to the event, it also is rather uncharacteristic. When news breaks about a school shooting, most people struggle to come to terms with the tragedy and begin their quest for answers to a number of questions. One of the most elusive answers is to the question of "why" the event has happened (Schildkraut 2012a).

In an effort to answer this question, two groups have emerged as key narrators of the school-shootings story. First, the mass media are responsible for breaking the news and providing the audience with information on the shooters, the victims, and the events. Once the audience receives this information, they then turn to the second group—politicians—to report on the response and get the "official reaction." In addition to seeking answers to why these events happen, members of society also rely on their elected representatives and political figures to help put the event in perspective, and to look for ways to prevent the next tragedy. Both of these key narrators are filtered through mass media, as journalists themselves frame and comment upon the tragedies, and as politicians reach their constituents and broader audiences via media reportage.

New Hampshire senator Kelly Ayotte recently weighed in on the tragedy in Newtown, stating, "Ultimately when we look at what happened in Sandy Hook we should have a fuller discussion to make sure that it doesn't happen again" (Kelly Ayotte, quoted in Associated Press 2013). While a similar sentiment has been echoed following other mass shootings in schools, both the media and politicians continue to focus on three major themes—guns, mental health, and violent media. This discourse may be supplemented by considerations of individual and sociological causes, including the roles of family, religion, and community. These latter topics, however, play a supporting role to the stories' main cast of issues around which to frame school massacres.

While these stories are presented to the public in a neat, succinct news package or article, the reality is not quite so simple. Rarely can events so unpredictable and difficult to explain be reduced to a simple narrative; yet this doesn't stop the media and politicians from trying. This chapter explores the discursive construction of school-shootings stories, from how the media covers these events to the themes interwoven through the political rhetoric. Specifically, we examine three prominent school shootings—2012's Sandy Hook as well as its equally infamous predecessors Columbine (1999)[2] and Virginia Tech (2007)[3]—and how relatively short-lived, random events have turned into unprecedented "media spectacles" (Kellner 2003, 2008a, 2008b) and moral panics (Burns and Crawford 1999; Schildkraut, Elsass, and Stafford 2013; Springhall 1999).

## We Interrupt This Program
## with Breaking News of a Shooting . . .

When news of a school shooting breaks, the media rush to the scene to begin a barrage of coverage that can last days and even weeks. News stations, particularly twenty-four-hour news networks such as CNN, Fox News, and MSNBC, cover every facet of these stories during their wall-to-wall coverage (Elsass and Schildkraut 2013). Newspapers capture audiences with sensationalized headlines and are able to generate more stories between printings through their digital counterparts (Elsass and Schildkraut 2013). The end result is that these relatively uncommon events are highly sensationalized, thereby making them appear considerably more common than they are (Kellner 2008a; Surette 1992).

Following Newtown, journalist David Carr (2013) wrote that "[our] job as journalists is to draw attention, to point at things, and what we choose to highlight is defined as news." As most people will never experience a school shooting, the media become their only outlet to these phenomena (Jewkes 2004;

Mayr and Machin 2012; Robinson 2011). Researchers have shown that for up to 95 percent of the general public, any information they receive, particularly about crime, comes via the media (Graber 1980; Surette 1992). It then appears that the media must operate under the motto, as Uncle Ben told Peter Parker in *Spiderman*, "with great power comes great responsibility" (Ziskin, Bryce, and Raimi 2002). Yet does this happen?

In a 2013 article, *New York Times* opinion columnist Ross Douthat tackled this quandary. In his analysis of partisanship in the media, Douthat (2013) suggests that the mainstream media act "as a crusading vanguard while denying, often self-righteously, that anything of the sort is happening." Though this statement was made in the context of the nation's fiscal crisis, he goes on to link it to the recent Newtown shootings:

> The trouble is that when you set out to "lead" a conversation, you often end up deciding where it goes, which side wins the arguments and even who gets to participate. (Douthat 2013)

This trouble is often the result of the discord between journalistic neutrality and editorial choices (Douthat 2013). He discusses two particular editorial choices that are especially relevant to the public's understanding of school shootings.

First, Douthat (2013) notes some stories receive continuous, or "wall-to-wall," coverage, while others are buried. Columbine, for instance, became the biggest news story of its year, as well being one of the most followed stories of the entire decade (Pew Research Center for the People and the Press 1999; Robinson 2011). Similarly, the shootings at Virginia Tech were the biggest story of a news week that included coverage of the war in Iraq, a Supreme Court ruling on abortion, and the upcoming presidential election (Pew Research Center for the People and the Press 2007). Sandy Hook was the second most-followed story of 2012, falling a close second to that year's presidential election (Pew Research Center for the People and the Press 2012). The end result is that the media focus on several high-profile cases, which can give viewers a misinformed understanding of the frequency of occurrence (Burns and Crawford 1999; Kellner 2008a; Muschert 2007a; Muschert and Ragnedda 2010; Newman 2006). In reality, school shootings occur at an average of fewer than ten events per year (Schildkraut 2012a).

Beyond where the story ranks in terms of perceived importance, the sheer volume of coverage these events receive also greatly influences public understanding of these events, as the continuous coverage makes these events all but inescapable. For the first month following Columbine, for example, three of the major networks—ABC, CBS, and NBC—devoted a minimum of half of their evening-news coverage to the shooting, totaling 319 stories (Robinson 2011). Another study (Maguire, Weatherby, and Mathers 2002) found similar results when examining the first week of coverage of Columbine compared to thirteen other shootings. The same three major networks aired fifty-three stories and four hours of coverage on Columbine, while the remaining shootings *combined* totaled nearly the same amount of coverage (Maguire et al. 2002). Following the Virginia Tech shooting, particularly after NBC News released the shooter's multimedia manifesto, the backlash from the volume of coverage was so pervasive that NBC executives limited their coverage of the event to 10 percent of total airtime (Schildkraut 2012b). Prior to this, however, CNN and Fox News had registered 1.4 million and 1.8 million viewers, respectively, on the day of the shooting (Garofoli 2007). By comparison, these networks typically averaged 450,000 (CNN) and 900,000 (Fox News) daily viewers in the year prior to the shootings (Pew Research Center's Project for Excellence in Journalism 2006).

Following Columbine, over 10,000 stories about the shooting appeared in the nation's top fifty newspapers (Newman 2006), including 170 articles published in the *New York Times* alone (Chyi and McCombs 2004; Muschert and Carr 2006). More than 130 articles were published between the *Times* and the *New York Post* following Virginia Tech (Schildkraut 2012a). Coverage of Sandy Hook in the *New York Times* in the month following the shooting also exceeded 130 articles, excluding op-eds and blogs (Schildkraut and Muschert 2014). Increases in media coverage also can be observed through online-coverage statistics. Following Virginia Tech, for instance, MSNBC.com registered 108.8 million page views (Garofoli 2007). On an average day, the site registers around 400,000 page views (TheWebStats.com). What is perhaps most staggering about these numbers is that other shootings—such as the 1999 Conyers, Georgia, shooting (one month after Columbine); the 2008 Northern Illinois University shooting; or the 2012 Chardon, Ohio, high-school shooting—have failed to garner the same level of media attention. This confirms Kellner's (2003, 2008a, 2008b) theory of the "media spectacle" related to Columbine, Virginia Tech, and Sandy Hook, each of which have become iconic and archetypal of school shootings in their own right.

Douthat (2013) also notes that a conscious decision is made to cast one side as aggressors and the other as the aggrieved.[4] This is perhaps easier to discern when examining mass murder in schools, as there is a clear aggressor (the shooter) and aggrieved (the victims). With the media, however, the conscious decision is less about who is cast in which role and more about which actor gets the most coverage and airtime. While a considerable amount of coverage of the Columbine victims appeared across major news outlets—such as the *New York Times*, Associated Press, ABC News, CNN, and PBS News (Muschert 2007b)—the majority of the coverage centered on the shooters, Eric Harris and Dylan Klebold (Muschert 2007b; Schildkraut and Muschert 2014). One of the most iconic images published of the shooting was a still frame of the shooters in the school's cafeteria, which made the December 1999 cover of *Time* magazine (Schildkraut and Muschert 2014).

A similar disparity in coverage between the aggressor and the aggrieved also was noted in the case of Virginia Tech. In 113 articles examined from the *New York Times* and the *New York Post*, there were a total of 413 references (177 and 236, respectively) to the shooter, Seung-Hui Cho (Schildkraut 2012a). By comparison, there were fewer than one hundred references combined between the two papers for all thirty-two victims (Schildkraut 2012a). Additionally, in both Muschert's (2007b) and Schildkraut's (2012a) examinations of the coverage of these events, it was observed that the media created further disparity with their reporting of selected individuals. In each case, only a handful of victims received an increased amount of attention, whereas most victims received only one or two mentions, if they were covered at all (Muschert 2007b; Schildkraut 2012a).

While the coverage of the Sandy Hook shooting also clearly defined the aggressor (shooter Adam Lanza) and the aggrieved (the twenty first-grade students and six of their educators), this coverage visibly departed from the framework laid out by the earlier events (Schildkraut and Muschert 2014). Specifically, a considerably larger amount of coverage focused on reporting on the victims rather than the shooter (Schildkraut and Muschert 2014). While additional research is needed to understand the full impact of this new reporting trend, Sandy Hook marked one of the first shifts from "offender-centered reporting" to "victim-centered reporting" (Schildkraut and Muschert 2014, 22), a developing discourse that dovetails with effects to identify who (or what) is responsible for such attacks.

## Who Is to Blame?

Perhaps one of the more interesting discourses to have emerged following each of these school shootings is the idea that the cause of the event *must* be bigger than the shooters themselves. It is not acceptable just to say that one or two angry young men went into a school and committed homicide. Instead, the idea is that there has to be some greater reason why these events have occurred, in order to make what has happened understandable, or possibly even manageable.

While the media fuel this speculation, they often do so by serving as a vehicle for politicians, pundits, and the public to weigh in. The sources of these narratives have separated themselves into two different camps: proponents of individual causes and proponents of social causes.

## Individual Responsibility

It is possible that, although the answer cannot be as simple as "they were angry," the shooters themselves can be held responsible for their actions. What is perhaps more noticeable in this discourse, however, is that this accountability is perceived more as the result of some sort of individual defect that has turned these young males into killers. These arguments tend to deny the influence of the social world, and place the blame solely on the offenders. By doing so, it becomes unnecessary to acknowledge any shortcomings in the sociological structure, and less necessary to demand change in the prevailing structure.

One such sentiment suggests individual affect or personality defects as causative. For example, former vice president Dan Quayle, in the wake of Columbine, commented that "The overriding issue isn't really gun control—it's self-control" (in Seelye 1999). Vikki Buckley, the Colorado secretary of state at the time Columbine occurred, was quoted as saying, "Guns are not the issue. Hate, what pulled the trigger of violence, is the issue" (in Seelye and Brooke 1999). Similar sentiments followed Newtown: "A gun didn't kill all those children, a disturbed man killed all those children" (Scott Ostrosky, in Moss and Rivera 2012).

In other instances, it is not so much the presence of a negative characteristic as much as it is the absence of ones considered to be positive. One of the main points of argument in this instance is religion. This discourse was the most prominent following Columbine, particularly as the area is extremely religious and because there were rumors that two of the victims, Rachel Scott and Cassie Bernall, were killed for affirming their belief in God to the shooters (Muschert 2007b). Dan Quayle opined, "A child who loves God, honors his parents and respects his neighbors will not kill anyone" (in Seelye 1999). In an interview on *Larry King Live* following the event, then-Vice President Al Gore elaborated, saying:

> We have with our power of conscience, with our beliefs in God, if we have those, as most of us Americans do, we have the ability to—to overcome those impulses with higher ones. We have the ability to overcome evil with good. (in Walker 1999)

Interestingly, following the Virginia Tech shootings, discussion of religion was notably absent, with the exception of a single line in an editorial:

> Over the next few days, we'll ponder the sources of Cho Seung-Hui's rage. There'll be no shortage of analysts picking apart his hatreds, his feelings of oppression and his dark war against the rich, Christianity and the world at large. (Brooks 2007)

This statement, though not directly implicating religion (or a lack thereof) in the shooting, is indicative of how people dissect these events and their perpetrators looking for answers.

Following the Sandy Hook shooting, the minimal amount of discourse centered on how religion benefits those who are healing:

> It is a failure of community, and that's where the answer for the future has to lie. What religion has to offer to people at moments like this—more than theology, more than divine presence—is community. (Greg Epstein [Harvard's humanist chaplain], in Freedman 2012)

What is particularly interesting about the Sandy Hook case is that, unlike the town of Littleton, which was heavily skewed toward Christian evangelicals (Muschert 2007b), Newtown's residents held more diverse religious beliefs. More importantly, this suggests that Adam Lanza was potentially excluded from this community (which is discussed in the next section).

The shooters were not the only source of blame following these events. Perhaps one of the greatest lightning rods for criticism in the school-shootings discourse has been the National Rifle Association (NRA). Formed in 1871 to promote marksmanship and shooting as a sport, the NRA has grown into "America's longest standing civil-rights organization," seeking to protect the Second Amendment right to bear arms and promote firearms education (www. NRA.com). What is most interesting, and easily overlooked in this ongoing feud between the two sides, is that the NRA's responses to these shootings have not been markedly different from the responses from other parties.

In fact, the NRA was scheduled to hold their annual meeting and exhibition in Denver in the weeks following Columbine. Out of respect, the exhibitions were cancelled and only the annual business meeting was held (Seelye and Brooke 1999). In a statement presented at the meeting, NRA president Wayne LaPierre said, "We believe in absolutely gun-free, zero-tolerance, totally safe schools" (in Seelye and Brooke 1999). Similar statements also were made following the shooting at Virginia Tech. When asked about legislative improvements for reporting mental-health issues to background-check systems, LaPierre responded, "We are not an obstacle. We're strongly in support of putting those records in the system" (in Luo 2007). Still, when the public, the media, and politicians are looking to point fingers, the NRA has been an easy target.

## Collective Responsibility

Some proffered causes for school shootings are simply too broad to target just one individual or group. Instead, the focus shifts to social causes, and ultimately, the need for social change. These discussions imply that there is something wrong with the prevailing social environment. By extension, therefore, the only way to fix the "problem" of school massacres is to restructure parts of our collective sociology. As Utah senator Orrin Hatch mused after Columbine, "We all know this is a much more complex problem than guns" (in Bruni 1999).

One of the most prevalent social causes blamed for these mass shootings is community. This refers not only to community in the traditional sense of neighborhoods and towns, but also to the communities within communities, such as schools and their subcultures. Following Columbine, the typical culture of cliques seen in high schools around the nation was immediately fingered as one potential cause for the shooting. Like many other schools, Columbine placed a heavy emphasis on its athletic programs, and rumors suggesting that Harris and Klebold had specifically sought out "jocks" in their rampage did not help to dispel this myth (Larkin 2007).

The role of subcultures within schools was heavily blamed as the cause for Columbine. Harris and Klebold were named as members of the "Trenchcoat Mafia," which was rumored to be a group of misfits who didn't subscribe to the traditional high school culture of proms and pep rallies, and instead opted for "Goth rock" and black duster jackets or camouflage, military-style clothing (Frymer 2009; Larkin 2007; Springhall 1999). As one Massachusetts principal summarized:

> In these big high-powered suburban high schools, there's a very dominant winner culture, including the jocks, the advanced-placement kids, the student government and, depending on the school, the drama kids or the service clubs. But the winners are a smaller group than we'd like to think, and high school life is very different for those who experience it as the losers. They become part of the invisible middle and suffer in silence, alienated and without any real connection to any adult. (Carol Miller Lieber, in Lewin 1999)

Beyond the divide within the school's walls, some have mused that suburban communities also are to blame for the shootings. Columbine and other school shootings represented a shift of violence from an inner-city problem to a threat to the perceived safety of suburban and rural communities (Schildkraut et al. 2013). As one writer noted:

> Created as safe havens from the sociological ills of cities, suburbs now stand accused of creating their own environmental diseases: lack of character and the grounding principles of identity, lack of diversity or the tolerance it engenders, lack of attachment to shared civic ideals. Increasingly, the newest, largest suburbs are being criticized as landscapes scorched by unthoughtful, repetitive building, where, it has been suggested, the isolations of larger lots and a car-based culture may lead to disassociation from the reality of contact with other people. (Hamilton 1999)

Another problem associated with suburban communities is the lack of parental presence. In many instances, children of suburban families become latchkey kids as one or both parents commute into the nearest big city for work. Politicians campaigning on family values after Columbine, including George W. Bush, seized the opportunity to ponder this impact: "The fundamental issue is, Are you and your wife paying attention to children on a day-by-day, moment-by-moment basis?" (in Seelye 1999).

While the community design of Littleton, Colorado, was targeted as a cause for the Columbine shootings, an opposite discourse emerged following the Sandy Hook shooting. Newtown has been touted as a picturesque community, the kind of community that is ideal to raise children. With its sprawling homes (some even complete with picket fences and a dog in the yard), Newtown has even been described as "tak[ing] its child-friendly, Norman Rockwell ambience seriously" (Dwyer and Rueb 2012). In discourse following the Sandy Hook shooting, the ideal-community aspect was most prominently featured in coverage about healing and restoration, rather than as a catalyst for Lanza's rampage. As with many other facets of the story, Newtown's community aspect was portrayed as a case where they did everything right.

While high schools break into fragmented groups, and suburban communities have been credited with furthering such isolation, colleges and universities also have been labeled as ostracizing environments for school shooters. While institutions of higher education also are considered to be communities, they do not function in the traditional sense of the word. Due to their size and heterogeneity (in respects to demographics, majors, and a collection of other factors), postsecondary schools are bound to create barriers to forming strong ties to one's "community." For Cho, this isolation was furthered by his social disorder (selective mutism) and a disdain for mainstream student culture at Virginia Tech (Schildkraut 2012b).

## "Round Up the Usual Suspects"[5]

Beyond the specific individual and social causes that have been pinpointed in the political discourse, three specific culprits have emerged as the trifecta of causes of school shootings: violent media, mental health, and guns. These issues not only are consistent in discourses following each of these events, but also transcend the individual, community, and even macro-social levels of concern. What is perhaps most interesting, as Dr. Jeffrey Fagan notes, "Any one of these three risks separately does not produce a violent event. It's their convergence and interaction that produces an event" (as quoted in Stolberg 1999). It is, as Muschert (2007a) notes, the "perfect storm" for school shootings. Thus, in the public discourse about school massacres, these have emerged as the three-ring circus of blame, so to speak.

### Violent Media

A causal factor appearing in reportage of school massacres has been a focus on the shooters' reported consumption of violent media. In an editorial following Columbine, Bob Herbert (1999) summarized how our culture regards violence in the media:

> Welcome to America, a land where the killing is easy.... We make it exciting. We celebrate it, romanticize it, eroticize it, and mass-market the weapons that bring murder within easy reach of one and all. It's no big deal. Just pick up that handgun and drive down to the video store for a couple of exciting flicks about killing women. And if somebody cuts your car off along the way, shoot him.... We are addicted to violence. It sustains and entertains us.

Details released as part of the Columbine investigation indicated that both boys, but particularly Eric Harris, were fans of "Goth rock," such as Rammstein, KMFDM, and, most notoriously, Marilyn Manson. Manson was, in fact, scheduled to have a concert in Denver just after the shooting, but cancelled the concert date once he was linked to the shooting and people began boycotting the show. In an op-ed piece in *Rolling Stone* magazine, it was Manson (1999) who actually turned the tables on the media:

> From Jesse James to Charles Manson, the media, since their inception, have turned criminals into folk heroes. They just created two new ones when they plastered those dip-shits Dylan Klebold and Eric Harris' pictures on the front of every newspaper. Don't be surprised if every kid who gets pushed around has two new idols. We applaud the creation of a bomb whose sole purpose is to destroy all of mankind, and we grow up watching our president's brains splattered all over Texas. Times have not become more violent. *They have just become more televised.* (Emphasis added)

Although there were few, if any, links between Cho and Lanza and their consumption of violent media, this did not stop people from speculating that it was still a cause. Some posited that Cho drew his inspiration from the South Korean film *Oldboy*, which features a scene in which the main character exacts retribution on his tormentors (Hendrix 2007; Schildkraut 2012b). Cho was never linked to any violent video games. Lanza was rumored to have played *World of Warcraft* (Lichtblau 2013); this, however, has never been confirmed. It also is possible that this speculation is actually the byproduct of the media's linking of James Holmes, the perpetrator from the Aurora, Colorado, movie theater shooting just five months earlier, to the same game (Lichtblau 2013). Still, even without concrete evidence, politicians seized the opportunity to call out the media. Following Newtown, Chris Christie, the governor of New Jersey, stated

> I don't let games like Call of Duty in my house. You cannot tell me that a kid sitting in a basement for hours playing Call of Duty and killing people over and over and over again does not desensitize that child to the real-life effects of violence. (in Lichtblau 2013)

What seems to escape this discourse is the consideration of all of the people who consume these different media and *don't* become school shooters. Marilyn Manson has sold over 50 million albums worldwide (Blabbermouth.net 2010). The 1994 film *Natural Born Killers* grossed over $11 million in its opening weekend alone (BoxOffice.com, n.d.). It has been estimated that around 10 million people played *DOOM*, the game of choice for Columbine shooter Eric Harris, during the first two years of its 1993 release (*DOOM*, n.d). More recently, *Call of Duty: Black Ops 2* sold over 11 million units in its first week of release (Kain 2012).

Still, despite the millions of consumers who flock to these products for entertainment and don't, as Agger (2007) noted about Cho, "pump three bullets per victim," these coincidences have somehow become a soapbox for some on why violent media need to be outlawed. David Geffen, a record executive and film producer, questioned this platform, noting:

> Why not blame the libraries? They're full of violent books. If you're looking for violence, what about the evening news? America is bombing Yugoslavia; it's on every day. It's not a movie, it's real. (in Broder 1999)

Perhaps Alicia Silverstone's character Cher in the movie *Clueless* said it best: "Until mankind is peaceful enough not to have violence on the news, there's no point in taking it out of shows that need it for entertainment value" (Rudin et al. 1995).

## *Mental Health*

A second factor associated with school shootings is the frequent discussion of mental illnesses or disorders on the part of the shooters. Reports circled that Columbine shooter Eric Harris had been taking the antidepressant Luvox at the time of the shooting, which commonly is used to treat obsessive-compulsive disorder. Despite the fact that Harris wrote caustically about his hatred of his peers at Columbine, it was not until the coverage of the Virginia Tech shooting that the mental-health debate became more prominent. Inquiries into shooter Seung-Hui Cho revealed that he had a lengthy history of mental-health issues. Aside from the selective mutism (and a later diagnosis of major depression) that had plagued him since his family emigrated from South Korea when he was eight, Cho had left a number of clues about his mental state along his path at Virginia Tech. His writings became increasingly violent, and his behavior so bizarre that one professor had him removed after other students stopped attending class out of fear (Virginia Tech Review Panel [VTRP] 2007). He was extremely withdrawn, claimed to have a girlfriend named Jelly (a model), and in the rare instances he did attempt to communicate with anyone, usually a female student on campus, he did so through his alter ego "Question Mark" by leaving random scrawling on their dorm room message boards (VTRP 2007).

Following an incident in December 2005, in which the Virginia Tech Police Department (VTPD) were called to Cho's dorm after he randomly appeared at one student's door dressed in sunglasses and a hat, Cho threatened suicide to one of his suitemates, who then called the VTPD (VTRP 2007). Cho was taken to the station, where he was screened for mental illness by a member of the local community-service board (VTRP 2007). The screener determined that Cho was mentally ill, refused to seek treatment voluntarily, and posed an imminent danger to himself or others; the screener contacted a magistrate to secure a detention warrant (Bonnie, Reinhard, Hamilton, and McGarvey 2009; VTRP 2007). Cho was then transferred to St. Alban's Behavioral Health Center, where he underwent several examinations by independent, licensed mental-health professionals prior to a commitment hearing (Bonnie et al. 2009; VTRP 2007). Despite that these additional psychiatrists deemed Cho "an imminent danger to himself as a result of mental illness," the special justice presiding over the commitment hearing still ordered Cho to undergo outpatient treatment as a result of overcrowding at the state's facilities (VTRP 2007; see also Bonnie 2009).

At the time, the Virginia code (see § 37.2–819) required that anyone who had been admitted to a mental-health facility (either voluntarily or involuntarily) or who had been detained by a legal order must be reported to the Central Criminal Records Exchange (CCRE) (Schildkraut and Hernandez 2013). For Cho, his stint at St. Alban's was never reported, and subsequently, when he went to purchase his firearms, he was not flagged in the background-check system (Roberts 2009). When this information surfaced, then-Governor Timothy Kaine signed an executive order in Virginia requiring immediate reporting to the CCRE (Schildkraut and Hernandez 2013), while additional legislation to improve reporting was passed in twelve other states (Brady Campaign Press Release 2011). The following year, President George W. Bush signed into law the NICS Improvement Amendments Act and designated nearly $1.3 billion in federal grants to improve, update, and establish reporting systems (Schildkraut and Hernandez 2013).

Following the Newtown shooting, it was reported that shooter Adam Lanza had Asperger's syndrome, which is a high-functioning form of autism. This concern was immediately thrust into the discourse of the event and prompted fear and worry in others with the condition. In reality, as one doctor noted, "aggression in autism-spectrum disorders is almost never directed to people outside the family or immediate caregivers, is almost never planned, and almost never involves weapons" (Dr. Catherine Lord, as in Harmon 2012). Further, research has shown that no Asperger's patients (of those studied) had ever used a weapon and only about 2 percent had been aggressive toward someone outside their family (Harmon 2012). Still, as Lori Shery, president of an Asperger's advocacy group, noted:

The media's continued mention of a possible diagnosis of Asperger syndrome implies a connection between that and the heinous crime committed by the shooter. They may have just as well said, "Adam Lanza, age 20, was reported to have had brown hair." (in Harmon 2012)

## Guns

There is perhaps no greater or more controversial culprit in the blame game of school shootings than firearms. In the aftermath of these events, the NRA and like-minded gun proponents have suggested that more guns, and subsequently fewer restrictions on guns (such as easing campus bans prohibiting concealed weapons), would help to protect the good guys from the bad guys. Following Columbine, Charlton Heston, who then was president of the NRA, suggested that "If there had been even one armed guard in the school, he could have saved a lot of lives and perhaps ended the whole thing instantly" (in Verhovek 1999). Despite the presence of a school resource officer on campus the day of the shooting, Minnesota governor Jesse Ventura added that Columbine "supports conceal-and-carry because of the fact that what happens when a group of unarmed individuals are confronted with people with weapons like this, you have no defense" (in Verhovek 1999). While pro-gun advocates were virtually silent following Virginia Tech—as the main discourse, even when guns were involved, focused on mental health—the debate was immediately recharged after Sandy Hook. Wayne LaPierre, current president of the NRA, responded to the shooting by saying, "The only thing that stops a bad guy with a gun is a good guy with a gun" (in Bilton 2013). He then suggested that every school should have armed guards by the time classes resumed in the spring (Bilton 2013).

Conversely, those in opposition have claimed that it is the ease and availability of guns that led to the shootings in the first place. Some even suggest that besides being unrealistic in terms of manpower and financial resources, placing armed security guards or law enforcement at every single school nationwide would do nothing to prevent such attacks:

There were two armed law enforcement officers at that campus [Columbine], and you see what happened—15 dead. (Senator Dianne Feinstein, in Bilton 2013)

People like Mr. LaPierre want us to believe that civilians can be trained to use lethal force with cold precision in moments of fear and crisis. That requires a willful ignorance about the facts. Police officers know that firing a weapon is a huge risk; that's why they avoid doing it. In August [2012], New York City police officers opened fire on a gunman outside the Empire State Building. They killed him and wounded nine bystanders. (Rosenthal 2012)

The volatility in the back-and-forth argument between gun-control and gun-rights activists continued to grow as the state of New York passed one of the strictest gun-control packages within a month of the Sandy Hook shooting, while President Obama convened a panel on mass violence, led by Senator Joe Lieberman. With the support of the usual champions—California senator Dianne Feinstein, New York congresswoman Carolyn McCarthy, and New Jersey senator Frank Lautenberg—a number of gun-control measures were introduced. Still, given the partisan divide of Congress, it is unlikely that many of these measures will be enacted into law, as seen following Columbine (Schildkraut and Hernandez 2013; Soraghan 2000).

## A Rhetorical Ouroboros?[6]

In the movie *National Lampoon*'s *Van Wilder* (Abrams, Levy, and Becker 2002), the main character opined, "Worrying is like a rocking chair. It gives you something to do, but it doesn't get you anywhere." While this may seem to be an outrageous proposition in the context of school shootings, it does put the discourse in a perspective of sorts. In the aftermath of school shootings such as Columbine, Virginia Tech, and Sandy Hook, legislative bill after legislative bill are rushed to the floor, yet few (if any) pass. Following Columbine, more than 800 bills aimed at regulating gun ownership and gun shows were introduced, yet only about 10 percent of these bills were enacted into law (Soraghan 2000). It didn't bode well for legislators that the very issue they were trying to address had been figured out by high schoolers (Schildkraut 2012b). In a 1998 class paper, Eric Harris identified the gaps in the Brady bill for the control of gun sales that eventually enabled him (or more precisely, his friend) to purchase guns: "the biggest gaping hole is that background checks are only required for licensed dealers … not private dealers … private dealers can sell shotguns and rifles to anyone who is 18 or older" (Jefferson County Sheriff's Office 1999, 26, 538).

After Virginia Tech, and following the passage of the NICS Improvement Amendments Act, the majority of the funds made available were never claimed and millions of records still have not been added to background-check systems; these gaps leave many people who should be disqualified eligible to legally purchase firearms (Brady Campaign Press Release 2011; Witkin 2012). These lapses in reporting also enabled other mass shooters, including Jared Loughner (who recently pled guilty to the Tucson, Arizona, shooting of Arizona congresswoman Gabrielle Giffords and others, despite spending a year and a half classified as "incompetent to stand trial") and James Holmes (who shot seventy people at a midnight showing of *The Dark Knight Rises* in Aurora, Colorado; nine months after the shooting, he has decided to use the insanity defense) to purchase their guns legally. These reporting systems, however, are predicated on whether a person has seen a professional, either as an inpatient or outpatient, and has been declared to have a mental illness; it fails to account for the millions of people who go undiagnosed each year (Schildkraut and Hernandez 2013). It also stigmatizes those with mental illnesses who do not try to purchase weapons but instead try to lead normal lives. As David Shern, the chief executive of Mental Health America, noted, "This is a classic example of a well-intentioned effort that's going to have almost no effect and, in fact, is going to do harm" (in Luo 2007).

There are two glaring issues with this continued reaction. The first is that, as Howard Kurtz (2012) astutely notes, "the news business, with few exceptions, pays little attention to the gun issue except in the immediate aftermath of the latest mass shooting in Columbine, Virginia Tech, Tucson, Aurora, or Newtown." As quickly as the media latches onto the issue, something else captures its attention and they move on. The second is the adequate addressing of existing laws. Though he received a tremendous amount of criticism, NRA president Wayne LaPierre raised this issue (Lichtblau and Rich 2012). Why should politicians continue to crank out new legislation instead of enforcing the existing bills in place from the previous tragedy that failed to prevent the current event? This is the cyclical challenge that likely will not be solved.

Still, the disproportionally high fear of school shootings leads many—parents, students, faculty, politicians, and the media—to worry about when the next event will occur and who will be the target. Following Columbine, schools across the nation saw a surge in metal detectors and identification badges. These are "feel-better" responses, but do not actually guarantee that a gun will not get into the school (see Addington 2013). At airports across the nation, people have been able to get firearms as large as .40 caliber through TSA security-screening checkpoints, despite heightened procedures following the September 11 terrorist attacks (see, for example, Quinn 2010).

What escapes all of the chatter about school shootings is how *unlikely* it is that a person will be the victim of a school shooting. Between the 1992–1993 and 1997–1998 school years (pre-Columbine), more than 50 million children attended schools across the United States (Sanchez 1998). During that same time period, 226 kids were killed in school-shooting-related incidents (Bernard 1999; Donohue, Schiraldi, and Ziedenberg 1998). This means that the probability of any student becoming the victim of a school shooting during these years was at less than *one in five-ten thousandths* (that is, < 0.0005). These same children had a greater chance of being struck by lightning (Donohue et al. 1998; Sanchez 1998). But, as Lloyd Christmas (Jim Carrey) pondered in *Dumb and Dumber*, "So you're telling me there's a chance?" (in Krevoy et al. 1994). Regardless, this statistic does not stop people from worrying that they or their children will be the next victim and trying to reduce the possible risk that is assumed. The problem is that once you reduce the odds to one in a million, the next obstacle is reducing them to one in ten million. Despite the fact that there is never a risk factor of zero, it doesn't keep people from worrying, even though it gets them nowhere.

## So What Is the Answer?

It is clear that we will never truly know "why" these events have happened. The people who can answer such a question are not here. The Virginia Tech shooter, Cho, left a detailed manifesto in which he rambled on about his disdain for wealthy kids and hedonism (Schildkraut 2012b). For Columbine, there potentially is a similarly documented response straight from the killers. These tapes, infamously dubbed "The Basement Tapes," have been sealed from the public and won't be released until 2026 (at the earliest) out of fear of copycat attacks (Schildkraut 2012b). So until we can hear it straight from the killers' mouths, we are left to speculate as to their motive. Sandy Hook, however, presents an even greater challenge, as Adam Lanza doesn't appear to have left the same video diary as his predecessors. This gap appears to only fuel the fire of speculation, rather than allowing society to focus elsewhere.

Given the reliance of the public discourse on media reporting of such tragedies, we are perhaps left with more questions than answers regarding the potential causes (and therefore implied remedies) for such cases. Clearly, the three-ring circus of violent media, guns, and mental illness are insufficient, even in combination, to explain the complexity of school massacres. The following quote from an editorial by Maureen Dowd illustrates the ridiculous simplicity of characterizing an event such as Columbine as solely related to gun availability and policies (regardless of whether the argument is that there are too many or too few restrictions on firearms):

> As Jesse Ventura said, if only the concealed weapons law had passed in Colorado, students and teachers secretly packing heat could have cut down those

two outcasts. The problem is not that bad guys have guns; it's that good guys don't. (Dowd 1999)

Similarly, in combination, violent and fantasy media, guns, and uncontrolled rage cannot be fingered as the cause, as illustrated in another quote from Dowd's op-ed:

> Just blame Marilyn Manson, Oliver Stone, the Internet, video games, Magic cards, Goths. Here's a good sound bite: Software makes people go nuts, not hardware. Guns don't kill people; trench coats kill people. Guns don't kill people; people who have not reached closure with their anger kill people. (Dowd 1999)

It is not our position simply to point the finger at the news media or politicians, and it is obviously pointless to expect the media industry and political apparatus to disregard the relevance of shocking school massacres. As self-reflective media personnel commented after the Columbine incident, it's impossible for media *not* to cover such cases.

> [T]he Sheriff speaks directly with a female reporter at KUSA [unnamed in transcripts] and he suggests that the media coverage sparks the possibility of copycat attacks. "Well, you just wonder how much—when the attention like this media attention gets on it, that this is broadcast all over the United States and other people get the same idea...." The reporter responds, "And the conflict is that you can't not cover it. But then again, you know, the dilemma is that 15 seconds of fame of whatever the motive is." Stone concludes, "Yes, I understand." (Savidge et al. 1999)

Similarly, the public expects its leaders to comment on such cases, and therefore public leaders walk a similar line in their responsibility to step up as leaders and spokespersons for their constituencies, and perhaps also to advance their political agendas. After all, public figures will frequently attempt to connect their agendas rhetorically to the events, an action which capitalizes on the affective intensity of a riveted audience. As John Velleco commented, "Unfortunately, there are going to be politicians who are going to climb over the bodies of the victims and pursue an agenda" (in Brooke 1999). Clearly the news media and politicians are both necessary to the functioning of civil society; however, such cases also make both their necessity and limited nature clear.

Even for academicians, the complex causes of school massacres are extremely difficult to pinpoint, for various reasons. First, there are relatively few cases of school massacres, and therefore it is impossible to identify a set of nomothetic causes from the examination of a small number of cases. Second, in the case studies that have been conducted, the causes seem to vary from case to case. Therefore, no set of causes has been identified as sufficient to produce a school massacre.[7] It is true that the "big three" of violent media, guns, and mental illness often figure into the situation; however, these are insufficient to explain school massacres in themselves. Case in point is the fact that millions of persons may consume violent media, own firearms, and have mental illnesses, often at the same time, yet school massacres are rather rare.

How, then, to clarify the causes of these troubling events? We argue that what is needed is a protracted, extended discourse about school shootings and related massacres, one that explores their cultural meaning and causes. Given the new media's relatively short attention cycle for any specific issue, this examination apparently cannot take place in the news media. In addition, given the wide array of areas on which politicians must comment, it is unrealistic to expect such public figures to spend a long time on violence, as it will always be superseded in short order, with public attention and/or media attention shifted elsewhere.

However, such a slow and protracted exploration of relevant issues is taking place in various scholarly disciplines in the social sciences, education, and humanities (see Muschert 2007a and 2010 for a review). But if such exploration is going on in the academic realms, why does it not then bleed over into the popular, mass-market discourse of news media and politicians? The divide persists more sharply in the United States between the so-called ivory tower and more popular modes of public discourse. In part, the academic discourse in the United States is frequently divorced from the public and political discourse, and academics are rarely professionally rewarded for informing news media and politicians. In short, these parties simply do not converse with one another very frequently, and therefore there is little opportunity for academics to inform journalists and politicians as to their findings and thinking about issues, just as there little chance for the opposite conversation to take place. What is needed in the case of school massacres is a discussion among these parties regarding the complex individual, community-level, and sociocultural causes of school massacres (and violence more generally) (see Henry 2000 and 2009; Muschert 2007a and 2010; Muschert et al. 2014).

Nonetheless, there may be glimmers of hope. Over the last decades, many academic disciplines have taken strides to make their expertise more public, and politicians and policymakers are increasingly insisting on evidence-based policies and/or independent evaluation of policy outcomes. It is our hope that this trend toward sharing information and cross-fertilizing academic, media, and political discourses will continue, especially in the case of mass violence in various locations, including schools. Such an extended and protracted discussion is necessary, because without intelligent and informed analysis of social problems such as school violence, policies may be ineffective (or even counterproductive) in preventing and mitigating the issue, without which we are in danger of continuing to live in disproportionate fear of such tragedies.

## Notes

1. In this event, twenty-year-old Adam Lanza forcefully entered Sandy Hook Elementary School in Newtown, Connecticut, and opened fire. The shooting left twenty first-grade students and six educators, including the school's principal, dead. Lanza also had shot and killed his mother Nancy prior to the rampage.

2. On April 20, 1999, Columbine seniors Eric Harris (age eighteen) and Dylan Klebold (age seventeen) opened fire on their school. They shot and killed twelve students and one teacher before committing suicide in the school's library.

3. On April 16, 2007, Virginia Tech senior Seung-Hui Cho (age twenty-three) shot and killed two students in the West Ambler Johnston dormitory on campus. After a two-hour break, during which he mailed his now infamous multimedia manifesto to NBC, Cho opened fire in Norris Hall, killing an additional thirty students and faculty. He killed himself as police gained entry to the building.

4. For a discussion of the complexities of assigning culpability to youthful offenders, see Cerulo (1998), Muschert and Janssen (2012), Spencer (2005), and Spencer and Muschert (2009).

5. In Warner and Curtiz (1942).

6. An ouroboros is an ancient symbol that represents cyclicality. In its current form, it is the idea that there is no beginning or end to a discussion following school shootings, and that this discussion does not lead to any progress toward a solution.

7. Muschert (2007a) points out that individual access to guns are the only necessary cause for school shootings to occur. However, similar attacks have taken place without guns, and have involved bombs (as in the 1927 Bath, Michigan, school massacre) or knives (as occurred in various places in China in 2012, on the same day as the Sandy Hook massacre).

# Chapter 5

# Guys and Guns (Still) Amok

*School Shootings, Domestic Terrorism,*
*and Societal Violence in the Age of Obama*

**Douglas Kellner**

WITH THE BRUTAL MASSACRE OF TWENTY CHILDREN AND SIX TEACHERS AND administrators at the Sandy Hook Elementary School in Connecticut on December 14—following the assassination of innocents in an Oregon mall earlier in the week—2012 may be remembered in part as the year when mass shootings spiraled out of control and shocked the nation. As President Obama declared with tears in his eyes in a televised address the night of the Connecticut tragedy: "As a country, we have been through this too many times. Whether it's an elementary school in Newtown, or a shopping mall in Oregon, or a temple in Wisconsin, or a movie theater in Aurora, or a street corner in Chicago—these neighborhoods are our neighborhoods, and these children are our children." With a resolute look, Obama declared: "And we're going to have to come together and take meaningful action to prevent more tragedies like this, regardless of the politics."

School shootings attract maximum media attention. Shooters, craving publicity and the public eye, gravitate toward schools, which may be why the Sandy Hook shooter chose an elementary school, whose pupils are the most innocent and vulnerable, and whose slaughter would gain maximum media attention. In April 2007, Korean American student Seung-Hui Cho went on a rampage at Virginia Tech, killing thirty-two and wounding seventeen in what was the worst mass shooting in US history. His writings and videotaped pronouncements revealed that he imitated images from films and enacted a vengeance drama like that of the Columbine School shooters, whom he cited as "martyrs," in a clear example of "copycat killers."[1]

The February 14, 2008, shootings at Northern Illinois University featured former student Steven Kazmierczak, who leaped from behind a curtain onto a stage in a large lecture hall. Armed with a barrage of weapons and dressed in black, he randomly shot students in a geology class, killing five before he shot himself. While his motivation is still unclear, he created a highly theatrical spectacle of violence reminiscent of the Columbine and Virginia Tech shootings.

The epidemic of school shootings continued throughout 2012. On February 10, 2012, a fourteen-year-old student shot himself in front of seventy fellow students in Walpole, New Hampshire, while on February 27 a former classmate gunned down three students and injured six at Chardon High School in Ohio. On March 6, 2012, in Jacksonville, Florida, a twenty-eight-year-old male high school teacher, after he was fired from his job, shot and killed the headmistress; and on April 2, 2012, in Oakland, California, a forty-three-year-old former student shot seven people and wounded several others at Oikos University. In 2012, mass shootings took place in movie theaters, malls, Sikh temples, and elementary and high schools, as well as universities.

The Aurora, Colorado, shooting during a midnight showing of *The Dark Knight Rises* killed twelve and wounded seventy-eight. Evidently, no public space is now safe in the United States, as the epidemic of male violence and mass shootings proliferate.[2] The shooters are also increasingly modeling themselves as military killing machines. In December 2012, both the Connecticut and Oregon killers loaded themselves up with lethal weapons and body armor, and planned assaults in public places where they were likely to get maximum media attention and days of celebrity infamy. The Oregon mall murderer was reported to have run through the mall screaming "I am the shooter" before firing his AR-15 semi-automatic assault rifle (similar to the one used in Sandy Hook), which mercifully jammed after two people were killed and one wounded, leading the shooter to aim the gun at himself and take his own life.[3]

Perhaps for the first time in decades, serious discussions in the public sphere emerged after the Sandy Hook slaughter concerning the need for gun control in an out-of-control gun culture as well as for better mental-health care in a society in which mentally disturbed young teenagers and men have been producing an epidemic of mass murder. In the media frenzy in the face of mass shootings, we need to better understand that we face a crisis of masculinity in the country, and that young alienated males are increasingly turning to guns and murder to construct their identities and resolve their personal crises.[4]

By "crises in masculinity," I refer to a dominant societal connection between masculinity and being a tough guy, assuming what Jackson Katz (2006) describes as a "tough guise," a mask or façade of aggressive assertiveness, covering over vulnerabilities. The crisis has erupted in outbreaks of violence and societal murder, as men act out rage, taking extremely violent forms such as political assassinations, serial and mass murders, and school and workplace shootings.

In this chapter, I argue that the cycle of mass shootings throughout 2012 and previous decades suggests that young men are constructing media spectacles to achieve celebrity, attempting to overcome their alienation and failures by turning to weapons and gun culture and carrying out mass murders. I suggest that our media/celebrity culture has helped produce an epidemic of predominantly male copycat killers who resolve their crises of masculinity through immersion in gun culture and carry out deadly mass shootings in public places. Unless we begin to have national discussions on the dangers of gun culture, alienated men, mental health problems, and societal crises as the context to discuss mass shootings and then take serious action to address the problems, we are condemned to repeat endlessly the cycle of the mass murder of innocents.

Admittedly, the problem of mass shootings and social violence is complex and involves multiple aspects that require different kinds of social and political action to address the problem. Yet while there are multiple causes to specific acts of gun violence, there are discernible factors that play important roles in each event. In the following chapter, I will first interrogate the Sandy Hook Elementary shootings in the context in the United States of an outburst of mass shootings by alienated males during the past years; I will then present analyses of some of the key aspects of the crises of masculinity and factors which help produce gun violence that are generally overlooked in mainstream media discussions. Next, recognizing that the sources of mass shootings are complex and that multiple measures are necessary to address an issue, I will offer some reflections on why we urgently need discussion and action on gun-safety reform, concluding with some suggestions concerning long-term steps toward dealing with the problems of crises of masculinity and gun violence.

## The Sandy Hook Slaughter and Media Spectacle

On Friday, December 14, 2012, reports circulated that scores of children and adults working at the Sandy Hook Elementary School in Newtown, Connecticut, had been killed by a gunman. In the following days, the story completely dominated the cable news channels and network news reports, newspapers, the Internet, and social networking outlets. Initial information turned out to be wildly false: Within hours of the initial reports of the shootings, wire services and television networks identified the shooter as twenty-four-year old Ryan Lanza; by the next day, it was reported that the shooter was actually his brother Adam Lanza. Initial reports had the shooter killing his mother, Nancy, said to be a school teacher at Sandy Hook Elementary, and then slaughtering students in her classroom, with suggestions that the shooter had committed matricide and—in all-consuming hatred of his mother—killed those she loved the most, her students. It was initially stated that Adam Lanza had been allowed to enter through the school security system, while the next day authorities claimed that he shot his way into the school and that his entrance was thus forcible. Yet, it was soon revealed that the shooter's mother was not a teacher, that the schoolchildren murdered were not her students, and that the mother was killed at home, apparently before the mass shooting at the school. The unfolding accounts of the shooting created a puzzle concerning why the shooter chose the elementary school to act out his male rage and carry out his spectacle of carnage.

The initial reports painted the mother as a well-regarded homemaker who loved gardening and her children, and whose home her neighbors regarded as neat and attractive. For years, Nancy Lanza had functioned as a single mother after a divorce from her husband, Adam's father. By the weekend, media reports also highlighted that the mother was a gun collector who took her children to rifle ranges to practice shooting, that she apparently never let any neighbors or tradespeople into her house, and that the arsenal of handguns and assault rifles found in the school where the shooting occurred had been legally purchased and registered by the mother.[5]

Media reports at first claimed that the shooter had used Glock and Sig Sauer semiautomatic handguns in his killing spree, but the state coroner reported the next day that an AR-15 Bushmaster semiautomatic assault rifle had been used in the killings, that extremely lethal bullets and a high-speed gun magazine firing rounds had been deployed, and that hundreds of bullets had been shot. It was also reported that the young children were so bullet-riddled that none had survived the carnage, although several adults shot in the school had survived and were taken to hospital emergency rooms.

Contradictory reports also circulated concerning the shooter. Adam Lanza was evidently a loner who apparently had few, if any, friends, and was barely remembered by classmates. While he was described by some who remembered him as "smart," and as "one of these real brainiac computer kind of kids,"[6] he left no traces on the Internet, just as there were no pictures of him in his school yearbooks and few images of him otherwise available. While the police reported that they had taken his computers from his home after the shooting, and had "very good evidence" that would explain the why and the how of the killings, police reported over the weekend that the shooter's home computer had been "smashed," thus intensifying the mystery concerning why the shooter carried out his rampage at Sandy Hook Elementary.

Over the weekend of December 15–16, the media spectacle of the Sandy Hook shootings focused on the victims, their families, the interfaith memorial service that President Obama attended, and how the people of Newtown were coping with the tragedy. These themes continued to play out over the next week as funerals for the victims began, allowing a chance to memorialize the lives of the individual victims and their families. Heroes appeared, such as the principal and teachers, who reportedly gave their lives to protect the children. Little new information appeared about the shooter, his family, and his mother, whose murder began the killing spree that day.

The issue of gun control became a major media story of the day, with cable news channels focusing on public outrage and the demand for strict gun control, starting with banning the sale of assault rifles and requiring background checks on all gun sales. Congressmen; families of children shot at Columbine, Virginia Tech, and Newtown; and members of the public appeared on the news, demanding urgent change in the gun laws. Politicians, including those who had previously opposed gun-law reform, promised swift action. In the immediate aftermath of the tragedy, there appeared to emerge serious debate on gun control that created possibilities for the first federal action on reform since the Clinton years.

Yet the mainstream corporate media and US public sphere so far refuse to see the gun crisis as a crisis of masculinity, of young men who attempt to resolve their personal crises through guns and acts of violence. In every case of mass shootings, young men turn to guns, get involved in gun culture, and then act out their fantasies through acts of aggression involving shooting and killing, usually innocent victims unrelated to the shooter. The Sandy Hook slaughter involved a case where the shooter killed his mother, for as yet-unspecified reasons, and then went on a rampage, indiscriminately shooting children at a grade school in his district. Obviously, this was a young man in crisis, but the media reduced his problems to unspecified "mental-health" issues, as if mental health were the key variable to the problem of school shootings.

Obviously an out-of-control gun culture and mental-health crises are both important factors in the epidemic of school shootings, but so is a crisis of masculinity as more and more men spiral out of control. I am writing this paragraph just after watching a MSNBC report around 9:45 a.m. on December 19, 2012, that indicated that in the past day Oklahoma public schools had been shut down because of a "credible threat" to school safety; in Utah, a student had been detained because he was found with a gun at school, which he claimed his parents had told him to take to school to protect himself; in Ohio, a male student had been arrested when his car was found to be full of knives, a revolver, and ammunition; while in Maryland, a male student had been arrested after drawings and diagrams outlining possible gun-murder scenarios were found. This two-minute report on out-of-control young men found to threaten others with gun violence could be happening every day, but it is apparently so common that it rarely garners much media attention. Reflection on the threats and actions carried out by men out of control signifies a serious crisis of masculinity in the United States today and the need to take immediate action.

Minutes after the MSNBC report on December 19, President Obama appeared on television and made a dramatic announcement that he had appointed Vice President Joe Biden to head a task force consisting of cabinet secretaries and outside organizations to come up with proposals by January that would inspire "very specific" initiatives on gun violence early in Obama's next term, insisting that "this time, the words need to lead to action."[7]

Further, Obama argued that a consensus was beginning to build around very specific measures on gun safety, stating: "A majority of Americans support banning the sale of military-style assault weapons.[8] A majority of Americans support banning the sale of high-capacity ammunition clips. A majority of Americans support laws requiring background checks before all gun purchases so that criminals can't take advantage of legal loopholes to buy a gun from somebody who won't take the responsibility of doing a background check at all."

Dramatizing the explosion of gun violence throughout the United States and emphasizing that gun violence is a facet of everyday life, and not just occasional media spectacles of mass shootings, President Obama stated in a White House Briefing Room statement on December 19:

Since Friday morning, a police officer was gunned down in Memphis, leaving four children without their mother. Two officers were killed outside a grocery store in Topeka. A woman was shot and killed inside a Las Vegas casino. Three people were shot inside an Alabama hospital. A four-year-old was caught in a drive-by in Missouri and taken off life support just yesterday. Each one of these Americans was a victim of the everyday gun violence that takes the lives of more than 10,000 Americans every year—violence that we cannot accept as routine.

So I will use all the powers of this office to help advance efforts aimed at preventing more tragedies like this. We won't prevent them all, but that can't be an excuse not to try. It won't be easy, but that can't be an excuse not to try.

And I'm not going to be able to do it by myself. Ultimately, if this effort is to succeed, it's going to require the help of the American people. It's gonna require all of you. If we're going to change things, it's going to take a wave of Americans—mothers and fathers, daughters and sons, pastors, law enforcement, mental-health professionals, and, yes, gun owners—standing up and saying, enough on behalf of our kids.

It will take commitment and compromise, and most of all it will take courage.

Obama thus made his strongest pledge so far that he and Biden would lead the way to achieve meaningful gun-safety reform in his second term. Interestingly, after his forceful comments on going forward with concrete actions on an out-of-control gun culture, the White House press corps spent the rest of Obama's news conference peppering him with question after question about battles with the Republicans over the debt crisis and the so-called fiscal cliff, not once mentioning the problem of gun safety. The performance of the press showed the relative indifference on behalf of the mainstream corporate media to significant problems like gun violence and their obsession with political infighting in Washington.

Yet the Newtown tragedy deeply influenced the public, and discussions about gun violence and the need for beefed-up gun control intensified during early 2013 in the public, Congress, and media. There were mounting reports that the NRA was losing its grip on Congress and the public after having contributed millions of dollars to defeat Obama and spending even more on congressional candidates, only about 50 percent of whom won in the 2012 elections.[9] There appeared to be a backlash against the NRA; an increasing number of people spoke up against it, including many of its own members, who called for reasonable limits on gun access. New York mayor Michael Bloomberg, a gun-safety activist who had contributed millions to defeat right-wing politicians supported by the gun lobby in the 2012 election, promised that he would spend millions more to counter NRA propaganda and support of pro-gun politicians, and to help create a counterbalance to its sphere of influence.[10]

On December 21, as the people of Newtown rang twenty-six bells in commemoration of the death of twenty-six beloved people exactly one week after the shooting and President Obama held a moment of silence in the Oval Office, NRA executive vice president Wayne LaPierre called in the press for a thirty-minute lecture on "Guns in America," arguing that armed police officers in every school was the solution to school shootings. Combative and defiant, LaPierre claimed that it was "monsters" who were doing the killing, erasing the categories of people and guns, and attacked Hollywood films, video games, and the country's mental-health services for causing violence in society. LaPierre was interrupted twice by protestors, first by a banner held by Tighe Barry of Code Pink standing in front of him and the TV cameras with a large sign stating "NRA killing our kids," before he was hauled away. Then, after LaPierre resumed his speech, Medea Benjamin of Code Pink stood up holding a banner reading, "NRA: Blood on your hands," and was also pulled out of the auditorium by security forces.

After his tirade, LaPierre was immediately criticized by many, with Sen. Frank Lautenberg (D-NJ) insisting that: "The NRA leadership is wildly out of touch with its own members, responsible gun owners, and the American public who want to close dangerous loopholes and enact common-sense gun safety reform." New York mayor Michael Bloomberg called LaPierre's comments "a shameful evasion of the crisis facing our country. Instead of offering solutions to a problem they have helped create, they offered a paranoid, dystopian vision of a more dangerous and violent America where everyone is armed and no place is safe."

Critics noted that the NRA argument that people are safer owning guns is bogus and that research indicated that having a gun in your home made it twenty-two times more likely that you would be a victim of a gun crime; further, research revealed that "people who carried guns were 4.5 times as likely to be shot and 4.2 times as likely to get killed compared with unarmed citizens."[11] Thus, NRA gun discourse went against academic research as well as common sense and is becoming increasingly discredited.

Following his impassioned argument, LaPierre was assailed throughout the country.[12] While LaPierre's speech might appear tone-deaf and angered both NRA critics and some members, it plainly showed that the main function of the

NRA is to boost the gun industries which pay it to serve as their PR and lobbying agency.[13] The NRA thus was involved in a fierce struggle to make sure that no arms were removed from the streets so that the gun industry could maximize its profits. The gun lobby was also spreading fear that the government was coming to take away peoples' precious weapons, and accordingly weapon sales of all sorts were booming, especially semiautomatic assault rifles that were under legitimate scrutiny and might well be restricted.

The NRA is correctly perceived as an arm of the right wing of the Republican Party whose candidates it had supported for years, although not so successfully in the 2012 election. The night before LaPierre's fiery speech, the Republican Party's inability to pass an alternative plan to President Obama's proposals to address the fiscal crisis brought the "fiscal cliff" perilously close, with pundits proclaiming that it would be "Cliffmas" this year with the overwhelming majority of citizens facing higher taxes in January if Congress and the President did not come up with a fiscal plan to resolve the debt crisis. There appears to be a parallel between the Republican Party refusal to compromise on taxes and the NRA refusal to compromise in the least on gun safety, suggesting that both the Republicans and the NRA have been taken over by extremist factions who are incapable of political compromise and thus democratic decision-making. Clearly, both groups are currently putting their right-wing ideologies and visceral hatred of taxes and gun reform before the public interest and the public opinion of the majority of citizens.

With the NRA making it clear that there could be no rational compromise on the issue of gun control, and Congress unable to forge a consensus concerning the debt crisis, the country was looking at an impasse as it faced a not-so-merry Christmas and a frightening New Year. The end of the world prophesized for December 21 by the Mayan calendar was instead finally correctly interpreted as the end of one Mayan calendar cycle and the beginning of a new one; there wasn't much hope that the new political cycle beginning in January would be a promising one, however, as the country was further polarized by the intransigence on taxes and gun control by the Republicans and the NRA.

## Time for Gun Safety AND Mental-Health Reform NOW!

Will the brutal massacre of children and administrators at the Sandy Hook Elementary school in Connecticut finally initiate a serious discussion of the burning need for a conversation about gun-safety reform in the United States that aims at practical steps for curbing gun violence? The many shocking mass shootings in 2012 all elicited declarations of intent to tackle the out-of-control epidemic of gun violence, but no meaningful action followed. After the shooting of Arizona congresswoman Gabrielle Giffords in 2011, President Obama promised "sound and effective steps that will actually keep those irresponsible, law-breaking few from getting their hands on a gun in the first place." However, no resolution emerged, although a more intensive background check on those purchasing firearms was promised by the Justice Department. Likewise, while Obama cited the need for stricter gun laws in summer 2012 after the Aurora, Colorado, movie-theater shooting, no action had been taken on the federal level to promote gun-safety reform until the Sandy Hook massacre seized the attention of the media and the conscience of the nation. Previously, under the Obama administration, gun laws around the country had become more lax, allowing people to carry concealed weapons. In addition, there are more places where people are allowed to openly carry guns, while weapon sales have boomed.[14]

Could it be different this time? The mass slaughter of children in school is unprecedented and should concern every thinking and feeling person. The 2012 election is over and Obama and his administration have four years to carry out meaningful gun-safety-reform legislation. During the past election, Republicans were widely defeated, and, in particular, extreme conservatives lost in race after race, losing six out of seven contested seats in the Senate to liberal Democrats. Clearly, the public is fed up with conservative Republicans' politics, like their insistent opposition to any and all gun-control measures. The voting public may be ready for "change that matters" in gun laws.

Perhaps President Obama's emotional speech at a Sandy Hook Memorial service on Sunday, December 16, could mark a turning point in the national attitude toward gun control. In a heartfelt speech full of Biblical references and resonances, Obama insisted that we *must* do something and take up the challenges of mass shootings:

> Can we say that we're truly doing enough to give all the children of this country the chance they deserve to live out their lives in happiness and with purpose? I've been reflecting on this the last few days, and if we're honest with ourselves, the answer's no. We're not doing enough. And we will have to change.
>
> Since I've been president, this is the fourth time we have come together to comfort a grieving community torn apart by mass shootings, fourth time we've hugged survivors, the fourth time we've consoled the families of victims.
>
> And in between, there have been an endless series of deadly shootings across the country, almost daily reports of victims, many of them children,

in small towns and in big cities all across America, victims whose—much of the time their only fault was being at the wrong place at the wrong time.

We can't tolerate this anymore. These tragedies must end. And to end them, we must change.

We will be told that the causes of such violence are complex, and that is true. No single law, no set of laws can eliminate evil from the world or prevent every senseless act of violence in our society, but that can't be an excuse for inaction. Surely we can do better than this.

If there's even one step we can take to save another child or another parent or another town from the grief that's visited Tucson and Aurora and Oak Creek and Newtown and communities from Columbine to Blacksburg before that, then surely we have an obligation to try.

In the coming weeks, I'll use whatever power this office holds to engage my fellow citizens, from law enforcement, to mental-health professionals, to parents and educators, in an effort aimed at preventing more tragedies like this, because what choice do we have? We can't accept events like this as routine.

Indeed, in the aftermath of the Sandy Hook slaughter, throughout the media and public sphere, there have been calls to return to the ban on assault rifles carried out by the Clinton administration in 1994; the ensuing Bush/Cheney administration had allowed the ban to expire in 2004. The shooters in the Oregon mall and Sandy Hook Elementary School shootings, both in December 2012, carried AR-16 assault rifles and high-speed gun magazines, allowing hundreds of high-velocity bullets to be fired rapidly.

Firearms similar to the Bushmaster rifle, which was identified as the murder weapon in the Sandy Hook massacre, had been deployed as well in other recent mass shootings, thereby leading to debates whether such rapid-fire semiautomatic rifles should be banned. The Bushmaster assault weapon is targeted toward men, and the Bushmaster website even makes a connection between owning the gun and being a "man":

> Visitors of bushmaster.com will have to prove they're a man by answering a series of manhood questions. Upon successful completion, they will be issued a temporary Man Card to proudly display to friends and family. The Man Card is valid for one year.
>
> Visitors can also call into question or even revoke the Man Card of friends they feel have betrayed their manhood. The man in question will then have

to defend himself, and their Man Card, by answering a series of questions geared towards proving indeed, they are worthy of retaining their card.[15]

This blatant connection between hard masculinity and Bushmaster rifles makes clear part of the reason why so many young men in crisis turn to guns as a means of becoming a "real man." It raises the question why men need a "Man Card" to validate their masculinity, and why they think buying an assault rifle makes them men. The Bushmaster Firearms International Logo seems to offer an answer in what appears as a bright-red Chinese dragon coiled up as a snake with what appears to be an erect penis protruding from its base.[16] Obviously, the Bushmaster Man is manly, fully erect, and ready for action and must have his gun handy and ready at all times, reminding me of the old Beatles song "Happiness Is a Warm Gun," with its refrain, "bang, bang, shoot shoot."

A little more than a week after the Sandy Hook slaughter, Christmas Eve, 2012 saw another shooting: In a suburb near Rochester, New York, on a beachfront strip off Lake Ontario, paroled ex-felon William Spengler Jr. killed his sister, with whom he lived, set the house on fire, and then used his Bushmaster assault weapon to kill two firefighters and seriously wound two others before using a weapon to take his own life. The assassin left behind a typewritten note that indicated his mind-set and plan: "I still have to get ready to see how much of the neighborhood I can burn down and do what I like doing best—killing people."

**Figure 5.1 Bushmaster Firearms International, LLC.**

| Type | Subsidiary |
|---|---|
| Founded | 1973 |
| Headquarters | Madison, North Carolina, U.S. |
| Owner(s) | Freedom Group |
| Website | http://bushmaster |

Guns, however, were becoming a controversial commodity in the economy and marketplace, as well as in the public sphere. On the Monday after the Sandy Hook shootings, private-equity firm Cerberus Capital Management announced that it was selling off its shares in the firearms company that made the Bushmaster, after the California State Teachers' Retirement System (CalSTRS), the second-largest pension fund in the country, threatened to sell its share of Cerberus unless the firm sold the company that produced the Bushmaster and other assault weapons. Walmart pulled Bushmaster rifles from its online store as furor grew over the sales of ammunition and guns online with no background check, but the giant chain continued to sell rifles in its stores and sales were reportedly booming of semiautomatic assault weapons throughout the country, a trend that continued through the Christmas holidays.[17]

Such deadly assault weapons as the Bushmaster, used by the military, are properly seen as weapons of mass destruction and the shooters involved in mass shootings should be viewed as terrorists. After 9/11, the country came together and agreed on harsh measures concerning domestic security in airports and airlines; similarly, after Sandy Hook, there was initially intense concern for school safety and the need to protect the public against gun violence. Interestingly, before Sandy Hook, the NRA and the gun lobby talked incessantly of "gun rights" and the Second Amendment to attack any efforts at gun-law reform, and the media went along with this discourse, whereas now the term "gun safety" and protecting the public against gun violence has become a national discourse.

In light of such awesome and destructive firepower capable of producing mass murder and horrific carnage, surely a consensus could be reached that there is no rational reason to let private citizens run amok with deadly semiautomatic assault weapons, such as the rapid-fire assault weapons that were used in Oregon and Connecticut to kill innocents in a mall and a public school. Likewise, following the Sandy Hook shooting, calls multiplied for more intensive background checks and even gun registration, with the aim of limiting gun ownership among criminals and people with mental-health problems. It is scandalous that as many as 40 percent of guns in the United States are sold privately at gun shows or other venues and that there are no background checks in these cases; the payoff here is that over 80 percent of gun crimes are committed by those who had no background checks before obtaining their weapons.[18] Further, the existing database for mental-health and criminal prohibitions against selling guns to specific individuals is not even functional in many states, creating a "Wild West" situation in the United States, in that seemingly anyone can buy a gun.[19] Such unrestricted gun sales are a clear and present danger to safety in the United States and must be addressed by those seeking a secure and rational society.

While there are definitely serious mental-health issues involved in the epidemic of mass shootings in the United States,[20] it is definitely a mistake to reduce the problem to mental health since *all* of the mass murders in 2012 have involved males deeply immersed in gun culture who used guns to perpetrate mass murders. Until we understand the depth of the problem of the crisis of masculinity and an out-of-control gun culture in the United States, and take rational steps to control them, we are condemned to repeat endlessly the cycle of the murder of innocents.

Media pundits and anti-gun-control conservatives often diminish the mass shootings to mental health, saying simply, "he's crazy," without looking at the intersection of mental health, guns and guns culture, and the crises of masculinities. For instance, in the widely-carried NRA speech referenced earlier, Wayne LaPierre denounced the mass shooters as "monsters," as if using such a word would end discussion about gun-safety reform. Such people not only reduce mass shooting to mental-health categories, but when specific gun-control measures are proposed, they divert discussion by claiming it's primarily an issue of mental health. For instance, freshman senator Heidi Heitkamp (D-ND), who had received an "A" rating from the National Rifle Association, stated on TV that: "To me, one of the issues that I think comes—screams out of this—is the issue of mental health and the care for the mentally ill in our country, especially the dangerously mentally ill. And so we need to have a broad discussion before we start talking about gun control."[21]

Indeed, the nexus of mental-health issues and unrestricted gun possession is a key variable in all of the mass shootings. Thus, as Newark, New Jersey, mayor Cory Booker recommends to seriously address gun violence, we need the National Instant Criminal Background Check System (NICS) to be deployed for all gun sales, ending the gun-show/private-dealer loopholes and making all guns subject to background checks, including mental-health checks. Implementing NICS would require mandating criminal-background and mental-health databases so that adequate information could be used to keep weapons out of the wrong hands. Further, as Booker advocates, we must tighten anti-trafficking laws, passing laws "that makes gun trafficking a clear, substantial, and practically enforceable federal crime," with stronger penalties for illegal gun sales and possession, which currently, "as recently noted by the bipartisan coalition Mayors Against Illegal Guns, carries the same punishment as for the trafficking of chicken or livestock."[22]

Crucially, all of the mass shootings of recent years involved semiautomatic assault weapons and high-capacity magazines; hence, it is obvious that these weapons of mass destruction need to be banned. Killers can buy unlimited amounts of ammunition and even guns unchecked over the Internet. James Holmes, the Aurora, Colorado, theater shooter, had reportedly bought over 6,000 rounds of ammo from the Internet, as well as an arsenal of guns from local gun shows.[23] No assault munitions, guns, or perhaps even gear used by the police or military should be sold over the Internet, and there should be heavy penalties for illegal sales of this material.

While there was intense media discussion and calls for urgent gun-safety reform during the early months of 2013 following the Sandy Hook Elementary shooting, so far there has been no significant legislation on the national level, as of fall 2013, and the pro-gun constituency of the Republican party that controls Congress makes it unlikely that serious reform will take place in the immediate future. While the Obama administration pressed for gun-law reform that would mandate and expand background checks while banning assault rifles and high-capacity cartridges, the NRA and gun lobby has so far continued to block legislation on the national level.[24] Although a bipartisan committee in the Senate attempted to advance a bill that would expand background checks, so far it has been blocked and there has since been little concrete action on the gun-safety issue on the national stage. On the state level, however, there have been many significant gun-safety laws passed in states including New York, Connecticut, Maryland, and even Colorado and significant debates to change local gun laws throughout the country, although there continue to be fierce debates over changes on the state and local level.

However, it would be a mistake to wait and expect politicians on the national or local level to solve the problem of mass shootings and gun-safety reform. This is an issue that concerns every individual who cares about their fellow citizens and wants to see a reduction in gun violence. We need a national discussion to pressure politicians on the national, state, and local level to move toward seeing the real extent of the problem of gun violence, and the need for serious steps to address the cycle of mass shootings. The debate over school shootings and gun violence would include multiple dimensions such as mental-health issues, crises of masculinity, and a culture of violence in the media and other sectors of US life.

## Crises of Masculinities, Mass Shootings, and Media Spectacle

I would argue that in order to carry forth meaningful discussions of the scope of gun violence and mass murder in the United States, we need to better understand how a wide range of school shootings and acts of domestic terrorism have multiple dimensions and need to be addressed by a diverse range of responses. Indeed, school shootings and domestic terrorism have proliferated on a global level. In 2012, there have been school shootings in Finland, Germany, Greece, and other countries as well as in the United States.[25] Although each case of gun violence has specific causal features and context, in all cases men acted out their rage through the use of guns and violence to create media spectacles and become celebrities-of-the-moment. In the following sections, I will argue that dealing with problems of school and societal violence will require reconstruction of male identities and critique of masculinist socialization and identities, as well as altered gun laws, stricter gun control, and better mental-health service.

The mainstream corporate media have rarely, if ever, seriously discussed the crisis of masculinity and its connection with gun violence and mass shootings. Invariably, when shootings or acts of social violence are mentioned in the corporate media, the word "male" is rarely, if ever, used. In the concluding discussions of this chapter, I want to suggest some of the connections between crises of masculinity, gun culture, and mass shootings and how a reconstruction of masculinity and different models of male socialization are necessary to seriously address the problem of mass shootings and social violence in the contemporary United States.

In the following discussion, I argue that media culture, gun culture, gang culture, sports, and military culture produce ultramacho men as an ideal, generating societal problems from violence against women to gang murder (see Katz 2006 and Kellner 2008). As Jackson Katz urges, young men should renounce these ideals and behavior and construct alternative notions of masculinity. Katz concludes that reconstructing masculinity and overcoming aggressive and violent macho behavior and values provides "a vision of manhood that does not depend on putting down others in order to lift itself up. When a man stands up for social justice, nonviolence, and basic human rights—for women as much as for men—he is acting in the best traditions of our civilization. That makes him not only a better man, but a better human being" (Katz 2006, 270).

Major sources of violence in US society include cultures of violence produced by poverty as well as many other factors, including a masculinist military, sports, and gun culture; ultramasculine behavior in the corporate and political world in a predatory environment of neoliberalism; school bullying and fighting; general societal violence reproduced by media and seen in family and everyday life; and escalating violence in prisons. In any of these cases, an ultraviolent masculinity can explode and produce societal violence, and until we have new conceptions of what it means to be a man that include intelligence, independence, sensitivity, and the renunciation of bullying and violence, societal violence will no doubt increase.

Hence, in diagnosing violence in the schools we need a broader critical theory of societal violence and the specific factors that produce gun violence. As Henry Giroux points out, "it is crucial that educators, parents, politicians, and others show how the gun lobby and its culture of violence is only one part of a broader and all-embracing militarized culture of war, arms industry, and a Darwinian survival-of-the-fittest ethic, more characteristic of an authoritarian society than a democracy" (2013, 177).

Both Larkin (2007) and Giroux (2013) point out how a culture of bullying in schools contributes to school shootings. Likewise, Lee Hirsch's film *Bully* (2011) has called attention to the phenomenon of bullying in schools, by showing intense bullying taking place on school buses, playgrounds, classrooms, and neighborhoods. Focusing on five victims of bullying from various regions in the United States, two of whom committed suicide, Hirsch's film puts on display shocking physical mistreatment of high school students by their peers. Yet Hirsch's *Bully* avoids the issue of guns and of jocks who systematically terrorize countercultural youth or those who are different, making it appear that the bullies are just individuals who antagonize other individuals, rather than seeing the problem of bullying as related to the structure of schools, separation of youth into different groups, and crises in masculinities.[26]

Sports culture is another major part of the construction of American masculinity that can take violent forms. In many of the high school shootings of the 1990s, so-called jocks tormented young teenage boys, who then took revenge in asserting a hyperviolent masculinity and went on shooting rampages. Ralph Larkin (2007, 205ff), for instance, provides a detailed analysis of "Football and Toxic High School Environments," focusing on Columbine. He describes how sports played a primary role in the school environment, how jocks were celebrities, and how they systematically abused outsiders and marginal youth like Columbine shooters Eric Harris and Dylan Klebold.

The "pattern of sports domination of high schools," Larkin suggests, "is apparently the norm in America" (2007, 206). Larkin notes how football has become incorporated into a hypermasculinized subculture that emphasizes physical aggression, domination, sexism, and the celebration of victory. He notes that more "than in any other sport, defeat in football is associated with being physically dominated and humiliated" (2007, 208). Further, football is associated with militarism, as comedian George Carlin noted in his classic routine:

In football the object is for the quarterback, also known as the field general, to be on target with his aerial assault, riddling the defense by hitting his receivers with deadly accuracy in spite of the blitz, even if he has to use the shotgun. With short bullet passes and long bombs, he marches his troops into enemy territory, balancing this aerial assault with a sustained ground attack that punches holes in the forward wall of the enemy's defensive line.

In baseball the object is to go home! And to be safe! (Carlin, cited in Larkin 2007, 208)

Larkin argues that football culture has "corrupted many high schools," including Columbine where "the culture of hypermasculinity reigned supreme" (2007, 209). Larkin concludes that: "If we wish to reduce violence in high schools, we have to de-emphasize the power of sports and change the culture of hypermasculinity. Football players cannot be lords of the hallways, bullying their peers with impunity, sometimes encouraged by coaches with adolescent mentalities" (2007, 210).

Hypermasculinity in sports is also often a cauldron of homophobia; many of the school shooters were taunted about their sexuality and responded ultimately with a berserk affirmation of compensatory violence.[27] Indeed, hypermasculinity is a problem for young men beyond high school and college. Professional sports like football, boxing, and wrestling promote hypermasculine images of men and tough-guy behavior, as do body-building culture, some forms of gym culture, and informal sites of male-bonding like fight clubs.[28] Pro football players are our modern gladiators, highly trained and armored to go out every week and "kill" the other side.[29] Televised sports programs promote violent sports and reward hypermasculine winners.

Hypermasculinity is found throughout sports, military, gun, gang, and other male subcultures, as well as in the corporate and political world, often starting in the family with male socialization by the father. These attitudes are reproduced and validated constantly in films, television programs, and media. Media culture is full of violence; the case studies in Chapter 3 in *Guys and Guns Amok* of violent masculinity show that Oklahoma City bomber Timothy McVeigh, the two Columbine shooters, and many other school shooters in the 2000s were deeply influenced by violent media culture. In particular, Cho at Virginia Tech was a failed film writer who left a dossier full of violent cinematic images and arguably orchestrated the Virginia Tech massacre as a cinematic media spectacle (see Kellner 2008) in which he was director, producer, writer, and star. There are reports that Norwegian shooter Andreas Breivik, Adam Lanza, and other mass shooters were fans of the military first-person-assault video game *Call of Duty*, a program used by the military to train recruits.[30]

I do not, however, want to claim that either a film or a video game "causes" mass shootings, as influences of media culture are but one factor in a complex nexus of societal influences that include gun culture and other societal influences. Yet, while media images of violence and specific books, films, TV shows, video and computer games, and other artifacts of media culture may provide scripts for violent masculinity for young men to act out, it is the broader culture of militarism, gun culture, violent sports, ultraviolent video and computer games, subcultures of bullying and violence, and the rewarding of ultramasculinity in the corporate and political worlds that are major factors in constructing hegemonic violent masculinities. Media culture itself obviously contributes to this macho ideal of masculinity, but gender is a contested terrain between different conceptions of masculinity and femininity, and between liberal, conservative, and more radical representations and discourses (Kellner 1995 and Kellner 2010).

Crises in masculinity are grounded in the deterioration of socioeconomic possibilities for young men and are inflamed by economic troubles. In a time of neoliberal capitalist economic crisis, young men without a positive economic future and prospects for good jobs turn to guns for empowerment. Their rage is intensified by gun culture and declining economic prospects. Gun carnage is also encouraged in part by media that repeatedly illustrate violence as a way of responding to problems. Explosions of male rage and rampage are also embedded in the escalation of war and militarism in the United States, from the long nightmare of Vietnam through the military interventions in Afghanistan and Iraq.

In this context of escalating societal violence, adoption of a more rational policy regarding access to guns is one part of addressing this problem. It was initially heartening that people appalled by the Virginia Tech shootings campaigned to close loopholes for gun shows enabling the purchase of firearms without adequate background checks, as was the case of the girlfriend of one of the underage Columbine shooters. Yet failure to act to close these loopholes, or to reverse ending the ban on semiautomatic assault weapons in succeeding years, has been disheartening.

We also must examine the role of the Internet as a source of ammunition and firearms, where anyone can assume a virtual identity and purchase lethal weapons. It is perhaps not coincidental that the Virginia Tech and Northern Illinois University shooters both bought their ammunition from the same online business,[31] and it is incredible what one can now find on the Internet promoting guns and male violence.[32]

However, escalating gun violence and random shootings is a larger problem than gun control alone. Underlying causes of rampant gun violence include increasing societal alienation, frustration, anger, and rage against schools, universities, workplaces, public spaces, and communities. To address these problems, we need better mental-health facilities, improved monitoring of troubled individuals, and more secure institutions.

Schools and universities, for example, have scrambled to ensure counseling and monitoring programs to help troubled students, offering safety plans on how to address crises that result in violence. Many institutions have increased video surveillance. Schools themselves should be assessed on how well they provide a secure learning environment and counseling for troubled students. Schools can also teach nonviolent conflict resolution and media literacy courses that critique media representations associating power and gun violence with masculinity and should cultivate alternative images to the ultraviolent images of masculinity circulating in media.

To be sure, in an era such as ours of ongoing war, poverty, and societal violence, male rage shootings will no doubt be a problem for years to come. It is essential, therefore, that we address the issue of crises of masculinity and social alienation, and not reflexively resort to using simplistic jargon—"he's just crazy"—to explain away the issue. Mental illness is a complex phenomenon that has a variety of dimensions and expressions.

It is also important not to scapegoat the Internet, media, computer games, prescription drugs, or any single factor that may very well contribute to the problem, but is not the single underlying cause. Rather, we need to admit to both the complexity and the urgency of the problem of school shootings, and enact an array of intelligent and informed responses that will produce a more peaceful and humane society. In the concluding section, I will present further suggestions of the sort of social reconstruction and cultivation of new sensibilities necessary to address challenges of mass shootings and domestic terrorism.

## Scapegoating, Social Reconstruction, and a New Sensibility

After dramatic school shootings and incidents of youth violence, there are usually attempts to scapegoat media culture. After the Virginia Tech shootings, the Federal Communication Commission (FCC) issued a report in late April 2007 on "violent television programming and its impact on children" calling for expanding governmental oversight on broadcast television, but also extending content regulation to cable and satellite channels for the first time and banning some shows from time slots when children might be watching. FCC commissioner Jonathan S. Adelstein, who was in favor of the measures, did not hesitate to evoke the Virginia Tech shootings: "particularly in sight of the spasm of unconscionable violence at Virginia Tech, but just as importantly in light of the excessive violent crime that daily affects our nation, there is a basis for appropriate federal action to curb violence in the media."[33]

In a *Los Angeles Times* op-ed piece, Nick Gillespie, editor of *Reason*, noted that the report itself indicated that there was no causal relation between watching TV violence and committing violent acts. Further, Gillespie argued that given the steady drop in incidents of juvenile violence over the last twelve years, reaching a low not seen since at least the 1970s, it was inappropriate to demonize media culture for acts of societal violence.[34] Yet, in my view, the proliferation of media culture and spectacle requires renewed calls for critical media literacy so that people can intelligently analyze and interpret the media and see how they are vehicles for problematic representations of race, class, gender, sexuality, power, and violence.

In the wake of the Columbine shootings, fierce criticism and scapegoating of media and youth culture erupted. Oddly, there was less finger-pointing at these targets after the Virginia Tech massacre, perhaps because the Korean and Asian films upon which Cho modeled his photos and videos were largely unknown in the United States, or perhaps because conservatives prefer to target jihadists or liberals as nefarious influences on Cho (Kellner 2008). I want to avoid, however, both extremes, neither demonizing media and youth culture, nor asserting that it is mere entertainment without serious social influence. There is no question that the media nurture fantasies and influence behavior, sometimes sick and vile ones. Achieving mental health in our culture requires that we are able to critically analyze and dissect media culture and not let it gain power over us. Critical media literacy empowers individuals so that they can establish critical and analytical distance from media messages and images. This provides protection from media manipulation and avoids letting the most destructive images of media gain power. It also enables more critical, healthy, and active relations with our culture. Media culture will not disappear and it is simply a question of how we will deal with it and if we can develop an adequate pedagogy of critical media literacy to empower our youth (see Kellner 2004).

Unfortunately, there are few media literacy courses offered in schools in the United States from kindergarten through high school. Many other countries such as Canada, Australia, and England have such programs (see Kellner and Share 2007). In previous studies, I have argued that designing schools for the new millennium that meet the challenges posed by student alienation and violence and that provide skills which students need for a high-tech economy requires a democratic reconstruction of education (Kellner 2004, 2006, and 2008).

I would also argue that to address problems of societal violence raised in this chapter requires a reconstruction of education and society, and what Herbert Marcuse referred to as "a revolution in values" and a "new sensibility."[35] The revolution in values involves breaking with values of competition, aggression, greed, and self- interest and cultivating values of equality, peace, harmony, and community. Such a revolution of values "would also make for a new morality, for new relations between the sexes and generations, for a new relation between man and nature" (Marcuse 2001). Harbingers of the revolution in values, Marcuse argued, are found in "a widespread rebellion against the domineering values, of virility, heroism and force, invoking the images of society which may bring about the end of violence" (ibid).

The "new sensibility" in turn would cultivate the need for beauty, love, connections with nature and other people, and more democratic and egalitarian social relations. Marcuse believed that without a change in the sensibility, there can be no real social change, and that education, art, and the humanities can help cultivate the conditions for a new sensibility. Underlying the theory of the new sensibility is a concept of the active role of the senses in the constitution of experience that rejects the Kantian and other philosophical devaluations of the senses as passive, merely receptive. For Marcuse, our senses are shaped and molded by society, yet constitute in turn our primary experience of the world and provide both imagination and reason with its material. He believed that the senses are currently socially constrained and mutilated and argues that only an emancipation of the senses and a new sensibility can produce liberating social change.

This is not to say that masculinity per se, or the traits associated with it, are all bad. There are times when being strong, independent, self-reliant, and even aggressive can serve positive goals and resist oppression and injustice. A postgendered human being would share traits now associated with women and men, so that women could exhibit the "manly" traits listed above and men could be more loving, caring, emotional, vulnerable, and other traits associated with women. Gender itself should be deconstructed; while we should fight gender oppression and inequality, there are reasons to question gender itself in a more emancipated and democratic world in which individuals create their own personalities and lives out of the potential found traditionally in men and women.

Since guns are identified with hypermasculinity and societal violence, a reconstruction of masculinity could help individuals and society deal with the ongoing American obsession with guns and resultant outbreaks of gun massacres. Developing new masculinities and sensibilities and overcoming alienation of students and youth is of course a utopian dream, but in the light of growing societal violence, domestic terrorism, and indiscriminate mass shootings, such a reconstruction of education and society is necessary to help produce a life worthy of human beings.

# Notes

1. Ralph Larkin (2011, 336) has noted that: "All of the rampage [school] shootings outside North America were influenced by the Columbine shootings. Columbine received international coverage and generated debates world wide among adolescents between sympathizers and those who vilified the acts of Klebold and Harris.... Many of the European rampage shootings, including the two in Finland, and two of the three in Germany, emulated Columbine. Robert Steinhauser wanted to exceed the body count of Columbine, which he did."

2. For an ever-expanding "Time Line of Worldwide School and Mass Shootings" since 1996, see www.infoplease.com/ipa/A0777958.html (accessed on December 20, 2012). For a global "list of rampage killers," see http://en.wikipedia.org/wiki/List_of _rampage_killers (accessed on December 26, 2012). For information on specific mass shootings, including guns used and a map of the shootings, see "Mother Jones Guide to Mass Shootings" at www.motherjones.com/politics/2012/07/mass-shootings-map (accessed on January 26, 2012).

3. Mariano Castillo and Holly Yan, "Details, but No Answers, in Oregon Mall Shooting," *CNN*, December 13, 2012, at www.cnn.com/2012/12/12/justice/oregon -mall-shooting (accessed on February 9, 2013).

4. See my analysis of connections between crises of masculinity, an out-of-control gun culture, and media spectacle in Kellner (2008).

5. Questions were later raised concerning why Nancy Lanza purchased such an arsenal of assault weapons, took her child to target practice with her, and did not keep her gun collection secured, allowing her son Adam to use her arsenal for mass murder. It was reported that many people in her community of Newtown were angry with Ms. Lanza and did not include her in their memorials of the murdered victims; see Kevin Sullivan, "In Newtown, Nancy Lanza a Subject of Sympathy for Some, Anger for Others," *Washington Post*, December 19, 2012, at www.washingtonpost .com/national/in-newtown-nancy-lanza-a-subject-of-sympathy-for-some-anger-for -others/2012/12/19/5a425f1c-4a1e-11e2-ad54-580638ede391_story.html (retrieved December 20, 2012). A later *Washington Post* story gave a more detailed account of Adam Lanza's solitary life, indicating that Adam was alone in life except for his relation to Nancy Lanza, who homeschooled him, and that when his father remarried, Adam broke off relations with both his father and brother. See Marc Fisher, Robert O'Harrow, and Peter Finn, "A Frustrating Search for Motive in Newtown Shootings," *Washington Post*, December 22, 2012, at www.washingtonpost.com/national/a-frustrating-search -for-motive-in-the- madness/2012/12/22/1cbe1cbc-4956-11e2-820e-17eefac2f939_story .html (accessed on December 22, 2012). As I conclude this study in fall 2013, documents

have not yet been released which would explain why Adam Lanza killed his mother and then went on a rampage at Sandy Hook Elementary.

6. This phrase was used in media accounts of the rampage, and the following YouTube shots one of Adam Lanza's acquaintances using the phrase; see www.youtube .com/watch?v=qcCRhj2qZ5w (accessed September 8, 2013).

7. See Ewen MacAskill, "Obama Puts Gun Control Centre Stage as Biden Appointed to Lead Task Force," *The Guardian*, December 2012, at www.guardian.co.uk/world/2012 /dec/19/obama-gun-control-biden-task-force (accessed at February 1, 2013).

8. As it turns out, December 2012 polls indicated a majority of Americans do not support banning assault rifles, whereas there was a strong majority supported background checks and a significant majority supported banning high-capacity ammunition clips, so it appears that US gun-safety reform will begin with reforms supported by the majority; see "After Newtown, Modest Change in Opinion about Gun Control. Most Say Assault Weapons Make Nation More Dangerous," Pew Research Center for the People and the Press, December 20, 2012, at www.people-press.org/2012/12/20/after-newtown -modest-change-in-opinion-about-gun-control/ (accessed January 30, 2012).

9. See Matea Gold, Joseph Tanfani, and Richard Simon, "Gun Lobby's Grip Loosens on Congress," *Los Angeles Times*, December 19, 2012: A1, and Peter Wallsten and Tom Hamburger, "Even before Newtown Tragedy, NRA Was Losing Democratic Support," *Washington Post,* December 19, 2012, at www.washingtonpost.com/politics/even-before -newtown-tragedy-nra-was-losing-democratic-support/2012/12/19/9b32738a-4952 -11e2-ad54- 580638ede391_story.html (accessed December 21, 2012).

10. Michael M. Grynbaum, "Bloomberg, Incensed by Shooting, Vows Stiffer Fight to Rework Gun Laws," *New York Times*, December 20, 2012, at www.nytimes .com/2012/12/21/nyregion/bloomberg-vows-stiffer-fight-to-overhaul-us-gun-laws .html?pagewanted=all (accessed January 27, 2012).

11. Ewen Callaway, "Carrying a Gun Increases Risk of Getting Shot and Killed," October 9, 2009, at www.newscientist.com/article/dn17922-carrying-a-gun-increases -risk-of-getting-shot-and-killed.html (accessed December 27, 2012); see also *American Journal of Public Health*, DOI: 10.2105/AJPH.2008.143099 (accessed December 27, 2012).

12. Newspapers were even more scathing, with Rupert Murdoch's *NY Post* featuring a giant headline GUN NUT, while its competitor the *New York Daily News* ran a headline describing the NRA's Wayne LaPierre as "CRAZIEST MAN ON EARTH." A *New York Times* editorial was less incendiary, describing LaPierre's "mendacious, delusional, almost deranged rant." In general, the media was angry because a press conference was announced and LaPierre did not take any questions, using his twenty-five-minute free network airtime to present a sales pitch for guns as the only solution for gun violence, while attacking the media, video games, the mental-health system, and other targets for allegedly being responsible for gun violence. For discussion of media response to LaPierre's speech, see Matt Williams, "Wayne LaPierre's Newtown Statement Pilloried by US Newspapers," *The Guardian*, December 22, 2012, at www.guardian.co.uk /world/2012/dec/22/nra-lapierre-statement-pilloried-newspapers (accessed on December 23, 2012).

13. For a striking report on how the gun industry funds the NRA that functions as the industry lobby, see "National Rifle Association Receives Millions of Dollars From Gun Industry," at www.vpc.org/press/1104blood.htm (accessed on December 26, 2012).

14. On the failure of Obama and other leaders of the Democratic Party to address gun control during the 2008 presidential election, see Derrick Z. Jackson, "Missing on Gun Control," *Boston Globe,* February 19, 2008, at www.boston.com/bostonglobe /editorial_opinion/oped/articles/2008/02/19/missing_on_gun_control/ (accessed on April 4, 2012). Adam Winkler recently claimed that: "Few presidents have shown as little interest in gun control as Barack Obama.... It's as if 'avoid gun control at all costs' has become a plank in the Democratic Party platform." Cited in Mitchell Landsberg, "NRA Is Restless Despite Clout. The Group Is So Worried about Obama That It Is Willing to Ignore Romney's Past." *Los Angeles Times,* April 13, 2012: AA7.

15. See the Bushmaster website at www.bushmaster.com/press-release-050710.asp (accessed December 18, 2012).

16. The logo was accessible on the Wikipedia Bushmaster site on the top right-hand side when I accessed it on December 22, 2012, at http://en.wikipedia.org/wiki /Bushmaster_Firearms_International.

17. Walmart had previously been the subject of campaigns against the easy availability of assault weapons and ammunition; see George Zornick, "How Walmart Helped Make Newtown Shooter's AR-15 the Most Popular Assault Weapon in America," *The Nation,* December 17, 2012, at www.thenation.com/article/171808/how-walmart-helped -make-newtown-shooters-ar-15-most-popular-assault-weapon-america (accessed on December 21, 2012).

18. Cory Booker, "It's Time to Emphasize Pragmatic and Achievable Gun Law Reform," *Huffington Post,* December 21, 2012, at www.huffingtonpost.com/cory-booker /gun-law-reform_b_2346911.html (accessed on December 27, 2012).

19. Michael S. Schmidt and Charlie Savage, "Gaps in F.B.I. Data Undercut Background Checks for Guns," *New York Times,* December 20, 2012, at www.nytimes .com/2012/12/21/us/gaps-in-fbi-data-undercut-background-checks-for-guns .html?pagewanted=all (accessed on December 27, 2012). Unfortunately, there has not been recent research on how many guns are purchased without background checks or obtained from underground and illegal sources, and the NRA and gun lobby has blocked funding of such research.

20. Mental health professionals argue that only 5 percent of shootings in the contemporary United States are attributed to those with diagnosed mental-health issues, and that such people are more likely to be an object of violence rather than its subject. See Michael Menaster, David Bienenfeld, et al., "Psychiatric Disorders Associated With Criminal Behavior," *Medscape,* April 12, 2012, at http://emedicine.medscape.com /article/294626-overview (accessed on January 20, 2013).

21. Sean Sullivan, "Lines Drawn in Gun-Control Debate," *Washington Post,* January 6, 2013, at http://articles.washingtonpost.com/2013-01-06/politics/36208427_1_checks -on-gun-buyers-gun-control-gun-laws(accessed at January 20, 2013).

22. Booker, "It's Time to Emphasize Pragmatic and Achievable Gun Law Reform."

23. See Douglas Kellner, "Media Spectacle and Domestic Terrorism: The Case of the *Batman/Joker* Cinema Massacre," *The Review of Education/Pedagogy/Cultural Studies*, 35, no. 1 (2013): 1–21. On the ease with which guns and munitions can be bought over the Internet, see Michael Luo, Mike McIntire, and Griff Palmer, "Seeking Gun or Selling One, Web Is a Land of Few Rules," *New York Times*, April 17, 2013 at www.nytimes.com/2013/04/17/us/seeking-gun-or-selling-one-web-is-a-land-of-few-rules.html?pagewanted=all&_r=0, accessed on July 9, 2013).

24. By mid-April 2013, the writing was on the wall that no meaningful gun-safety legislation would be passed by the current Congress despite writing a bipartisan bill to strengthen background checks in April 2013 that as much as 90 percent of the public supported and that had some bipartisan backing; see Dan Roberts, "Gun Control Hopes Fade as Joe Manchin Admits: 'We will not get the votes today.'" *The Guardian*, April 17, 2013, at www.guardian.co.uk/world/2013/apr/17/gun-control-hopes-fade-senators (accessed on July 9, 2013). When the bill to strengthen background checks was voted down in the Senate shortly thereafter, it appeared the NRA and gun lobby had won another big victory; see Dan Roberts, "Gun Control Reform: All but Three 'No' Senators Received Pro-Gun Cash," *The Guardian*, April 18, 2013, at www.guardian.co.uk/world/2013/apr/18/pro- gun-groups-donated-senators(accessed on July 9, 2013).

25. In China, the same day as the Sandy Hook slaughter, a man attacked twenty-three school children with a knife, but none were killed, highlighting the more lethal violence used by angry men on gun rampages in the United States; see Carlos Tejada, "China Grapples with Latest Attack on School," *Wall Street Journal*, December 17, 2012, at http://online.wsj.com/article/SB10001424127887324407504578182904026663998.html (accessed on December 20, 2012).

26. See Larkin 2011, 330ff., who documents the rise of bullying since the 1980s and the role of jocks and those who champion hypermasculinity against youth who do not confirm to the dominant male stereotypes.

27. Yet as the Penn State football scandal revealed in 2011–2012, a deified football culture can also lead sports and university leaders to cover over sexual abuse of young men and women, as has the Catholic Church. See Henry A. Giroux, "From Penn State to JPMorgan Chase and Barclays: Destroying Higher Education, Savaging Children and Extinguishing Democracy," *Truth Out*, July 24, 2012, at http://truth- out.org/opinion/item/10301-from-penn-state-to-jpmorgan-chase-and-barclay-destroying-higher-education-savaging-children-and-extinguishing-democracy (accessed on July 30, 2012), and "Henry Giroux on Penn State, College Athletics, and Capitalism: Solidarity Is 'Impossible' When Sports Are Driven by Market Values," *Truth Out*, July 24, 2012, at http://truth-out.org/news/item/10496-henry-giroux-on-penn-state-college-athletics-and-capitalism-solidarity-is-impossible-when-sports-are-driven-by-market-values (accessed on July 30, 2012).

28. On men and fight clubs, see Henry A. Giroux, "Private Satisfactions and Public Disorders: *Fight Club*, Patriarchy, and the Politics of Masculine Violence," at www.henryagiroux.com/online_articles/fight_club.htm (accessed on January 3, 2013).

29. There have been steadily growing serious injuries in pro football in recent years and calls to better protect players; see Kevin Cook, "Dying to Play," *New York Times*, September 11, 2012, at www.nytimes.com/2012/09/12/opinion/head-injuries-in-football .html?_r=0&pagewanted=print (accessed on January 3, 2013).

30. See "Report: Newtown Gunman Adam Lanza Spent Days In Basement Playing *Call Of Duty*," *CBS News New York*, December 19, 2012, at http://newyork .cbslocal.com/2012/12/19/report-newtown-gunman-adam-lanza-spent-days-in -basement-playing-call-of-duty/ (accessed on December 26, 2012), and Barney Henderson, "Connecticut School Massacre: Adam Lanza 'Spent Hours Playing *Call Of Duty*,'" *The Telegraph*, December 18, 2012, at www.telegraph.co.uk/news/worldnews /northamerica /usa/9752141/Connecticut-school-massacre-Adam-Lanza-spent-hours -playing-Call-Of-Duty.html (accessed on December 26, 2012). The Norwegian killer Anders Breivik was also reportedly a devotee of *Call of Duty*, which he reportedly played for hours on end. See Douglas Kellner, "The Dark Side of the Spectacle: Terror in Norway and the UK Riots," *Cultural Politics*, 8:01 (March 2012): 1–43.

31. See "Gun Dealer Sold to Both Va. Tech, NIU shooters," *USA Today*, February 16, 2008, at www.usatoday.com/news/nation/2008-02-16-gundealer-niu-vatech -shooters_N.htm (accessed on April 16, 2012). Interestingly, Eric Thompson's company, TGSCOM Inc., which sold Cho and Kazmierczak weapons through his website www .thegunsource.com, offered customers weapons at cost for two weeks to help citizens get the weapons they needed for their own self defense, see "Owner of Web-Based Firearms Company That Sold to Virginia Tech and NIU Shooters to Forgo Profits to Help Prevent Future Loss of Life," April 25, 2008, *TGSCOM Inc.* at www.thegunsource .com/Article.aspx?aKey=Guns_at_Cost (accessed on April 16, 2012).

32. See, for example, Barry Meier and Andrew Martin, "Real and Virtual Firearms Nurture a Marketing Link," *New York Times*, December 24, 2012, at http://t.co/Ixlio00V by nytimesbusiness 283397456211894273 (accessed on December 25, 2012). The article reminds us that a "Norwegian who killed 77 said later that he honed his shooting skills by playing many hours of *Call of Duty*." On the Norwegian shooter, see Kellner 2012.

33. Cited in Nick Gillespie, "The FCC's Not Mommy and Daddy," *Los Angeles Times*, May 2, 2007, A23.

34. In his book (2008) *Guyland. The Perilous World Where Boys Become Men*, Michael Kimble carries out a thorough and insightful mapping of the terrain of male culture in the contemporary United States, but does not address the problems of guns and culture, downplays the impact of video games and media culture (152ff), and does not adequately address the problems of hypermasculinity and violence.

35. See Herbert Marcuse, "A Revolution in Values" in Marcuse 2001, and on the new sensibility see my introduction to the volume of collected papers of Marcuse on *Art and Liberation* (2006).

# Chapter 6

# *Beyond Alienation and Anomie*

## *Gun Violence and Sociological Monstrosities*

### Mark P. Worrell

On March 5, 2001, Charles Andrew "Andy" Williams entered Santana High School in Santee, California, and shot fifteen of his fellow students, killing two and wounding thirteen more. In a recent interview with Miles O'Brien (2013), Williams says that he was incapable of "comprehending the finality" of his actions, that he was suicidal, and that his "grand plan was suicide by cop." In other words, the destruction of others was a means toward another end, the desire for self-destruction that he was incapable of inflicting upon himself. The explanation for this event follows the standard (even ritualized) formulations for other mass shootings in America: mental illness, alienation, bullying, drug and alcohol abuse, decadent youth culture, and so on. Liberals tend to seek institutional and organizational factors to comprehend mass killings, while conservatives blame the dissolution of traditional values and the receding power of God in an increasingly secular world. The point of liberal-conservative convergence, however, the blind spot or null point in the American episteme, is the spirit of anarchy: civil deregulation on the part of liberals and economic deregulation on the part of conservatives.[1] America is the land of anarcho-capitalism ruled by a spirit of limitlessness. That Williams was incapable of "comprehending the finality" of his actions is telling: the United States is, preeminently, the land of the Infinite, from foreign policy and military adventures, to financial and speculative magic, to religious fanaticism and cultural hype (Worrell 2013). After each mass shooting the public, media, and politicians engage in the time-honored ritual reactions, demands for changes are issued, and, as always, nothing is done to prevent further death. Social-media meme battles are telling with respect to the placement of blame and illustrate our collective paralysis. After the Sandy Hook tragedy, however, a language of "sacrifice" began to emerge.

Garry Wills says that Sandy Hook massacre was a "sacrifice we as a culture made, and continually make, to our demonic god."

> We guarantee that crazed man after crazed man will have a flood of killing power readily supplied him. We have to make that offering, out of devotion to our Moloch, our god. The gun is our Moloch. We sacrifice children to him—daily, sometimes, as at Sandy Hook, by directly throwing them into the fire-hose of bullets from our protected private killing machines, sometimes by blighting our children's lives by the death of a parent, a schoolmate, a teacher, a protector. Sometimes this is done by mass killings ... sometimes by private offerings to the god.... Adoration of Moloch permeates the country, imposing a hushed silence as he works his will. One cannot question his rites, even as the blood is gushing through the idol's teeth. The White House spokesman invokes the silence of traditional in religious ceremony. "It is not the time" to question Moloch. No time is right for showing disrespect for Moloch. (2012)[2]

Wills's interesting sociological and anthropological observation brings us back to the problem of the spirit of limitlessness. Are people (almost always male) with guns just lone, crazy killers in need of medication and friends or are they instrumental avatars of impersonal powers demanding obedience and tribute? Alienation and anomie are good concepts to start with in explaining rampage shooters, but we cannot rest content with an idea or two without losing sight of their synthetic capacities. How can we intellectually raise the problem of mass shootings to another scale of social reality (a "higher" perspective) whereby concepts like sacrifice, the impersonal, psyche, alienation, and so on, are preserved while also bringing them into a transformed synthetic unity whereby our resulting comprehension is deeper and further?

*    *    *

It is not surprising that media deploy critical words like "alienation" in uncritical ways to help explain things like mass shootings. Since the 1950s, "alienation" has been one of the standard tags used to define American life. Here, alienation is typically meant as the everyday notion of experiencing life as a social outcast or lonely outsider incapable of making sense of a strange world. The domain of critical sociology, by contrast, draws its theory of alienation directly from Marx's theory of the commodity and, before him, to Hegel.

When we confront the word "alienation" in Marx, we are usually reading a troublesome rendering of the German *entfremden* or *entfremdung* (e.g., Marx 1976, 203; Marx and Engels 1972, 104). *Entfremdung* signifies theft, mental debilitation, and the separation or estrangement of people from one another or between people and their products—think of *entfremden* as "to make alien" or the making of strangers. This definition clearly fits with Marx's criticism of capitalist productive relations, whereby finished products are not the property of the workers who produced them. As such, *entfremden* or *entfremdung* denote "separation from" or, better, a sense of "estrangement." But the idea of "alienation" as the presence of something extra (some excessive thing) at the center of our being is better comprehended in the (Hegelian) concept *entäusserung*, an idea that signifies *possession*[3] and *splitting* (see Inwood 1992, 36). It is undeniably the case that Marx more or less holds the patent for alienation theory; however, I would like to make the claim that Durkheim's implicit theory of alienation, while entirely sympathetic with Marx's, takes critical sociology further.

Durkheim's theory of social forces and organization (the foundation of his theory of alienation) can be summarized thusly: human assemblage produces a "surplus" that, when named or otherwise signified, crystallizes into sui generis, authoritative powers.[4] A normal and healthy society is the sublimated product of the synthesis of these energized representational streams converging and blending in myriad forms. Intersubjective reality represents an interdigitated fusion of material and collective mental forms (a system of ideas) in something that approximates a dynamic equilibrium in flux, undergoing continuous adjustment. Existence here is characterized by a submergence in collective life, the feeling of moral vitality, quasi-mystified individual consciousness,[5] the realization of actual individuality of the person by virtue of his or her attachment to a multiplicity of associations (from the intimate life of the family out to the abstract cult of humanity),[6] and the resulting limitation of desires and the regulation of aspirations.[7] Far from this ideal-typical model of society, American life "enjoys" a "morbid effervescence" of commodity fetishism and rampant materialism, atomization, the proliferation of impossible dreams[8] and foolhardy schemes, and a mania for violence and the stockpiling of the means of destruction.[9]

It might be argued that America has never been a coherent society, that the "DNA" of America was, from the beginning,[10] doomed to disorganization—where energy streams become disorganized and intersect in a multitude of weird, polar combinations,[11] undercurrents, and vortices, leaving individuals in a state of doubt, anxiety, ambivalence, conflict, and so on, alternating between mania and depression, where people are left to their own devices in determining their routes of action and modes of conduct, and imprisonment in a lifetime of dead-end labor. In this vein, Durkheim's *Suicide* posits not only a taxonomy of self-destructiveness but also discloses four elementary modalities of alienation relevant to the contemporary American situation.

Egoism (Selfism) = estrangement, separation, or detachment (the corresponding emotions are melancholy, indifference, and a repugnance toward the exterior world in the Stoic form and skeptical disillusionment in the Epicurean form); egoism may be active or passive, the latter representing a forced (voluntary or involuntary) separation of the member from a group; this passive form may develop in an active direction where the individual comes to desire and prefer separation from contaminating otherness.

Anomie (Deregulation) = splitting, being divided against oneself, or being doubled in self-opposition (the corresponding emotions are violent anger in its active regressive form, maniacal excitement in its active progressive form, disgust in its passive regressive form, and weariness in its passive progressive form).

Altruism (Otherness) = "possession" (the corresponding emotions are fanatical enthusiasm and sadness or despair sometimes mixed with hope). Obligatory altruism is essentially "negative" in that it seeks to avoid the stigma associated with avoiding sacrifice, whereas optional altruism is "positive" in that it seeks to gain a measure of prestige in, for example, seeking sacrifice; of course, the positive and the negative are merely two sides of the same metaphorical coin and, as such, aspects blend and combine in myriad ways. The acute form of altruism represents an ideal-typical purity where there is literally no longer a self—it is completely absorbed in the life of the Other.

Fatalism (Overregulation) = servitude or bondage (the corresponding emotions are futility, anger, and the spirit of revolt or resigned capitulation).[12] The twin aspects of Fate (*Moira*) are Necessity (thou must) and Right (thou should).[13]

Decisively, these four primary "spirits" combine in myriad composite forms to provide the underlying dynamic bases of any society—they are the four horsemen that drive the "positive hell" of social life. Well-regulated societies represent an objective synthesis of these contradictory currents (double polarities)[14] and are characterized by a coherent reality where members are "inoculated" against the impulse toward self-annihilation and homicide. Diseased societies, by contrast, are characterized by a cacophony of contradictory commands issued by negative drivers—i.e., the "spirits" of egoism, anomie, altruism, and fatalism. Modern, capitalist societies, according to Durkheim, suffer from what he called the "disease of the infinite"—the fusion of egoism (the "infinity of dreams") and anomie (the "infinity of desires"). We will focus on anomie and then turn our attention to the modalities of alienation in order to explore veiled transits and convergences that fuse anomie with other toxic currents that constitute the "annual tribute" of mass killings.

* * *

The American bias is toward examination of the abstracted psyche (mass murderers are simply "crazy") but, as Durkheim notes, the psyche is itself an infinity and sociology cannot venture off into the infinite. The infinite cannot be grasped by critique. Moreover, if we want to comprehend the sociology of gun violence, we will be forever stymied by looking through the peephole of the psyche. Besides, that which is essential with respect to the psyche is precisely its social determinants. The psyche is infused with the social.[15] The psyche is a condensate that "drips" out of the collective order. If society is "crazy" it will mass-manufacture "crazy" people. If violence is considered prestigious and sanctified, people will act violently in order to participate in the positive or negative prestige of violence and thereby approach sanctification.[16] Few nations today have gone as far as the United States to glorify and sacralize war, violence, and mass destruction. We are, after all, a "gunfighter nation" (Slotkin)[17] and war is now a full-time, multidimensional occupation (Worrell 2011). It should come as no surprise, then, that the imperial spirit of limitlessness, mass death, and indiscriminate killings (witness drone attacks that kill off more than one hundred bystanders in order to "nail" one bad guy) should be reflected back into the internal core of its system in the form of mass killings of innocent civilians. Much of this is reflected in the life of Adam Lanza.

Labeling the Sandy Hook Elementary shooter, Adam Lanza, as mentally disturbed or disabled is not the end of analysis but only the beginning. When we examine the broad contours of Lanza's life (as seen, for example, on PBS's *Frontline* 2013), what stands out most dramatically is the problem of unceasing change[18] from one school to another and alternating integration with isolation;

just when the child would become somewhat integrated, his mother would move him to another school, enforcing his detachment from others. The one constant element of his life was his mother but she represented not stability (a point of contact with reality) but the guarantee of ceaseless change and instability. Whereas Andy Williams could not fathom the "finality" of his actions, Lanza, it seems, conceived all too well of the finality of his actions: this is the end. When "the disease of the infinite" manifests itself in its singular, exasperated, enraged, and armed form, we have something like an Adam Lanza. If Lanza was "crazy" it was because the organization of his life was anomic.

It is unlikely that the United States will solve its gun-violence problem because (a) we are trapped at the inane level of debating whether it is guns killing people or people killing people; (b) the state is almost completely dominated by special interests which depends for their pleasure on the spirit of anomie; and (c) we indulge in ego-centered, reductionist psychobabble. Only in the unlikely event that American pundits, critics, and analysts work themselves up to the sociological plane and discover that it is a diseased *society* that kills off its own members, that it commands them to die and destroy, will we begin to solve the problem by regenerating a new social system.

Adam Lanza and people like him obey and disobey commands that most of us never even hear. Is it because they are "crazy" that they "hear voices"? Virtually all of us are subjected to the same commands as mass shooters, but the social organization of our lives means that those commands are either disavowed altogether or sublated into "positive" or socially approved injunctions. Lanza's mother wanted only the best education for her son but created an unendurable and unending nightmare (her plans for his transfer to another college was, apparently, the final straw). Other kids in the same situation would have used, for example, an electric guitar to "slay" the world and put their misery behind them, but Lanza used a gun to accomplish the same thing: the end of mother, the end of schools, the end of everything and the embrace of nothing.[19] Adam Lanza was an unwilling subject in the kingdom of anomie, who apparently reached his limit and struck back wildly, irrationally, and murderously.

If we examine extreme cases of destructiveness, of the self or other, we will find that they lie at the terminal point of a fluid continuum connecting them with normal, everyday conduct.[20] For example, the extreme form of altruism (the acute form represented by the religious fanatic who engages in voluntary human sacrifice for the well-being of his or her imagined God) is related to the spirit of selfless generosity necessary for any society to function. When a Williams or a Lanza become unhinged and go on a rampage, our ritualized collective response serves to localize, personalize, and translate the event into a mental-health problem. In a very real sense, our scripted and ritualized responses are elements in the cult of anomic violence that guarantees the recurrence of mass killings.[21] Rituals make people, places, and things sacred (pure or impure, positively or negatively) and objects of a future cult; we should avoid transforming the "gun rampage" into a "pillar of fire" and permanent feature of American life. Wills is correct to frame these killings as a form of sacrifice: people, it seems, must die periodically if the spirit of anomie is to reign supreme. Lanza (we shall presume) wanted to put an end to his suffering at the hands of the people and impersonal forces that he imagined made his life miserable. However, in so doing, he ironically did his master's bidding. Lanza and killers like him, seen from the sociological point of view, are but personifications and instruments of abstract social forces.[22] In short, anomie, in the form of Adam Lanza, killed twenty-seven people on December 14, 2012, at Sandy Hook Elementary School. Adam Lanza was not merely a killer but anomie's willing *executioner*. Nonetheless, there was something more there than anomie. Indeed, pinning everything on "anomie" would not offer much in the way of an original insight.[23] Had Lanza merely shot his mother and then himself, we could probably rest at the concept of anomie to tell us what we want to know regarding the big picture; however, the sheer scope of the crime suggests something more, on the order of terror. Lanza's "gun rampage" that resulted in the senseless, mass slaughter of children suggests an alloy of elements. The possibilities are bewilderingly complex.

*   *   *

Where anomie reigns, one is sure to find its polar opposite, fatalism, playing a supporting and alternating role.[24] Likewise, where there is egoism of one variety or another, one is sure to find altruism lurking about in some kind of transfigured (and perhaps "transcendental") form.[25] There are myriad underground tunnels and vertices that create transits for ideas and currents to flow and coalesce into hybrids and sui generis composites. This, of course, applies to the register of modalities of alienation as well. Where one finds the "estrangement" of egoism and the unreal "splitting" and anger of anomie[26] one is in contact with the "possession" of altruism; likewise, where we find the "double" or "splitting" associated with anomie we are sure to find a measure of futility in the form of feelings of being trapped or life as a dead end. It was not simply anomie that made Adam Lanza come unhinged and go on a shooting rampage, he was also "possessed," in that some overpowering idea "mounted" him, converting him into an instrument ("the disease of the infinite" fused with an altruistic current). We often find this mind-set in the fanatic: For example, a suicide bomber (the ideal typical case of murder-suicide) is often portrayed as a fanatic,[27] but "fanatic" alone does not quite tell us what we want to know about somebody like Adam Lanza. When we interrogate the "spiritual" fusion of anomie and altruism with an eye toward extreme violence resulting in the perpetrator's own death (like a school shooter or suicide bomber) we are seeing the "spirit" of piacularism at work (Worrell 2013).[28]

Piacularism is a relatively obscure concept best explicated at the end of Durkheim's work on primitive religions (1995 [1912], 392–417). At first glance, piacularism, which emphasizes collective ritual mourning in the face of tragedy, would throw us off the track of the lone rampage killer. Indeed, piacularism is most obviously a potential reaction on the part of victims of a shooting spree rather than the perpetrators. However, when we dig a littler deeper we can construct a matrix of piacular forms: on the one hand, the piacular proper which represents collective rites of mourning and reaction that put the members of a society into contact with positive sacred energies. If, however, we turn to the negative and individuated form of the piacular, we find the criminal acts of the rampage killer bent on destroying as much of society as he can. Incidentally, between these two polar endpoints we find, for example, the terrorist in the form of a suicide bomber who acts "alone" but for the betterment of their Other, the suffering community of oppressed of which he or she is a member. The piacularism of the rampage killer who strikes periodically in American life must be qualified and reconstructed to emphasize its specialized, individuated, and negative form, as opposed to the positive and collective form of the piacular rituals that will follow in the wake of the shooting spree. The seeming paradox that the piacular applies to both the good and blameless group of victims and to the evil perpetrator can be resolved when we recall that the lone maniac is not as "alone" as he appears at first sight.[29]

We ask again: how can the lone gunman with no moral cause to kill and no social collaboration constitute a manifestation of the piacular, which is eminently social? A suicide bomber, for example, represents a single "instrument" of death but dies for some "cause" and for his or her community or God, its collective representation and transcendental third term. Can the same be said for the lone gunman who senselessly kills in the name of apparently nothing? How does nihilism (nothing-ism) pertain to the vital energies of life? If we turn back to suicide we find that what appears to be a lone act, uncoordinated from any central authority, is in reality a social fact not only statistically, but that the cohort of voluntary self-killers constitute, unconsciously, an actual class of subjects each obeying commands to dispose of themselves. We already know in advance more or less how many people are going to kill themselves every year and we can predict when the rate of self-destruction will rise and fall: "Life's vanquished form a long cohort of captives that society drags behind its chariot" (Halbwachs 1978 [1930], 297). Moreover, despite the spike in "spectacular" rampage killings in recent years, we can predict how many mass shootings and deaths resulting from these events will occur this year and next—indeed, since the early 1980s the incidents of mass shootings reveals no great change (Walker 2012). How "alone" is the suicide victim in his or her act? How "separated" from negative moral authority is the lone rampage killer?

In *The Sunset Limited*, playwright Cormac McCarthy makes a nice contribution to the sociology of suicide when his character "Black" wonders if it is not the case that all suicidal types are the "natural kin" of White, who represents a classic example of the Stoic. People who occupy certain coordinates within a social system will find themselves in communion with social monstrosities issuing commands to kill or die. Obviously, millions of Americans are in contact with those same imperatives every day but they disobey the commands, they choose to live and to not harm their fellow human beings. Unfortunately, a regular number of those individuals, from year to year, will heed the command to kill and die. While we know approximately how many will turn their weapons on society and how many victims will be killed, we do not know who in particular will be pulling the triggers until after the fact. These apparently lone killers, however, are members of a virtual community of like-minded individuals. It must be remembered that a disorganized and dysfunctional social system is no less energetic and forceful than a healthy society—every one of Durkheim's books, in fact, addresses at some place or another the frenzy of the unregulated crowd or mob that rapidly degenerates into a "monstrosity" or terrifying beast. If we seek to eliminate the eruption of monsters like the rampage shooter, then we must focus on the monstrous social system in which they are produced and which they represent as irrational symptoms. The rampage killer is not a brain problem, a family-values problem, or a Jesus-deprivation problem, but rather a structural problem afflicting late-capitalist America. Societies do not simply die off from old age, they are killed off by active forces such as predatory finance, austerity, gross class inequality, warmongering, hatred in countless forms, egoism, hypermaterialism, and massive deregulation of the whole social order. The real question is not why does a person go on a random shooting spree but rather, given the condition of the current social order, why don't more people lash out destructively?

Attempts to mend the psyche without wholesale reconstruction of society is futility itself. In fact, it would appear to the naïve consciousness that fixing the individual would be infinitely easier than fixing the whole of society (and pharmaceutical corporations would emphatically agree), but trying to solve gun violence without an overhaul of the entire social system would be like fighting forest fires with garden hoses. The theoretical constellation that is "the piacular" (in its individuated and negative form) enables us to move beyond any isolated and partial concept. The negative piacular draws together the mystical dream construct of the estranged egoist who erects a substitute fantasy world for itself—a futile attempt at self-duplication or Othering. The piacular also connects this mysticism with the "self torture" of limitlessness (*apeiron*) and insatiability of desire. The piacular also connects these two aspects of unreality with the fanatical terror and destructiveness of the sociological "altruist" who desires the obliteration of the existent.

## Notes

1. Paradoxically, religious conservatives "enjoy" civil anarchy because they imagine it brings them closer to the end times and the day of reckoning (Wolin 2008, 117), while upper-middle-class liberals enjoy the material benefits of speculative accumulation and low-wage service.

2. See also Rex Berry's editorial in the *Tulsa World* (2013).

3. In a very real sense, being a recognized and accepted member of society means that there is not only a commanding voice "above" us telling us what we should and should not do but also an *alien* presence alive *within* us somewhere—indeed, the voice "above" and the "thing" within share a connection. Sometimes, and at some points in our lives, we are blissfully unaware that some kind of foreign object resides at our core (we seem to vibrate sympathetically on the same frequency) while, under other conditions, we are made painfully aware of the radical otherness of a thing that has taken possession of us. Interestingly, it is often when we are unsuccessfully trying to do what we are supposed to do or when we resist external commands that the alien thing becomes a toxin: bad conscience, guilt, shame, or anxiety. When we become aware of the alien "thing" at the center of our self we come face to face with the problem of alienation and the contradiction of being both an individual and a member of society—the dialectic of private existence and social functions.

4. This "surplus" is entirely in line with Marx's analysis of value as a "phantom objectivity," that is, a nonmaterial yet objectively real thing, or a form of collective consciousness (Worrell 2009) grounded in any number of "productive functions" including work and, especially for Durkheim, ritual.

5. Society, says Durkheim, "is full of mystery for the individual. We constantly have the impression of being surrounded with a host of things in the course of happening whose nature escapes us. All sorts of forces move themselves about, encounter

one another, collide near us, almost brushing us in their passage; yet we go without seeing them until that time when some impressive culmination provides a glimpse of a hidden and mysterious event which has occurred under our noses, but of which we had no suspicion and which we begin to see only in terms of its results" (1961, 89). We see here the connection between Durkheim and the Lacanian-Žižekian notion of reality as a kind of "virtual reality" where fictions and fantasies work to support our existence in the world.

6. Like rock or mountain climbing, the individual needs three points of contact at all times in order to stand on his or her own two feet: family, the daily grind at school or work, and the weekend association. Anatomically, we are bipeds, but socially we must be minimally tripedal in order to "enjoy" life.

7. The American mentality finds individuality and intense collective life mutually exclusive but, as Durkheim notes, the words "individual" and "individuality," though similar in spelling, mean radically different things and are even opposed to one another in some respects (Durkheim 1973, 54–55). America is not the land of individuality but antisocial egoism. In a sense, "individual" means not dividable, whereas an "individual" is not only divided but multiplied (cf. Simmel 1971, 259).

8. "The Impossible Dream (The Quest)" composed for *Man of La Mancha* could very well be the unofficial theme song for the United States.

9. The stockpiling of the means of destruction applies to both the personal (tactical) and collective (strategic) levels. Since WWII, the United States has dumped nearly $10 trillion into the nuclear-armaments program alone (Zak 2013) and gun ownership in America has been declining since the mid-1970s, but the United States is nonetheless awash in perhaps as many as 320 million firearms (Tavernise 2013).

10. Fischer says, "Today less than 20 percent of the American population have any British ancestors at all. But in a cultural sense most Americans ... [are their product] no matter who their own forebears may have been" (1989, 6). Those original folkway streams that greatly determine contemporary life to this day as transformed "survivals" are contradictory at best and outright pathological in many ways. Reading Fischer's work through Durkheimian optics is highly revealing.

11. Superimpositions, alternations, and syntheses number among the possibilities.

12. As Simmel indicates, resignation should not be thought of as merely a passive form of surrender but can be an active form of proving strength in the face of defeat as well as a maneuver enabling a transit from the realm of fate toward the retention of the nobility of the ego (1955, 113–114).

13. For more on fate, see Harrison (1966) and F. M. Cornford (2004 [1912]).

14. Moral life, says Durkheim, is the contradictory synthesis of polar oppositions (1961, 124–125). Dialectically, we see that, for example, egoism and altruism are simultaneously consequences of disorganization, "raw materials" of social organization (they are "reconciled" in social reality), and autonomous forces ("informing causes") issuing commands and expecting obedience/recognition.

15. Durkheim's "idealism" (like Marx, he was what we would call a constructionist or, clumsily, a materialist-idealist) breaks with Hegel and Feuerbach in that, for Durkheim, external determination is self-determination. See Durkheim's analysis of Kantian "autonomy" (1961).

16. Note the recent deaths of "personified guns" (ex–Navy SEAL Chris Kyle and "gun guru" Keith Ratliff). Kyle was famous for being the "greatest" sniper in history with more "confirmed kills" than anyone previously, while Ratliff hosted a YouTube channel devoted to firearms to which nearly 3.5 million viewers subscribed. These were not merely "guys with guns" but were collective representations or beacons of the American gun culture. They were "the gun" itself in human form.

17. Even as firearm ownership in the United States condenses into fewer hands, popular culture is still undeniably saturated by gun violence and conflict resolution at the end of a barrel.

18. Change is only a problem within a social system that lacks a moral consistency and effective regulation (Durkheim 1961, 62).

19. It is also very interesting that these big spectacle rampages occur almost exclusively on school campuses. It is as if anomie "knows" where to strike to reach the heart of social discipline and moral order. The "conservative" war on education and the rampaging gun maniac are both, in their own ways, servants of anomie. The present era of "magical capitalism" aims to melt society down into pure anarchy and attacking the school, monetarily or with bullets, represent an unconsciously coordinated war on moral order and stability.

20. This is one of Durkheim's most important insights: "suicides do not form, as might be thought, a wholly distinct group, an isolated class of monstrous phenomena, unrelated to other forms of conduct, but rather are related to them by a continuous series of intermediate cases. They are merely the exaggerated form of common practices" (1951 [1897], 45).

21. Focusing only on the most "spectacular" forms of mass shootings of the Columbine, Virginia Tech, and Sandy Hook type, we find a definite increase in the rate of "gun rampages" in the United States since the early 1980s (Follman 2013).

22. When a society is well regulated and ordered, then our conduct is regular and orderly. There would be, then, "scarcely a moment in the day when we are not acting as instruments of the social order" (1961, 132). However, when a society finds itself in disarray (a "negative heaven" as opposed to the "positive hell" of normal society), we become instruments not of the social "order" but of the unsynthesized and unmediated "sociological monstrosities" that result from and further drive disorder. The naïve consciousness and popular conceptions of devils and demons is but a distortion and mystification of objectively real forces animating any social order.

23. A Google search of "Adam Lanza" and "anomie" yields nearly 16,000 results.

24. See Durkheim's discussion of "primitives" and children on the subject of alternations between, and superimpositions of, anomie and fatalism (1961, 131–138).

The convergence of anomie and fatalism can be termed *archaism*. We see the spirit of archaism in the likes of Dominionism, a kind of political-theological modern primitivism blended with infantilism. The commingling of rebelliousness and bureaucracy, indicative of authoritarian political regimes, is also highly interesting (1961, 130).

25. See, for example, Durkheim's discussion of nineteenth-century Jews in France and the Stoics (1951 [1897]). Though unnamed, Durkheim's reference to the Stoic ideal type is a reference specifically to the *sage*. The Stoic-Altruist transit can be thought of as a form of mysticism that projects a great being to function as a model for the virtuous life—also setting up the very real problem of futility (and fatalism) at never attaining sage-like virtue (Sellars 2006, 41).

26. The experience of being "beside oneself" is the ideal-typical expression of this "splitting" and capitalism, the very heart and soul of American society (Žižek calls capital the Thing par excellence of modernity), which revels in its capacity to produce doubles and that "magical" ability to be, like money, in two places at the same time. A fundamental experience of modern life is feeling torn or divided, and being presented with simultaneously too many courses of action and too few.

27. From the Latin *fanaticus*, "inspired by a god."

28. Incidentally, a Google search for "Adam Lanza" and "piacularism" yields zero results.

29. When we think of the distinction between religion and magic, we note that both the priest and the magician (representing the poles of the alter and the ego, the positive and the negative) participate in the same moral energy conceived of in its twin essence. Mana, as you will recall, is ambivalent, double, manifesting in totems and taboos.

# Chapter 7

# Fear, Punitive Anger, and Guns

## The Social Psychology of Vindicatory Firearm Ownership

### Robert L. Young

Aₗₜₕₒᵤgₕ MASS MURDERS—SUCH AS THOSE THAT OCCUR IN PUBLIC SPACES, work settings, and on high school and college campuses—grab headlines and even spur political action, the number of deaths resulting from such attacks constitutes a minute portion of the total gun killings in America each year. For example, in 2009, US homicides totaled just under 14,000, of which 67 percent were committed with guns (FBI 2011). Although these numbers add up to the highest annual murder rates in the industrialized world, a significantly larger number of deaths occur each year as a result of suicides. Approximately 37,000 Americans committed suicide in 2009, and approximately half of them ended their lives with guns (Centers for Disease Control and Prevention 2013). Thus, combined, more than 27,000 Americans die each year as a result of intentional shootings. Regardless of whether such attacks are directed outwardly in the form of homicide or inwardly in the form of suicide, the popularity and lethality of guns as a means of ending life is undeniable.

Many years ago, I heard a story that went something like this: A social scientist was traveling through the Appalachian Mountains, trying to understand why the homicide rate was so high in that part of the country, when he came upon a crusty old backwoodsman to whom he posed a simple question: "Why do you think there are so many murders in this area?" "Well," replied the old man, "I guess there must be lots of folks 'round here need killin'." Like many forms of caricature humor, most people find this story mildly amusing because it seems to capture the stereotypical image of the ignorant, hard-edged, "straight-shooting," and marginalized hillbilly. The joke simply would not work if the researcher were said to have gotten the same response from a local resident encountered, for example, strolling along the beach in West Hampton Dunes on Long Island. However, the notion that some people simply deserve to die is hardly a marginalized belief anywhere in contemporary America, and that belief is especially common among gun owners. According to the 2012 National Opinion Research Center's General Social Survey (Smith et al. 2013), 83 percent of Americans who reported personally owning a gun also supported the death penalty, compared to 61 percent of those who did not own a gun. Of course, many if not most gun owners would argue that it is precisely because of the threat of such violent criminals that they need a gun for protection, and I do not doubt that they believe that. However, unless we are to assume that those who oppose the death penalty are less concerned about violent crime than those who support it—and there is considerable evidence that that is not the case (for example, Williams and McGrath 1976; Stinchcombe et al. 1980; Young 1985; Young and Thompson 1995)—then fear of crime is not an adequate explanation for the capital punishment/gun connection. I would suggest that a better explanation, which is the focus of this chapter, is that both gun ownership and support for the death penalty are reflections of a generally punitive orientation that is rooted in anger rather than fear.

I will focus on gun ownership rather than gun deaths, on the assumption that the high level of firearm ownership, such as we have in the United States, is an important part of the gun-violence problem. I will argue that gun ownership, like support of capital punishment, is often an angry and essentially aggressive response to what is perceived as a dangerous world. Briefly, the core of the idea is that thinking about crime makes some people angry, which in turn produces the impulse to punish those responsible for crimes. Such individuals are thus drawn to guns as a means not only of protection from, but also retaliation against, potential attackers. On the other hand, thinking about crime makes other people apprehensive or afraid, which are emotions that produce the impulse to flee, shield oneself from, or avoid confrontations with criminals. Those individuals are thus likely to formulate responses aimed at avoiding or placing barriers between themselves and potential attackers, such as staying away from certain places at night and buying extra door locks or home alarm systems. Although I am not suggesting that the emotions of anger and fear—and thus their primary responses—are mutually exclusive, I would argue that some individuals have a predominantly angry-aggressive response to crime and that those individuals are more likely than others to own guns.

## Emotionality and Coping with Crime

### *The Perception of Vulnerability and Fear*

In one of the most famous statements on the nature of sociological investigation, W. I. and Dorothy Thomas stated that situations perceived as real are "real in their consequences" (1929, 572). Nowhere is that more true than in the perception of crime. Indeed, the reality of violent crime in American, in many ways, is quite different than the perception created by popular-culture productions and news-media coverage (Gerbner et al. 2008). For example, a fact that would surprise most Americans is that the homicide rate in America has declined steadily from 1980, when there was a modern-day high of 10.2 murders per 100,000 people (Bureau of Justice Statistics 2011), through 2011, when there were 4.7 per 100,000 (FBI 2011). Despite this three-decade downward trend, the media-distorted image of America as an increasingly dangerous place, where the threat of criminal victimization lurks around every corner, has fueled the belief among large numbers of citizens that civil authorities can no longer be counted on to provide adequate protection from evildoers. At the same time, such organizations as the National Rifle Association have worked relentlessly and spent lavishly to convince us that private ownership of firearms is our best defense against such threats.

Although a large portion of gun ownership in the United States is related to the enduring influence of rural hunting cultures, a sizable number of Americans own guns primarily for protection (Young 1986). During the 1970s and 1980s, when violent crime rates were significantly higher than they are now, scholars began to focus on gun ownership as an important component of the overall problem of crime and violence. Understandably, many of those early studies focused on discovering the extent to which gun ownership was influenced by fear of crime. The results of those studies were often inconclusive and contradictory. Part of the problem was that while aggregate-level studies found positive correlations between crime levels and gun ownership (for example, Seidman 1975; Kleck 1979; Clotfelter 1981; McDowall and Loftin 1982), individual-level data (Wright and Marston 1975; Williams and McGrath 1976; DeFronzo

1979; Stinchcombe et al. 1980; Lizotte et al. 1981) showed that individuals who expressed the most concern about and fear of crime were no more likely than others to acquire guns for protection. Elsewhere (Young 1985 and 1991; Young and Thompson 1995), I have argued that those inconsistencies were in part the result of the collective focus on fear to the exclusion of other important cognitive and emotional processes relevant to understanding the social psychology of gun ownership. Here I will present a theoretical framework, and illustrative data, that conceptualizes gun ownership in relation to the perception of vulnerability and the related but distinct emotions of fear, shame, and anger.

## *The Fear Response*

Based largely on the work of neuroscientists, biologists, and psychologists, I would suggest, as a working definition, that fear involves *a strong emotional reaction to a perceived threat, which is associated with feelings of displeasure, excitation of the sympathetic nervous system, and an associated impulse to flee or hide.* The *fear system*, which prepares the organism for a flight response, is located in the lateral central amygdala area of the inner/ancient brain. Interestingly, this is very near the center of the *anger/rage system*, which I will discuss later, located in the medial amygdala. The neurophysiological manifestations of both fear and anger include several of the same familiar series of modifications in the autonomic nervous system, including increased heart rate and increased blood flow to skeletal musculature (Solms and Turnbull 2002, 126). Although the *production* of emotional states can be explained neurophysiologically, the *experience* of emotional states is in large part the result of the learned cognitive associations and causal attributions through which we interpret the meaning of our own visceral responses. That is, largely as a result of social experiences, we learn to fear—and thus try to avoid—the stimuli associated with certain situations, just as we learn to angrily confront those associated with other unpleasant situations.

In their discussion of responses to crime, Stinchcombe et al. (1980) suggest three common characteristics of fear-provoking stimuli, the first of which is their *concentration in space*. When it comes to crime, for example, we are likely to fear certain poor inner-city neighborhoods to a greater extent than more diffused areas of poverty in suburban or rural areas, because of the perception that violence is concentrated more heavily in the former. Thus, within those neighborhoods danger appears hard to avoid. The second characteristic is the association of such stimuli with *signs of danger*. Some urban areas are not only dense, but are also replete with physical dilapidation and signs of social disorganization, which are perceived as indications of danger. Finally, fear is enhanced by the perception of our *inability to mitigate or control the danger*. Hence, "street" violence, which is frequently portrayed as essentially random, is all the more fear-provoking because random events are unforeseeable and thus difficult to avoid.

Fear is further illuminated by the concept of *vulnerability*. Skogan and Maxfield (1981), for example, argue that the personal correlates of fear of crime are linked to the perception of physical vulnerability, whereas the social correlates are linked to what they call social vulnerability. Physical vulnerability is defined as the inability to resist and extreme consequences of physical attack, whereas social vulnerability refers to routine unavoidable exposure to and limited means for coping with victimization risks. Because of extreme physical vulnerability, for example, coming face-to-face with a zoo lion would be a terrifying experience for most people. Yet few of us would place zoo lions high on the list of things we fear, because we are not socially vulnerable to them; we can easily avoid them by simply staying out of their spaces. However, those who are socially vulnerable do tend to fear violent crime largely because, given their life spaces, it is difficult for them to avoid. Physically vulnerable individuals, on the other hand, are more likely than others to fear crime because violent criminals tend to be young males, against whom they would fare poorly in a physical confrontation. This suggests that, generally speaking, women and the elderly would be more fearful of crime because they are more physically vulnerable than are men and younger people, whereas poor people and ethnic minorities would have greater fear of crime because they are more socially vulnerable than wealthy and white Americans.

## The Anger Response

Experience tells us that emotions are largely subjective. Why else, for example, might the same piece of music or visual art be perceived as calming and pleasant to one person yet irritating and unpleasant to another? Likewise, the experience of fear and anger is largely subjective. Much like fear, anger involves a strong emotional reaction to a perceived threat, which is associated with feelings of displeasure and excitation of the sympathetic nervous system. However, unlike fear, anger is associated with the impulse to confront the threat and *fight*. According to neuroscientists, when we experience anger, what we perceive is activated in the anger-rage system, which is located in the medial amygdala area of the inner area of the brain and is associated with a fight response. Recall that the *fear system*, which prepares the organism for a flight response, is located in the nearby lateral central amygdala area. The balance between flight and fight responses thus appears to be determined by interactions between these two sections of the amygdala (Solms and Turnbull 2002, 126). From this neurophysiological perspective, what we perceive when we feel any particular emotion is our own internal *subjective* response to an event rather than to the event itself (Solms and Turnbull 2002, 107). From a social- and behavioral-science perspective, however, we know that factors such as socialization and learning predispose different people to respond to perceived threats in different ways. For example, boys are typically taught and expected to "stand up" to such threats, whereas girls are taught to avoid the kinds of people and situations that pose such threats.

Schachter and Singer (1962) argue in their cognitive theory of emotions that emotion-exciting events produce an undifferentiated state of physiological arousal. As soon as we recognize the stimulus that we think has provoked an emotional state such as anger, either immediately or through a studied appraisal of the situation, we attribute responsibility to that stimulus. This allows us to interpret our visceral experience and also gives direction to our anger. Moreover, even in the absence of fear or shame, anger—and its aggressive behavioral manifestations—can be brought on by prior feelings of disapproval, dislike or hatred for others, or a sense of injustice (Izard 1991, 235). Although I will not go into detail in describing the complicated and somewhat controversial topic of how thoughts (cognition) and feelings (affect) are connected, the physiological states associated with such emotions as fear, anger, and shame are well established, as are the connections between those emotions and certain types of thoughts. The difficulty of establishing a clear conceptual distinction between thinking and feeling, however, is illustrated by Bem's conceptualization of *belief structures* (1970), by which he distinguishes between nonevaluative and evaluative beliefs. When we perceive "some relationship between two things or between some thing and a characteristic of it," we are said to hold a belief (Bem 1970, 4). *Evaluative beliefs*, however, are those that define not only one's perception of such relationships, but also the value we place upon such perceptions. That is, evaluative beliefs are those that are imbued with an emotional component. For example, the belief that young African American men are more likely to be convicted of violent crimes is qualitatively different from the belief that young African American men are more dangerous than others. The relevance of this distinction for understanding crime cognition is illustrated in earlier work, in which I showed that both negative beliefs about human nature in general and beliefs associated with racial prejudice in particular are directly linked to a punitive orientation toward those accused, though not yet convicted, of homicide (Young 2006). Thus, if a highly prejudiced person views a local television report about violent crime and sees images of members of a disliked ethnic group being arrested for such crimes, it is likely that he or she will immediately attribute blame for such crimes to inherent characteristics of those individuals or groups and interpret his or her own arousal response as justified anger toward that group.

Although social psychologists have tended to focus on anger-creating situational factors, such as those that produce frustration, physiological arousal, negative emotions, or evaluative beliefs, clinical psychologists have begun to probe the dimensions of what they consider the "angry" personality. Their work suggests that among consistently angry individuals anger is not just associated with particular situations but is a habitual way of thinking. According to Fernandez (2008), anger is characterized by six independent dimensions, each of which is characterized primarily by one of two opposing anchors: (1) Direction, which manifested in either reflection of deflection, (2) Locus, which is either internalized or externalized, (3) Reaction, which is either resistant or retaliative, (4) Modality, which is either verbal or physical, (5) Impulsivity, which is either controlled or uncontrolled, and (6) Consequences, which are either restorative or punitive. Thus, any type of anger that produces a punitive response is likely to be characterized by deflection, externalization, retaliation, physicality and impulsivity. Although Fernandez's work is focused on anger as a habitual tendency of certain people, these same dimensions of anger also can also be applied to situationally-produced episodes of anger. In both cases, punitive anger can be characterized as a visceral, impulsive, act of retaliation directed toward an external target. Such anger manifests itself in both punitive attitudes and aggressive responses, such as gun ownership, which are designed not only to protect against violent crime but also to equip the angry individual with the means of successfully confronting and exacting revenge upon those who pose criminal threats.

*Shame and Anger*

The emotion of anger can be triggered by a limited number of experiences; most common among them are pain, restraint, being blocked or interrupted from goal-directed behavior, and a sense of injustice (Izard 1991). However, an implicit goal of many social interactions is the avoidance of perhaps the most feared of all emotions: shame. Although shame and guilt are often seen as related, Buss argues that "guilt is the result of a conflict between the ego and conscience," whereas shame is the result of conflict between "the ego and the ego-ideal" (1980, 157). Shame is the effect of perceiving the self as having violated one's ideal standards and thus having been disgraced. When others are assumed to perceive and judge us in ways that deviate significantly from our ideal self (Cooley 1902), or when we judge our own acts or thoughts as inadequate vis-à-vis our ideal self (Bem 1972), we experience shame. Because "self ideals" are constructed to a significant extent on the basis of gender expectations, the kind of judgments that make men and women feel ashamed can be quite different. Moreover, because shame is often hidden, even from the self, it can become a self-perpetuating component of feedback loops that can also involve other emotions. For example, Scheff and Retzinger (1997) argue that women typically experience shame-shame feedback loops, in which individuals become ashamed of being ashamed, which makes them feel more ashamed, and so on. This process often results in depression and withdrawal. Males, on the other hand, are more likely to experience shame-anger loops, in which they become angry about being ashamed, ashamed about being angry, and so on. This emotional loop tends to culminate in aggressive behavior. Although men can certainly feel shame as a result of anger, traditional gender-role expectations mean that expressions of anger are more likely to result in shame among women than among men, who have more typically learned to hide their shame beneath strong feelings and intense anger displays.

Gilligan (1997) also argues for a strong connection between shame and aggression among men. Based on his own experiences with and research on violent male offenders, he concludes that shame "is the primary or ultimate cause of all violence" (1997, 110). At least since Freud, indications or feelings of sexual inadequacy have been seen as a major source of shame among men. However, I would suggest that a more common source of shame is feelings of gender inadequacy—that is, fear of failing to live up to expectations associated with the traditional male gender role. Among the many traits that characterize that role are courage and/or lack of fear in the face of danger. To many men, indications of respect from others are a major source of validation of their sense of manliness. In fact, such respect is so important to some men that they are willing to kill or be killed in order to establish or regain it. Such an attitude is reflected in what Luckenbill (1977) calls the typical homicidal transaction, which starts with a perceived slight, or "disrespect," after which two men become engaged in a spiral of conflict aimed at maintaining or restoring face and demonstrating character. The ultimate perpetrator of the ensuing homicide is the one with the most ready access to a deadly weapon—typically a gun. Further evidence of the character-contest nature of these disputes is the fact that the presence of witnesses increases, rather than decreases, the odds of the encounter ending in homicide. Intimate knowledge of this dynamic inspired one of Gilligan's incarcerated respondents to comment: "You wouldn't believe how much respect you get when you have a gun pointed at some dude's face" (1997, 109).

Thus it appears that, among men in particular, fear often becomes an additional element in the shame-anger feedback loop. That is, many men fear the shame of not living up to the traditional male gender role of the brave and resourceful protector of home and loved ones, and this fear can be greater than the fear of being a victim of violent crime. For some, fear of violent crime becomes a source of shame, which begets an intensified anger toward real or imagined criminals who represent threats not only to their own safety and that of their households and families, but also to their images of themselves as men.

## A Theory of Differential Responses to Crime

The combination of heightened arousal, negative attributions, fear, shame, and indignation over perceived injustices resulting from crime provide the perfect cocktail for anger and punitive responses. Although this combination can produce anger in many people, it is likely that some are especially inclined to such reactions. In the United States, the quintessential form of a punitive response to perceived threats is the personal ownership of a firearm.

The ideas that support these propositions form the basis for a theory of differential reactions to crime, which is depicted in Figure 7.1. To summarize, although only a small percentage of Americans have direct experience with violent crime, most are constantly bombarded with news coverage of crime events and various cultural images of crime, delivered by the mass media and the entertainment industry. The personal and social characteristics of individuals influence both the quantity and quality of the images they consume. The effect those reciprocal images have on individuals depends, in large part, on their personal and social characteristics. Men and women, young people and older people, individuals of different financial means, and different ethnic groups both choose and are involuntarily exposed to different amounts and forms of crime information and images. Often those same individual and social characteristics also affect the extent to which people experience physical and social vulnerability. For example, women and older people tend to feel greater physical vulnerability, whereas poor people and members of racial and ethnic minorities tend to be more socially vulnerable to crime. Individuals who are more socially or personally vulnerable to criminal attack are more likely to fear crime. Those who are the most fearful of crime are more likely to respond to crime concerns by employing avoidance responses, such as keeping watchdogs, buying extra locks for doors, putting bars on windows, or installing home alarm systems. They are also more likely to alter their routine activities in order to minimize exposure to crime and criminals.

**Figure 7.1 Theory of differential reactions to crime**

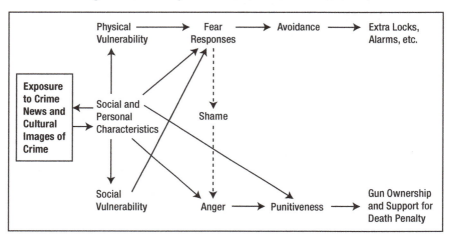

Although, relative to women, men report substantially lower levels of fear of crime, not all men are fearless when it comes to crime. However, unlike most women, men who are fearful are likely to feel ashamed of their fear, which makes them angry toward themselves for failing to live up to the expectations of the traditional male gender role. That anger, in turn, gets deflected onto the criminals whom they perceive to be responsible for their shame. Anger—whether born of shame, socialization, bigotry, or personal disposition—produces a punitive response to perceived crime threats. Such punitiveness is likely to manifest itself in support for harsh penalties against criminals and the personal ownership of firearms.

## Suggestive Data

Although a definitive test of the proposed theory is not possible, because valid measures of some of its key concepts are not available in existing datasets, recent survey data will be presented which point to the overall veracity of the model. The best data available for analysis are found in the National Opinion Research Center's General Social Survey (GSS) (Smith et al. 2013). As a result, I will provide what survey data I can from the combined 2000–2012 GSS in order to assess some key elements of the theory, and will refer to other studies in order to fill in the remaining empirical gaps. Because of the combined sample size of almost 12,000 respondents, all differences discussed below are statistically significant. Table 7.1 reveals the percentage of Americans in each of the theoretically relevant categories who report that they fear walking alone at night in their neighborhood. Consistent with Skogan and Maxfield's (1981) predictions, the results show that women, the more physically vulnerable group, are more likely than men to report such fear. However, contrary to Skogan and Maxfield's predictions, younger people report higher levels of fear than older people. This is quite likely the result of the fact that, even though younger people are less physically vulnerable than older people, they are more socially vulnerable and more frequently victimized, perhaps because they are more often out late at night and more likely than older individuals to participate in risky lifestyles (Ferraro 1995). Due to their proximity to high-crime areas, which produces a routinely higher degree of social vulnerability, African Americans and poor people typically report higher levels of fear than white Americans and those who are more affluent. Although social and physical vulnerability are conceptually independent factors, among some groups they are empirically correlated. Thus, more detailed assessment of their effects requires further research. In general, however, these data are consistent with the predicted influence of vulnerability on fear.

**Table 7.1 Fear of Crime and Support for the Death Penalty by Level of Physical and Social Vulnerability**

| Physical Vulnerability | Fear Walk Alone | Support Cap Pun |
|---|---|---|
| Males | 22% | 73% |
| Females | 54% | 64% |
| 18–30 years of age | 37% | 65% |
| 31–50 years of age | 32% | 69% |
| Over 50 years of age | 34% | 69% |
| Social Vulnerability | | |
| White Americans | 37% | 73% |
| African Americans | 50% | 45% |
| Income $25,000 or more | 34% | 71% |
| Income under $25,000 | 44% | 62% |

*Source:* NORC General Social Surveys 2002–2012
All comparison differences are statistically significant

Fear is important primarily as a motivator of efforts to avoid, rather than successfully confront, criminal attacks. Avoidance responses are designed to help the vulnerable avoid a direct confrontation with a criminal by staying away from them or placing barriers between themselves and potential victimizers. The latter strategy would include such measures as purchasing extra locks for doors or windows, burglar alarms, extra lights around one's home, or watch-dogs. In a previous study, based on data from the Detroit Area Study (Loftin 1979), I found a marginally significant effect of fear of crime on respondents' likelihood of purchasing such devices as special locks or bars for their doors and windows (Young 1985). Utilizing different data, Ferraro (1995) found that women who feared violent crime—rape in particular—were significantly more likely to report having constrained their behavior in various ways in order to avoid victimization. In contrast, fear of crime among women has been shown to have no effect on their ownership of firearms (Thompson et al. 1991). Thus, the results of prior work suggests that fear tends to be related to certain avoid-ance behaviors, but not to gun ownership.

The theory of differential responses to crime posits that anger about crime in particular is related to punitive responses. Unfortunately, the GSS does not contain a direct measure of such anger. However, scholars from a variety of disciplines acknowledge that anger produces an aggressive/fight response to perceived threats (for example, Bandura 1973; Berkowitz 1965; Averill 1979; Young 1985). In fact, experimental research by Lerner and Keltner (2001), which demonstrates that angry people make riskier choices than do fearful people, supports the notion that those who are angry about crime would be more willing to seek rather than try to avoid confrontations with criminals. The proposition that anger and fear produce divergent orientations is clearly supported by the GSS data. For each group comparison represented in Table 7.1, the group that reports the highest level of fear also reports the lowest level of support for the death penalty. For example, although only 22 percent of males fear walking alone in their neighborhood at night, 73 percent of them support capital punishment; whereas 54 percent of women report such fear, yet only 64 percent of them support the death penalty. The contention that anger and fear produce different responses to crime is also supported by the consistently higher level of support for the death penalty among groups who report the least fear of crime.

The most direct measure of the differential effects of fear versus anger is reported in Table 7.2. There we see that, of respondents who fear walking alone at night in their neighborhoods, only 14 percent report personally owning a gun, whereas 28 percent of those who do not report such fear own guns. By contrast, 28 percent of those who favor the death penalty own guns, while only 13 percent of death-penalty opponents own guns. The virtual mirror image of those percentages indicates that gun ownership is much more closely connected to punitiveness than to fear. Of course, correlation alone does not establish causality. Thus, we should also consider the possibility that the causal order of these relationships is reversed. That is, it is not an unreasonable interpretation of the results in Table 7.2 that fear among gun owners is lower because owning a gun makes people feel safer walking alone at night. Unfortunately, respondents were not asked if they took their guns with them on walks. Moreover, rather than suggesting that punitive people are more likely to acquire guns, these data could be interpreted as indicating that owning a gun makes people more punitive. Thus, although a definitive interpretation of these data is impossible without further research, the existence of a stronger punitiveness-gun connection than a fear-gun connection is quite clear. Perhaps the most conservative conclusion at this point is that anger is more likely than fear to motivate gun ownership.

**Table 7.2 Percentage of Gun Owners among Those Who Are Most Fearful versus Those Who Are Most Punitive**

| | Percent Who Personally Own Guns | |
|---|---|---|
| *Own Gun?* | *Most Afraid* | *Favor Death Penalty* |
| Yes | 14% | 28% |
| No | 28% | 13% |

*Source:* NORC General Social Surveys 2002–2012
All comparison differences are statistically significant

## Conclusions

Americans own guns for many reasons. Some were given or bequeathed to them by friends or family members, some acquired them for sport shooting or hunting, and some acquired them in response to their concerns about crime. Many individuals who own guns that were not acquired specifically in response to crime concerns are nevertheless willing, if not eager, to use them in response to such concerns. All of this creates a real but relatively minor methodological problem for this study. The theory and supporting evidence discussed in this chapter suggest that those who own guns and are willing to use them against potential criminals are more angry and punitive than other types of owners and non-owners. Unfortunately, using data from the General

Social Survey, we cannot differentiate those who own guns for dealing with criminals from those who own them for completely different reasons. Thus, for analysis purposes, those two groups are both classified simply as owners. Moreover, because there is no theoretical justification for expecting those who own guns for non-crime-related purposes to be more angry and punitive than nonowners, it is likely that the anger-punitiveness-gun connection found here is underestimated. That is, if we compared nonowners only with those who own guns in response to crime concerns, the observed effects would probably be even more pronounced than they appear to be here. Some readers might have wondered about a second methodological issue; namely, the data presented do not distinguish those who own handguns from those who own long guns, such as rifles and shotguns. Fortunately, I was able to distinguish handgun owners from other owners and perform all the analyses using only the handgun sample. However, because those analyses revealed the exact same patterns reported here, I chose to ignore that distinction in order to utilize the larger sample of gun owners. Finally, the data presented here are in the form of simple tabular analyses. That decision was made primarily for space limitations and for the sake of clarity for those readers who are not familiar with the more complex multivariate analysis techniques, which I and other researchers used in many of the studies cited in the text. Nevertheless, because of these issues, I do not claim that the data presented here provide definitive support for the theory of differential responses to crime that I have put forward. However, the findings presented here, combined with the results of a considerable volume of multidisciplinary research published elsewhere, suggest that the emotional correlates of gun ownership constitute an important element in the overall problem of gun violence.

That some Americans acquire guns for punitive motives should come as no surprise. After all, whether we wish to acknowledge it or not, the United States is one of the most punitive societies on the planet. More than two-thirds of the nations of the world, including all members of the European Union, have now abolished the death penalty "in law or practice" (Amnesty International 2013). The United States, however, is not among them. In fact, we are joined by China and Iran as the only countries to have been among the top five executioners in each of the past five years (Amnesty International 2013). Yet, despite our relatively frequent use of the ultimate punishment against convicted murderers, our homicide rate consistently ranks among the highest in the industrialized world. If, indeed, many gun owners believe that some people deserve to die—in some cases, even for attempting to steal property—and if even a modest portion of them are angry enough to be willing to pull the trigger, then it is not only criminals that we should fear. Recent events in Aurora, Colorado, Newtown, Connecticut, and numerous other American communities provide graphic evidence that a heavily armed society, in which guns have become almost as easy to buy as books, can be a very dangerous society. The following excerpt describing one tragic and avoidable death of a homeowner appeared in my hometown newspaper, even as I was writing this conclusion.

> Fort Worth police are investigating the circumstances under which a 72-year-old man armed with a handgun was fatally shot on his property by officers responding to a burglar alarm across the street.... Police spokeswoman Cpl. Tracey Knight said two officers encountered Jerry Waller at the back of his house near the garage early Tuesday morning and "felt threatened." ... Waller's wife told WFAA that, from what she could tell, her husband was shot six times. He had gone to see what was causing a ruckus outside the garage and carried a gun because he wasn't sure if someone was trying to break into a car in the driveway, Kathy Waller said. "Married 46 years, and then somebody gets a little trigger-happy and away they go," she told the station. (*Fort Worth Star Telegram* 2013)

As this case so clearly demonstrates, guns and the willingness to use them are not as much a product of feelings of vulnerability or fear of crime as they are of cultural scripts that call for aggressive responses in situations interpreted as threatening. Upon hearing a disturbance outside, rather than calling the police and further assessing the situation from the safety of his home, Mr. Waller grabbed his gun and moved toward the perceived threat. Although no criminals were present, the consequences of that move were tragic.

# Chapter 8

# *Ethos of the Gun*

## *Trajectory of the Gun-Rights Narrative*

### James Welch IV

T HE MORAL COMPASS OF GUN-RIGHTS ADVOCATES IS EXCEEDINGLY CLEAR, grounded in a narrative of American history and culture that dictates the way they react to efforts at gun regulation, however moderate. Despite the earnestness of emotional pleas and reasoned arguments, these regulatory efforts are perceived as an attack on an entrenched and longstanding element of American culture. The incompatibility of narratives between gun-rights and gun-control advocates makes democratic discourse over gun regulation all but intractable. Those who seek "common sense" solutions to the pathology of gun violence are frustrated by the focused will of the opposition, in part because they cannot wrap their heads around the mentality of the opposition. Therefore, I will attempt here to explore "the ethos of the gun" in an effort to render its incommensurability more permeable. The gun is a powerful symbol in American culture. The invention of firearms, along with other technologies of the Industrial Revolution, made the European settlement of America possible. All grand narratives, like the one enshrining gun ownership, are based in foundation myths. These myths supply adherents with compelling storylines that ground and stabilize their worldviews. Displacing a grand narrative is an arduous process, resulting in a terrifying sense of vertigo that resists and resents encroachment. The narrative provides security against a dangerous and unpredictable world.

Gun ownership is an adaptive strategy that arose from a specific set of needs and desires our ancestors held crucial for their survival. The ethos of the gun became part of the American creed of self-reliance, arising from the frontier spirit. This spirit arches over the evolution of American culture, from colonialism, to the Revolutionary War, the dispute over federalism, the civil disobedience of the Transcendentalists, legends of the Wild West, and through to the culture-war rhetoric of the present gun-rights narrative. Tracing this trajectory will offer insight into how the current sentiments of gun owners came about, and why they are so vehement in their beliefs. My purpose here is not to provide an account of the evolution of gun rights over the course of American history, nor is it to subject the popular narrative of gun ownership to historical verification or legalistic dispute. Instead, I wish to examine the narrative as a cultural mythology, deconstructing the historical, psychological, political, and sociological mechanisms embedded within it.

## The Frontier

The gun-rights narrative is a powerful tale that transpires centuries, a facet of the foundational myth of America. Guns were a tool of the pioneer, as important as any farming or building implement. They represented the ability to secure land, and with it hearth and home, both as means of defense and sustenance. The American settler is seen as the tamer of the wild, claiming their homesteads from cruel wilderness, repelling bears and Indians, and building atop their retreat. This powerful origin myth of the frontier spirit becomes conflated with the concept of liberty. Liberty for the colonists was a sacred ideal, providing a clear and simple foundation for this narrative. Liberty was the strategy the early settlers used to create a space of economic, political, and cultural security. In crucial ways, this liberty was accomplished at the end of a gun.

The ethos of the gun runs deep into the origins of American consciousness. The heroic characteristics of the settler—strong, self-reliant, resourceful, suspicious of strangers, dismissive of authority—were all survival mechanisms, necessary strategies that became immortalized in legend and lore. This narrative of the frontier spirit is born in a rural setting, where centralized government authority was often distant or entirely absent. The settlers had no choice but to rely on themselves and their immediate neighbors to establish localized and insulated order. They were expected to keep and bear arms for the common (local) defense. Their suspicion of authority was also predicated on the abuses of state power they had escaped in Europe. Disarming the populace was a common means of state control, both to prevent rebellion and to protect lands from unauthorized game hunting (Cornell 2006, 39). Although the era of the frontier is long gone, the frontier origin myth continues to hold sway over our identities as Americans. Origin myths have a timeless, sacrosanct character; they do not adapt to changing contexts, but rather recontextualize the continuum of history itself to conform to the established paradigm. America has undergone a great deal of change over its short history, yet to deny the validity of origin myth—that is, to say that the settlers were not as heroic as they seem, or that their experiences no longer have relevance to an urbanized, technologically sophisticated nation—is to literally become anti-American. These truths are not empirical or historical truths; they are the foundations for a belief system that dominates American cultural identity.

## The Revolution

The Revolution constitutes the establishment myth of America, supplying the second chapter in the ethos of the gun, built atop the Colonial origin myth. The success of the American Revolution was very much the product of an incredibly effective propaganda campaign, which constructed a narrative that mobilized the sentiments of a diverse colonial population and enabled them to repel what was arguably the preeminent military power of the day. One key to successful propaganda is the drawing of stark dichotomies, which in the case of the Revolution was "liberty" vs. "tyranny." This campaign painted the assertion of organized political, economic, and military power as a new threat to liberty. The frontier spirit of protection against beasts and savages was then redirected to oppose King George III and the Redcoats. The British hardly saw themselves in this light, however. According to their own narrative, they were protecting the motherland against upstarts who were ungrateful for the benefits of their expansive commonwealth. America's forefathers were able to shift the colonists' sentiment toward the British Crown from protector to oppressor. In doing so, the founders depicted their enemy as a cultural threat, whose domination would destroy everything the colonists held sacred.

Propagandists like Thomas Paine effected this change in sentiment by drawing from the foundations of the frontier spirit, the need to defend one's homestead against wilderness and outsiders, and redirecting their sense of self-protection against the British: "if a thief breaks into my house, burns and destroys my property, and kills or threatens to kill me, or those that are in it.... What signifies it to me, whether he who does it is a king or a common man...?" (Paine 1993, 55). Such rhetoric reinforced the American obsession with self-reliance and xenophobia, effectively hardwiring these traits into cultural consciousness for centuries. The settlers' suspicion of centralized authority, developed over decades of colonial autonomy, became stirred up once England began to look at the colonies as a potential revenue source to pay for its ongoing conflict with France.

> The first settlers in the different colonies were left to shift for themselves, unnoticed and unsupported by any European government; but as the tyranny and persecution of the old world daily drove numbers to the new, and as, by the favor of heaven on their industry and perseverance, they grew into importance, so, in a like degree, they became an object of profit to the greedy eyes of Europe. (Paine 1993, 79)

The task of the American propagandists was to take localized sentiment for individual or community self-protection and collectivize it as colonial self-protection. This was no small feat: The frontier spirit is quite prone to narcissism and parochialism. It does not wish to be interfered with, and therefore sees no obligation to interfere in the affairs of others. In order to mobilize the frontier spirit, tyranny became embedded as a core concept for American consciousness. Paine's rhetoric in *Common Sense* and the *American Crisis* repeatedly demonized George III and the British military leadership as aristocratic oppressors. Tyrants cannot be placated or compromised with; they only understand domination and thus can only be met with force. "Your lordship may hold out the sword of war, and call it ... *the last reason of kings*; we in return can show you the sword of justice, and call it 'the best scourge of tyrants.'" (Paine 1993, 58). His rhetoric also successfully integrated the self-reliance and autonomy of the colonists with the collective concept of Independence, allowing the frontier spirit to amalgamate into, as he put it, "common sense."

The frontier spirit was able to be mobilized against the British because there was already a paramilitary structure in place—the Militia. The militias embody this notion of liberty: Individual men banding together, protecting their mutual self-interest through voluntary force of arms. In the absence of a standing army, this was a very sensible colonial adaptation, a mechanism for organizing against local or regional threats. Every household was expected to own, maintain, and know how to use a musket. In fact, their homes were inspected to insure compliance. Householders engaged in organized training and were expected to respond to a call to arms within a minute's notice. Thus, the legend of the Minutemen was born. The Minutemen were instrumental in the narrative of the American Revolution, heralded in the story of Paul Revere's ride. America was founded on "the shot heard 'round the world," which was fired in protection of a militia's arms cache (Cornell 2006, 19–20). The narrative of tyranny describes this and other steps the British took to deprive the colonists of their firearms, helping establish the assertion that depriving the people of weapons is equivalent to depriving them of their liberty.

The myth of the militia persists as crucial to the establishment of America—ordinary men committing, of their free will, to sacrifice life and limb to the greater cause of liberty and independence. Like most establishment myths, the narrative of the Revolution is predicated upon overcoming obstacles and defying persecution. This persecution complex became an indelible facet of the American psyche, remaining constant while the identity of the persecutors themselves shifted over the course of history. The dark side of the frontier spirit is paranoia and xenophobia. Just as the oppression of bears and Indians was transferred into the oppression of the British crown, a parade of oppressors—internal and external, real and delusional—has been a consistent part of the American experience, incessantly triggering the need for defiant self-reliance. The Second Amendment is based upon the colonial necessity for self-protection within the myths of frontier and revolution, and that context continues to hold sway in the ethos of the gun.

## The Federalist vs. Anti-Federalist Debate

Once the British had withdrawn, the colonists were left to figure out how to put the principles of self-determination into practice in the establishment of a nation. The ethos of the gun became embroiled in the Federalist/Anti-Federalist debates over the Constitution. Anti-Federalist rhetoric continues to play out in contemporary debates over gun control. This is ironic, since the Anti-Federalists were opposed to the very Constitution now venerated by proponents of the gun-rights narrative. This rhetoric argued for the frontier spirit, arising from a dispersed populace who saw self-determination as an effective means of settling and controlling territory and was opposed to concentrations of political, military, or economic power. However, once nation-building had begun, reconciling fierce individualism with the need for a stable national identity presented a paradox for the country's founders. Defiance of authority, instrumental in repelling the British redcoats, now seemed to contradict establishing America as an authority herself, able to maintain internal and external security. The federal paradigm violated the frontier spirit just as England had, by exerting centralized control over individuals who had sacrificed much to win their freedom. In order to establish the United States, the founders created a system that attempted to balance this paradox.

The Federalists argued that

> the vigor of government is essential to the security of liberty; that, in the contemplation of a sound and well-informed judgment, their interest can never be separated; and that a dangerous ambition more often lurks behind the specious mask of zeal for the rights of the people than under the forbidden appearance of zeal for the firmness and efficiency of government. History will teach us that the former has been found a much more certain road to the introduction of despotism than the latter, and that of those men who have overturned the liberties of republics, the greatest number have begun their career by paying an obsequious court to the people; commencing demagogues, and ending tyrants.[1]

The Federalists believed that anarchy was the ultimate enemy of democracy. However, the Anti-Federalists were willing to take that chance: "If anarchy, therefore, were the inevitable consequence of rejecting the new Constitution, it would be infinitely better to incur it, for even then there would be at least the chance of a good government rising out of licentiousness."[2] They believed that "the new constitution in its present form is calculated to produce despotism, thralldom and confusion, and if the United States do swallow it, they will find it a bolus, that will create convulsions to their utmost extremities."[3]

The debate over a standing army is of particular relevance to the gun-rights narrative. In the myth of the American Revolution, America was established by military volunteers, who bore their own arms in their own self-interest. The Minutemen, however adept, were ultimately outclassed by regulars dedicated to military service. The Federalists argued for a well-trained standing army dedicated to the defense of the United States as a whole.

> The American militia, in the course of the late war, have, by their valor on numerous occasions, erected eternal monuments to their fame; but the bravest of them feel and know that the liberty of their country could not have been

established by their efforts alone, however great and valuable they were. War, like most other things, is a science to be acquired and perfected by diligence, by perseverance, by time, and by practice.[4]

The Anti-Federalists contended that a standing army represented nothing less that an instrument of tyranny. Within the frontier spirit, tyranny had become generalized to mean all forms of centralized authority, not solely the British Crown, as revolutionary propagandists intended. That spirit now became suspicious of the Constitution, which sought to establish America as the state, and thus potentially a new persecutor. The militia was held up as the essence of self-defense, as individuals tied to the land, responding to immediate crises. "It is asserted by the most respectable writers upon government, that a well regulated militia, composed of the yeomanry of the country, have ever been considered as the bulwark of a free people. Tyrants have never placed any confidence on a militia composed of freemen."[5] During peacetime, standing armies do a lot of standing around, needing an excuse to go into action. Idle hands often create crises of their own devising. A standing army is a powerful temptation for politicians, who too often incite warfare simply because an army allows them to do so.

Politicians are also prone to use a standing army to exert internal control over malcontents. The early history of the United States was rife with domestic rebellion. The frontier spirit demands action, with quick response to localized crises. As the former colonies became the United States, however, the role of individual liberty struggled to recontexualize itself. After the Revolution, the states had their own debts to pay and imposed revenue measures to meet these shortfalls. Shays's Rebellion constituted a reaction to these measures, organizing former Revolutionary soldiers within the militia network to effectively shut down the judicial system in the area to prevent it from enforcing debt collection. Here is familiar territory for the ethos of the gun: The assertion of individual will was enabled by the prevalence of gun ownership. Just as the colonists had rebelled against taxation without representation, Shays's forces utilized the power of the gun to demand redress of grievances. This pattern repeated over the early years of America, as local residents distressed at a federal mandate (almost always taxation) used the symbolic and organizational structure of the militia to circumvent legal, democratic mechanisms for resolving conflicts.

The right to rebel is deeply ingrained in the gun-rights narrative, arguing that liberty is perpetually under attack from any concentration of power. At the root of this is a philosophical understanding of the nature of power itself. For the American psyche, power is seen as an evil temptation. The Anti-Federalists were quick to point this out: "It is a truth confirmed by the unerring experience of ages, that every man, and every body of men, invested with power, are ever disposed to increase it, and to acquire a superiority over everything that stands in their way."[6] A bulwark against this tendency to create an arbitrary aristocracy is the right to free association, which privileges decentralized authority enforced through localized organizational structures, within which the individual is the main locus of control. Yet, insurrection constituted a direct threat to the establishment of the United States. The militia model, demonstrated in Shays's Rebellion and other incidents, asserted individual power at the expense of the stability of the state. Federalists were equally emphatic in identifying this danger:

> The important truth, which it unequivocally pronounces in the present case, is that a sovereignty over sovereigns, a government over government, a legislation for communities, as contradistinguished from individuals, as it is a solecism in theory, so in practice it is subversive of the order and ends of civil polity, by substituting VIOLENCE in place of LAW, or the destructive COERCION of the SWORD in place of the mild and salutary COERCION of the MAGISTRACY.[7]

The frontier spirit, while predicated on the establishment of security, was at the same time a threat to it. Thus, the American approach to power is an essential paradox. The moment of founding documented this paradox, providing for individual will within a collective framework. The balance between these two paradigms of security and society plays itself out in contemporary discourse over gun rights. The Bill of Rights presented a manifesto of Enlightenment ideals that placed implicit trust in the capacity for individuals to arrive at the common good.

For many Americans on the frontiers of the newly formed United States, the passage of the US Constitution itself represented a direct threat to liberty. Reliance upon central government flew in the face of all their experiences with state power and violated their sacrosanct sense of self-determination. In psychological terms, surrendering power to the government, even within the framework of the Social Contract, was deeply emasculating. More than violating some abstract political philosophy, the Constitution undermined the settlers' feeling of being in control, of being responsible and accountable for themselves. The national identity represented by the Constitution violated the frontier spirit in a fundamental way, as it sought to replace the frontier mechanisms for localized order with the more collective processes of representation, redress of grievances, and a uniform judicial system. These are the hallmarks of civilization, but for the early Americans, they represented the same oppression they had come to these shores to escape. Ironically, the very frontier spirit of self-reliance, upon which our foundation myths rest, turned against the founding of the country itself.

## Civil Disobedience and Transcendentalism

Despite protests, the United States was established and began to expand rapidly through the use of industrial technologies. By the mid-1800s, the Transcendental movement reacted to the problems of industrial expansion, reformulating the frontier spirit and the philosophy of self-reliance. Ralph Waldo Emerson (1836/1957a) called repeatedly for a return to communion with nature as a means for purging the evils of civilization. The transcendentalists believed that wisdom and morality were preexistent in the human mind, as an organ derived from natural processes. Society creates a false reality that takes men away from their true origins, through false teaching and the demand for conformity. "The world is nothing," declares Emerson, "the man is all; in yourself is the law of all nature ... in yourself slumbers the whole of Reason; it is for you to know all; it is for you to dare all" (1837/1957b, 79). The basis for self-reliance abides in the spirit of nature inherent in human instinct. "Truly it demands something godlike in him who has cast off the common motives of humanity and has ventured to trust himself for a taskmaster. High be his heart, faithful his will, clear his sight, that he may in good earnest be doctrine, society, law, to himself" (Emerson 1841/1957c, 161). This highly individualistic recontexualization of the frontier spirit in a rapidly modernizing nation comes to reject not simply centralized authority, but the whole of civilization itself.

Henry David Thoreau, the protolibertarian, put these lessons into practice through his social experiment at Walden Pond. In his account of the experience, *Walden*, he declared that it was impossible to hear a higher calling within industrialization. Civilization, he said, engenders hypocrisy, deception, and idleness as well as an obsession with consumption and creature comforts. Walden Pond represented simplicity and solitude. Thoreau's ability to survive comfortably there demonstrated the principles of innate self-sufficiency and the restorative properties of nature. It also provided a rationale for his hostility to altruism and philanthropy as forms of hypocrisy.

Thoreau's manifesto "Civil Disobedience" supplies gun-rights advocates with a clear statement of government's threat to individual liberty. "That government is best which governs not at all" (1937, 635). Government may be an expression of the people's will, but as this will becomes obscure, the state comes to serve its own interests, confusing its own will for the people's will. Oppression of the majority by an elite minority follows from this, and results in men serving the state as machines. Thoreau believed that all men reserve the right to revolution when the government is tyrannical, inefficient, or corrupt. He contended that progress toward democracy is progress toward true respect for the individual: "There will never be a really free and enlightened State until the State comes to recognize the individual as a higher and independent power, from which all its own power and authority are derived, and treats him accordingly" (1937, 659).

Emerson's and Thoreau's specific stances on gun control are more equivocal. Emerson's poem "Forbearance" recommends experiencing nature directly, instead of hunting it. Thoreau, despite all his survivalist rhetoric, makes a thoroughly compelling argument for vegetarianism in *Walden*. Nor did either of them emphasize the need for self-protection. While at Walden Pond, Thoreau welcomed strangers into his cabin and spoke highly of the camaraderie facilitated by the natural environment. Nonetheless, the transcendentalists supply a transitional point of the gun-rights narrative. The frontier spirit, originally defending against bears and Indians, then the British Empire and against the federal government, now becomes a generalized rejection of civilization itself. Embedded in the ethos of the gun is a fascination with anarchy and an affinity for lawlessness. Further, the ideals of self-reliance and self-determination hide an underside of simple selfishness. This is illustrated in "Civil Disobedience" when Thoreau enumerates the various taxes he should and shouldn't have to pay, according to his own use for them. He uses the roads, so he has no problem with the highway tax. However, having no children himself, he sees no need to pay revenues for public schools. There is a dualistic nature to frontier spirit: It encourages the virtues of strength and competitiveness, while discouraging the virtues of compassion and cooperation. The philosophy of transcendentalism influences the present-day advocates of gun rights, especially in hunters who praise the benefits of the outdoors and living closer to nature. Conversely, it supplies survivalists with their own rationale for separating from the evils of the civilized world, and, indeed, expecting for its collapse.

## Pioneers and the Wild, Wild West

Western expansion and the policy of manifest destiny provided an outlet for the frontier spirit for the rest of the nineteenth century. By constantly pushing westward, Americans were able to put off reconciling individual rights of self-determination with the needs of an expansive federal political and economic infrastructure. This period, glorified in film and legend, has had a great deal of influence over the gun-rights narrative and on the way gun owners perceive themselves and the clarity of their moral compass. The actual historical conditions of this period, which often were far from heroic, have little relevance to the gun-rights narrative. Beliefs, not facts, influence value systems and the narratives they are based upon.

The pioneers continued to play out the narrative of the original colonial settlers. They faced hardship and danger in order to make a life for themselves, away from the problems of industrialization and centralized authority, seeking the wide-open spaces that are the true source of liberty. In popular depictions of the pioneers, city folk are portrayed as weak, pampered, cowardly, greedy, and often deceptive—they have been corrupted by polite society. In the spirit of transcendentalism, being uncivilized is embraced as a positive antidote to urban corruption. In the film *Shane*, the main character explains the purpose of firearms: "A gun is a tool, Marian; no better or no worse than any other tool: an ax, a shovel or anything. A gun is as good or as bad as the man using it. Remember that."[8] Anarchy and lawlessness were held at bay because the true moral nature of man can only be revealed when he is true to himself, in a state of original liberty. In this narrative, morality is derived from a sense of personal responsibility.

However, lawlessness was often a problem for the old west. Without a centralized state to provide security, it was up to a few individuals with a clear moral compass to defend order in their towns. Order in this case is not the imposition of a judicial authority, but rather individual enforcement of the principles of freedom and justice. John Wayne's character in *The Shootist* declares the credo of the rugged individualist: "I won't be wronged, I won't be insulted, and I won't be laid a hand on. I don't do these things to other people, and I require the same from them."[9] It is the wildness of the west that demands self-reliance and personal heroism. Although marshals, sheriffs, and deputies attempt to protect the populace, each man is still considered responsible for his own security and can be mustered into posses to deal with collective threats. The conflict is readily reduced to simple dichotomy:

> Usually, the central plot of the western film is the classic, simple goal of maintaining law and order on the frontier in a fast-paced action story. It is normally rooted in archetypal conflict—good vs. bad, virtue vs. evil ... settlers vs. Indians, humanity vs. nature, civilization vs. wilderness or lawlessness, schoolteachers vs. saloon dance-hall girls, villains vs. heroes, lawman or sheriff vs. gunslinger, social law and order vs. anarchy, the rugged individualist vs.

the community, the cultivated East vs. West, settler vs. nomad, and farmer vs. industrialist.... Often the hero of a western meets his opposite "double," a mirror of his own evil side that he has to destroy.[10]

Although sheriffs are often depicted as having to curtail the mob mentality of their own citizens, this seems not to deter the gun-rights narrative. However, the old west does supply an easily identifiable context for the idea that "The *only* thing that stops a *bad* guy with a gun is a *good* guy with a gun." (LaPierre 2012). This context is highly accessible and familiar territory for most Americans, allowing them to quickly rationalize the ethos of the gun, including its encouragement of vigilante justice and obsession with the ubiquity of political corruption. Yet, on a deeper level, the gun-rights narrative is fundamentally dependent upon the ongoing failure of civilization to create security, and thus has a direct interest in preserving anarchy and lawlessness as a rationale for its own worldview. Here lies a crucial contradiction at the heart of the ethos of the gun—a simultaneous trust and distrust of human nature. The accessibility of firearms enables equilibrium of power; both good guys and bad guys can assert themselves as quickly and violently as they wish. In the gun-rights narrative, gun ownership is a constant, but responsibility is not. Responsible gun owners train themselves to be both safe and lethal, operating within a clear moral code that is predicated upon liberty and security, while the irresponsible wield their weapons wantonly, disrespecting life, liberty, and property. The narrative asserts that in a gun-regulated society, criminals will have greater access to guns than law-abiding citizens, thus allowing criminals to victimize the defenseless. This worldview depends on the failure of collective mechanisms of safety and security, through cooperation and mutual respect.

## The Culture War

Once the nation was settled from sea to shining sea, the frontier spirit and the creed of self-reliance based upon it reached a critical impasse. The imposition of centralized state power had been realized in the South, during Reconstruction and later in the civil-rights movement, when Northern abolitionist values were imposed on their agrarian traditions. For southern conservatives, this was proof positive that government power violated individual freedoms, which could be defended only by a well-armed population. Ironically, of course, one of these freedoms was the right to deprive others of theirs—but irony is the first casualty of fanaticism. While the conditions surrounding belief systems undergo constant change, it is vital that the fundamental beliefs remain stable. It is imperative that the frontier spirit feel surrounded by danger. At the beginnings of the narrative, these dangers were completely real and the mechanisms of self-reliance were sensible. However, as the realities of a modern, industrialized, multicultural America take shape, the paradigm of self-defense obsessively transfers itself onto a parade of new antagonists.

America is predicated upon resistance. Our antagonists have been internal and external—the untamed wilderness, traitors, Redcoats, Indians, outlaws—all obstacles to our personal self-fulfillment and our realization as a nation. The hostility of the founders toward these enemies continually renews itself in the form of new foes set upon upsetting our way of life and violating our core principles. The ethos of the gun is constantly recontexualizing normality through the ongoing shifting of its oppressors—unions, suffragists, communists, hippies, immigrants, gangsters, terrorists. The FBI and CIA are equally dangerous to liberty, as are the armed forces themselves—puppets of centralized authority. Sandwiched between these internal and external enemies of liberty, there seems little recourse but individual self-protection.

The fight-or-flight mechanism is a powerful conduit for the American spirit. It is much easier to create ongoing threats than it is to shift into a paradigm of mutual cooperation, because the domestication of the frontier spirit seems to violate our fundamental cultural identity. This is seen in the culture war, which categorizes the progressive movement as a form of national pathogen. A key figure in this phase of the ethos of the gun is Charlton Heston, who served as president of the NRA from 1998 to 2003. Heston was famous for holding up a Sharps rifle and declaring that it would have to be pried from his "cold, dead hands." This reinforced the narrative connecting current gun-rights advocates with the frontier spirit, solidifying the rationale that gun-rights advocates defend ancient American ideals against tyranny. During his NRA tenure, Heston gave numerous speeches on the culture war and the danger it represented to American traditions. A representative example was delivered at the Free Congress Foundation, a conservative think tank, on December 7, 1997, shortly before he began his first term. The speech is worth examining in detail, through excerpts and analysis.[11]

Heston begins by reminding the audience that Republicans belong to the party of Lincoln, which serves to connect freedom, symbolized by the Emancipation Proclamation, with the liberty espoused by conservative philosophy, including the liberty to own guns. However, the assault on American principles goes deeper than the Second Amendment.

I have come to realize that a cultural war is raging across our land . . . storming our values, assaulting our freedoms, killing our self-confidence in who we are and what we believe, where we come from.

Heston asks for a show of hands of gun owners in the audience. When he perceives hesitation, he launches into his main argument.

You are a casualty of the cultural warfare being waged against traditional American freedom of beliefs and ideas. Now maybe you don't care one way or the other about owning a gun. But I could've asked for a show of hands on Pentecostal Christians, or pro-lifers, or right-to-workers, or Promise Keepers, or school voucher-ers, and the result would be the same.

This move deftly creates a potent coalition from very diverse and heterogeneous interest groups. Libertarian ideology, which characterizes the sentiments of the most vocal gun owners, has very little in common with Christian fundamentalism. For example, fundamentalists have no problem with the assertion of state power to enforce their core values, over such issues as abortion, sexual orientation, creationism, birth control, or public prayer. Also, the Christian creed is explicitly opposed to violence, and presumably to armed uprising (despite its bloody history). However, what all of these groups have in common is a deep-seated persecution complex, a feeling that their beliefs and ideas are being subordinated to a new, foreign value system:

You have been assaulted and robbed of the courage of your convictions. Your pride in who you are, and what you believe, has been ridiculed, ransacked, plundered. It may be a war without bullet or bloodshed, but with just as much liberty lost: You and your country are less free.

What particularly alarms Heston is the insidiousness of the culture war, the way it makes people question their fundamental beliefs through unspoken social pressures. What is feared here is a cultural paradigm shift represented by the progressive movement of the 1960s and 1970s, which brought about civil rights, women's liberation, and a host of other revolutionary changes to the American identity. The attack on gun rights is the beginning of the slippery slope that will undermine "other rights not deemed acceptable by the thought police." The analogy of the Holocaust follows: "There may not be a Gestapo officer on every street corner yet, but the influence on our culture is just as pervasive." For those on the left, this may seem like complete hysteria, but it is taken very seriously, and again, without irony. However, they are reacting to the very real progressive strategy of attempting to alter American consciousness, to shift its overall worldview in a deep and permanent manner. Indeed, there is no other way to effect lasting social and cultural change, yet is it surprising that individuals feel threatened by that change of consciousness? Heston enumerates in detail the constituencies of this coalition:

> Heaven help the God-fearing, law-abiding, Caucasian, middle class, Protestant, or—even worse—evangelical Christian, Midwest, or Southern, or—even worse—rural, apparently straight, or—even worse—admittedly heterosexual, gun-owning or—even worse—NRA-card-carrying, average working stiff, or—even worse—male working stiff, because not only don't you count, you're a downright obstacle to social progress. Your tax dollars may be just as delightfully green as you hand them over, but your voice requires a lower decibel level, your opinion is less enlightened, your media access is insignificant, and frankly mister, you need to wake up, wise up and learn a little something about your new America ... in fact, why don't you just sit down and shut up?

It is not enough to be bewildered and confused, he says, to sit back and watch America changing around you—you must take affront. Under the guise of creating a more responsive, equalitarian America, progressives are in actuality bringing about its permissive, decadent ruin. "That's what happens when a generation of media, educators, entertainers, and politicians, led by a willing president, decide the America they were born into isn't good enough anymore. So they contrive to change it through the cultural warfare of class distinction." This statement enumerates the enemy constituency, who reject the time-honored truths contained in the origin and establishment myths that founded America, replacing it with a new world order. The mention of "class distinction" here is a direct jab at Marx, who has long been a common enemy of this coalition. For them, America is and always has been a "classless" society, that any distinctions of wealth and power are the natural, appropriate result of individual self-determination. They believe that the culture war is an attempt to replace this natural order by an intelligentsia who believe they can plan a society better than it can plan itself: "There are ruins around the world that were once the smug centers of small-minded, arrogant elitism. It appears that rather than evaporate in the flash of a split atom, we may succumb to a divided culture."

Heston goes on to liken his participation in civil-rights marches with Martin Luther King to his work defending gun rights with the NRA. This comparison may seem ludicrous, but in the ethos of the gun, it works on several levels. First of all, like so much of this rhetoric, it inverts the power equation of oppressor and oppressed. According to this narrative, progressives and minorities have taken hold of the reins of power, through media and government agencies, dominating the cultural environment so that traditional Americans are too ashamed to speak up for themselves. Second, the rhetoric takes the strategies of the civil-rights movement and appropriates them for use by this coalition. Now it is the white man who is put down by blacks and Latinos, deprived of his rightful voice in a democratic society. Gun ownership is central to this argument:

It's plain that our Constitution guarantees law-abiding citizens the right to own a firearm. But if I stand up and say so, why does the media assault me with such a slashing, sinister brand of derision filled with hate? . . . as if millions of lawful gun owners should genuflect in shame and seek absolution by surrendering their guns. That's what is now literally happening in England and Australia, of course. Lines—long lines—of submissive citizens, threatened with imprisonment, are bitterly, reluctantly surrendering family heirlooms, guns that won their freedom, to the blast furnace. If that fact doesn't unsettle you, then you are already anesthetized, a ready victim of the cultural war.

This conviction that the true goal of the gun-control lobby is to seize all weaponry continues to be a staple of gun-rights advocates. The vision of lines of downtrodden citizens relinquishing their precious firearms again brings up the specter of Nazi fascism and state control. For the gun-rights narrative, there can be no compromise or middle ground. Any attempt to regulate weapons sales or ownership is always set on eventually disarming society and disempowering its citizens. In fact, any reaction other than anger and alarm indicates that you have been rendered impotent by the culture war. This attitude effectively prevents gun-rights advocates from any kind of political negotiation; they are locked into a winner-take-all scenario of cultural domination. This coalition is working to preserve the very stability and moral compass of America from the forces of perversion. The stakes couldn't be higher.

Mainstream America is depending on you—counting on you—to draw your sword and fight for them. These people have precious little time or resources to battle misguided Cinderella attitudes, the fringe propaganda of the homosexual coalition, the feminists who preach that it's a divine duty for women to hate men, blacks who raise a militant fist with one hand while they seek preference with the other, and all the New-Age apologists for juvenile crime, who see roving gangs as a means of youthful expression, sex as a means of adolescent merchandising, violence as a form of entertainment for impressionable minds, and gun bans as a means to Lord-knows-what. We've reached that point in time when our national social policy originates on Oprah. I say it's time to pull the plug.

This call to action clearly delineates antagonists and protagonists, supplying a strong rationale for conflict between liberal and conservative, along with the rhetorical devices that have come into common usage on right-wing talk radio and the Internet. Further, moral high ground in this polarity is exceedingly straightforward:

> In a cultural war, triumph belongs to those who arm themselves with pride in who they are and then do the right thing. Not the most expedient thing, not the politically correct thing, not what'll sell, but the right thing. And you know what? Everybody already knows what the right thing is.

Absolutism is vital to the ethos of the gun. Perhaps the most heinous crime of the progressive movement is the introduction of relativism into the American cultural and political landscape. The advocating of underrepresented races and classes demands the ability to put oneself in the shoes of those with entirely different experiences and viewpoints, and allow that those viewpoints may have a self-contained validity of their own. Absolutists fundamentally reject the idea that normality or morality could have multiple meanings situated in such things as class, culture, race, gender, or sexuality. Instead, "the right thing" is said to be a matter of "common sense." The notion of common sense is foundational to the operation of American democracy, founded in the metaphysical Enlightenment idea that the ability to discern truth is universally embedded in the human mind. The founders asserted that through the discipline of reason, all individuals will arrive at a singular conception of what is real, true, and good. Transcendentalism echoed this assertion: Just as "we the people" are endowed with unalienable rights, we must also be endowed with the common sense to perceive the world in a similar fashion.

The danger of democracy, as a pluralistic system, is that the differences between individuals will lead to factionalism and conflict, making concerted action highly problematic. However, because everyone has common sense, cohesive action toward the common good can be accomplished through deliberation and debate. This was something of an article of faith among Enlightenment thinkers, and a rationale behind their arguments in favor of democratic rule. Yet, in practice, the notion of common sense often becomes a rationalization for individual ideologies and belief systems. Common sense has shifted away from its Enlightenment conception, based upon reason and deliberation, to one based on instinct and intuition. In this viewpoint, truth and the common good are arrived at by trusting one's gut, which contains the voice of conscience and even the wisdom of God. This is what Heston is referring to as the "long look in the mirror," the kind of soul-searching self-examination that is common practice in evangelical Christianity. This perception is not dependent upon education or critical-thinking skills. In fact, according to this viewpoint, education and rationality are themselves products of ideological indoctrination, which have contributed to the progressive movement's perversion of the American way. In this way, common sense serves to tautologically verify one's own notions of truth, and by contrast condemn and resist alternatives. Presumably, if those who disagree with you were themselves to look in the mirror, they would eventually see the error of their ways and return to "common sense." This method of constructing and validating truth is insulated and practically unassailable, and provides a powerful rationale for undermining the very processes upon which democracy is based.

> The maintenance of a free nation is a long, slow, steady process. And it is in your hands. Yes, we can have rules and still have rebels—that's democracy. But as leaders you must—we must—do as Lincoln would do, confronted with the stench of cultural war: Do what's right.... Defeat the criminals and their apologists, oust the biased and bigoted, endure the undisciplined and unprincipled, but disavow the self-appointed social engineers whose relentless arrogance fuels this vicious war against so much we hold so dear. Do not yield, do not divide, do not call a truce. Be fair, but fight back. It's the same blueprint our founding fathers left to guide us. Our enemies see it as the senile prattle of an archaic society. I still honor it as the United States Constitution, and that timeless document we call the Bill of Rights.

Although Heston does not explicitly call for armed revolution, he does state that possession of arms is an important facet of the defense of true American values. This defense is grounded in the foundation myths of the American Revolution and the Bill of Rights, where the ethos of the gun is enshrined. The timeless, eternal quality of the foundation myth and its formulation in the Constitution grounds the common sense intuitions of gun-rights advocates in the sacrosanct.

# Conclusion

In the years since Heston's speech was delivered, the rhetoric of the cultural war has, if anything, become more extreme, thanks to the proliferation of right-wing media outlets on radio, television, and the Internet. The power of the NRA has become so strong that support of any gun regulation whatsoever is tantamount to political suicide. The intimidation of the "victims" of the culture war was very short-lived. Nonetheless, the rhetoric of persecution continues to be a mainstay of the gun-rights narrative. In countless fundraising calls, blogs, websites, radio shows, and speeches, the NRA and its allies impress upon the membership that gun regulation, however incremental, is in actuality an effort to disarm the American people in direct contravention of the Second Amendment. It makes absolutely no difference whether or not such an effort exists. In the narrative of the gun, compromise is a sure sign of weakness and, ultimately, of complicity with the forces that are bringing America to ruin.

Gun-rights advocates have a paradoxical relationship with the concept of liberty so central to the ethos of the gun. Liberty is seen as a defensive strategy, a way of warding off tyrants and savages, a means of fiercely maintaining a bubble of security and self-determination around one's own person and property. This stands in contrast to a more collective approach to liberty. In a pluralistic society, which contains a diversity of cultural perspectives and value systems, collective liberty means that people with whom you disagree can potentially gain political and economic power. However, instead of adapting to a multicultural idea of collective liberty, the ethos of the gun remains firm. Liberty is thereby a privilege earned by "true" Americans whose philosophical heritage is derived from the foundation myths of the nation. This tradition is not interested in expanding liberty to others, only in defending their own liberty against perceived oppression. The gun is the last refuge of the righteous, a means of empowering those for whom conventional political and economic avenues have failed.

Throughout the history of the long debate over gun rights and the Second Amendment, the right to own, use, or regulate guns, along with the role of the militia, have changed sides repeatedly depending on the political exigencies of the day. The various militia rebellions claimed the right to bear arms, while others claimed the right to regulate them in the name of civil peace. Various Federalist and Anti-Federalist movements took turns rising up in arms and seeking to regulate the arms of the other, as grievances shifted between them. Abolitionists called for armed uprising to end slavery, while pro-slavery factions sought to deny them this right. After the Civil War, Ku Klux Klan members viciously opposed the right of blacks to form "well regulated militias" (Cornell

2006). These few examples demonstrate that the "timeless, sacred" quality of gun rights is simply used as a justification for arming or disarming political allies or enemies as needed.

In order to justify the necessity for firearms, the gun-rights narrative must continually reaffirm the frontier spirit, which makes self-defense essential and militia duty compulsory. Despite the fact that the frontier has long ceased to be a common experience for Americans, the staunchest gun advocates go to great pains to maintain a sense of the world as a dangerous, insecure place. It can be said that the progress of civilization is the growing capacity for conflicts to be resolved without resorting to violence, through systems of representation, justice, and competing economic interests. These mechanisms allow conflict and competition in society to be worked out abstractly, rather than physically. For many, however, this is a disappointment. The frontier spirit is quite manly and heroic; it continues to hold powerful sway over those who feel disaffected with modern society. Just as the transcendentalists had followed the call of nature, romantic notions of the pioneers or the Wild West become recontextualized into modern America. The rhetoric of gun rights describes civilization as a dysfunctional, insecure institution forever on the verge of anarchy and collapse. Individuals are threatened by home invaders, kidnappers, rapists, pedophiles, and serial killers, as often shown on TV. Numerous apocalyptic scenarios are posited—volcanoes, earthquakes, asteroids, terrorists, or dictators wielding nuclear, chemical, or biological weapons. Conversely, there are endless conspiratorial narratives that claim the American right to liberty is under attack from such shadowy forces as United Nations, the New World Order of the Illuminati, or the Bilderberg Group. All these internal and external threats are repeated and reinforced through multiple media outlets and have become common parlance of the gun-rights narrative. All are founded on the premise that civilized society on any collective scale is little more than a thin veil over the barbarism and tyranny that is the true nature of the mass of humanity.

At the core of this apocalypse mania is an unconscious desire and expectation for civilization to fail. On one level, this a disgust with the changes in American society, where "traditional" values have been disrupted by the influx of immigrants, urbanization, and globalization, the introduction of alternative cultural norms and religious beliefs, and a Marxist-inspired progressive movement that embraces cultural relativity and the revaluation of customary roles and classes. This disgust engenders isolation, faction, and resistance. Self-defense and defiance are fundamental to the ethos of the gun. But on a deeper level, the gun represents the last true vestige of what Nietzsche called the "will to power." The true threat that civilization poses to the ethos of the gun is a castration of the human spirit, founded in the warrior, the hunter, and the frontiersman. Its abstract mechanisms of collective security are seen as insidious instruments of control, promising safety and prosperity while anesthetizing our true power of individual self-determination. The collectivist ideals of the progressive movement, such as regulation, peace, and egalitarianism are seen as nothing more than excuses to turn human beings into sheep, dependent upon the government for everything. Again, it makes absolutely no difference that this narrative has little real basis in reality—endless anecdotal evidence is widely available, along with elaborate conspiracy theories to organize and validate it all. Any effort to regulate guns automatically plays into this narrative of collective control, and anyone who advocates gun control is seen as cultural elites or social engineers. For the gun-rights narrative, there can be no surrender and no retreat. The give and take of democratic deliberation is itself a relinquishing of liberty.

This leaves gun-control advocates with a serious dilemma and a need to reassess the assumptions they make about their opponents and the political process. The fundamental structure of American democracy is a product of Enlightenment principles, which emphasize reasoned debate between selfless representatives who sacrifice self-interest for the common good in an atmosphere of mutual respect. In any process of collective decisionmaking, it is inevitable that individuals will not always get their way and will have to cede to others' ideas. Furthermore, it is also possible that through deliberation and exposure to other ideas and viewpoints, individuals will come to change their ideas and evolve in their thinking. This is how democracy helps enable productive adaptation and transformation of society over time. However, as its critics have always asserted, democracy requires a great deal of maturity from citizens. History shows that Americans have repeatedly resorted to armed protest over public policy, rather than compromise their positions or modify their beliefs.

The paradigm of social change that has dominated the American left rests on the assumption that ordinary people, at least collectively, are honest brokers when it comes to public policy. Efforts to effect social justice and cultural change have focused upon combatting concentrations of political, economic, and military power. Multinational corporations are common targets for liberal ire, as are assertions of American state power, foreign and domestic. According to this paradigm, ordinary Americans are often manipulated by power elites in order to prevent democratic participation from interfering with vast accumulations of wealth and power by a few elites at the expense of the majority. In many ways, this sounds very much like the gun-rights narrative; however, that narrative redefines the "elite" not as the rich and powerful, but as bureaucrats and the intelligentsia—the so-called social engineers. This brilliant rhetorical move allies rich capitalists with the common man by equating deregulation with the idea of personal liberty. All government activity is seen as an abuse of power, whether it be covert activities of the FBI and CIA or social programs to aid the poor. This very simple, blanket dichotomy plays into the absolutism of the ethos of the gun.

Noam Chomsky, throughout his body of work, asserts that the American people, if given the true facts about the nature of state and corporate power, occluded through control of the media, would become outraged and reject the structures that keep this power in place. In light of the current popular political climate, Chomsky's assumption about the innate wisdom and discernment of "the American people" seems hopelessly naïve. Information about environmental abuses, torture, civil-rights violations, poverty, and evidence of other abuses of power are readily available from credible sources for all to see. Nonetheless, those who fanatically hold to the ethos of the gun freely choose to adhere to a paranoid narrative of conspiracy and persecution. The problem here is not the foxes guarding the henhouse; it's the inmates running the asylum.

Within the postmodern information age, the assumption that "The People" will come around to sensible outlooks and moral value systems is highly suspect. The inability to develop common-sense gun regulations stems from the capability of the gun-rights narrative to establish its absolutism, based upon timeless conception of human rights, enshrined in the sacred Constitution, and founded on the essential history of the nation. This narrative is all but immune to any reasoned argument. Gun-rights advocates operate under their own set of facts, statistical and anecdotal evidence, legal rationales, and philosophical principles. According to their narrative, it is the gun-control advocates who are paranoid and delusional. Any attempt to establish gun regulation must deal with this established narrative by positing a narrative that reaches people on a deep emotional and moral level. The gun-control narrative cannot be based upon reason alone, nor can it depend upon emotional outrage over any given mass killing, or crime statistics, but rather upon philosophical principles that have the same weight and foundational history as the gun-rights narrative. In many ways, the strength of gun rights has come about due to the failure to convincingly position compassion as a compelling philosophical voice in the discourse over guns.

Liberty best prospers in a climate of mutual respect. Violence is not an assertion of liberty; it is a violation of it. Guns were certainly necessary to the founding of America, but they served a greater purpose, that of creating a stable space for democracy to flourish. This is a dynamic and multivalent space of rhetorical flurries, political maneuvers, cultural clashes, and economic competition.

It is by no means peaceful, but there is little room for the gun here. The ethos of the gun, inherited from the Minutemen of yore, asserts that any collective form of government is both intrusive and incompetent. Government abuse must be countered with the threat of violence in order to be kept in check. However, the purpose of democratic institutions is to establish mechanisms for peaceable resolution of conflict, and to address the diverse concerns of the American people. We choose to fight our battles in the courts, the legislatures, the market, and peaceful demonstrations, because they are, after all, battles of ideas. Ideas can never be truly resolved at the end of a gun.

This is an unsettling development for those who desire a more direct expression of their will to power, but having faith in messy democracy does not mean that we all become sheep. Compassion seems incompatible with the will to power, yet it is deeply empowering. According to the ethos of the gun, compassion is naïve and weak, based upon misplaced faith in the goodness of human beings. We humans are, after all, prone to error, obsession, lust, and greed. There are indeed burglars, rapists, gangsters, serial killers, and terrorists among us, but we are hardly surrounded to the extent that we must barricade ourselves against them. Most of us are surrounded by neighbors—coworkers, colleagues, friends—all people we know and trust. The point of liberty is to extend this sense of neighborhood until it encompasses the whole nation. Idealistic, perhaps, but it is preferable to a state of mutual paranoia kept at bay through the fear of firearms. This state is certainly not what the Founding Fathers had in mind. What keeps criminals from assaulting you is not your arsenal, but a culture of cooperation and respect founded upon compassion. We choose not to fight because, in the long run, regarding each other as kindred spirits is more powerfully disarming than any police force or gun regulation could ever be. Gun regulation is instead part of the narrative of compassion, which in turn is an expression of democracy. The spirit of compassion and cooperation is also firmly rooted in the founding of our nation and the hearts of the people. Compassion must be comprehensively and consistently presented as a powerful counternarrative to the ethos of the gun.

## Notes

1. Alexander Hamilton, *Federalist No. 1.*

2. Letter from "Centinel," appearing in the *Independent Gazetteeer* on January 16, 1788.

3. Letter from "Philanthropos," appearing in the *Virginia Journal* and *Alexandria Advertiser*, December 6, 1787.

4. Alexander Hamilton, *Federalist No. 25*, published December 21, 1787.

5. Essay by "John Humble," published in the *North American Intelligencer*, January 16, 1788.

6. Essay by "Brutus," appearing in the *New York Journal*, October 18, 1787.

7. James Madison, with Alexander Hamilton, *Federalist no. 20*, December 11, 1787.

8. www.screenjunkies.com/movies/genres-movies/westerns/10-best-western-movie-quotes.

9. www.americancowboy.com/blogs/lfeldman/cowboy-quotes-movies.

10. www.filmsite.org/westernfilms.html.

11. The entire speech can be found at http://www.vpc.org/nrainfo/speech.html.

# Chapter 9

# *Policing the Second Amendment*
## *Unpacking Police Attitudes toward Gun Policies*
### Jennifer Carlson

## Introduction

"The problem is not that good guys have guns. The problem is that sometimes good guys—like police officers—die because the bad guys have guns."

*Mark Glazes, Mayors against Illegal Guns*

"The only thing that can stop a bad guy with a gun is a good guy with a gun."

*Wayne LaPierre, National Rifle Association*

In 2004, Police Chief Joseph M. Polisar of Garden Grove, California, called for a reauthorization of the federal assault-weapons ban, which was set to expire that year, in a column in *The Police Chief*, an industry magazine aimed at law enforcement. Citing broad support from the International Association of Chiefs of Police (of which he was president), he told readers that "Unless Congress acts, the firearms of choice for terrorists, drug dealers, and gang members will be back on our streets—where, once again, our officers will be outgunned by criminals."[1] The ban expired that year, but nine years later, in 2013, Vice President Joe Biden, appointed by President Obama as head of the task force on gun control, reiterated Polisar's concerns: "One of the reasons the assault-weapons ban makes sense, even though it accounts for a small percentage of gun deaths, is because police organizations overwhelmingly support it because they are outgunned on the street by the bad guys and the proliferation of these weapons."[2] President Obama and Vice President Biden maintain that law-enforcement agents are eager to have a conversation on gun control. As Obama stated in his 2013 State of the Union address, "Police chiefs are asking our help to get weapons of war and massive ammunition magazines off our streets, because they are tired of being outgunned." It seems straightforward that police would be natural allies in the push for gun-control legislation: As frontline workers in the battle against crime, police work carries one of the highest risks of on-the-job injuries and fatalities. For police officers, the problem of guns is personal; it is not just about lowering crime rates but also about protecting officers. As Police Chief Rusty York of Fort Wayne, Indiana, explained in 2009, "the fact that we have these relatively cheap, assault weapon-type firearms out there, it's not only a hazard to the public, but in particular to police officers."[3]

Yet public law enforcement does not unanimously support increased gun control. In the wake of Obama's calls for gun restrictions, some law-enforcement organizations and officers have in fact spoken in favor of increased gun rights. A number of sheriffs and sheriff organizations, including the umbrella pro-gun organization Constitutional Sheriffs and Peace Officers Association, have maintained that they are unwilling to enforce what they call "unconstitutional" gun laws. As the California State Sheriffs' Association (CSSA) writes in an open letter to Joe Biden, "It is the position of CSSA, in accordance with the Constitution of the United States and the statutes of the state of California, that law-abiding persons who meet the established requirements have the right to acquire, own, possess, use, keep and bear firearms. This right shall not be infringed."[4]

As debate rages on regarding gun legislation in the wake of the Newtown, Connecticut, shootings, a fracture is visible among American law enforcement: Unlike in the early 1990s, when public law enforcement appeared in national media as dependable allies of gun-control advocates, today public law enforcement seems to be as divided as the general public regarding the role of guns in civilian hands. The goal of this chapter is to provide a preliminary sociological framework to understand this division in police attitudes on gun politics in terms of two different cultures of policing, each with its own assumptions about the significance of guns in policing and the relationship between police and civilians.

After reviewing the surprisingly scant literature on police attitudes on gun policies, I turn to the contradictory significance of guns—as objects worn by both criminals and cops—in police work. After showing how guns both endanger and empower police, I describe two distinct logics of policing, embedded in particular moments of punitive neoliberalism, that resolve the contradictory nature of guns in two distinct ways. These policing cultures emerge from two dynamics at play in American neoliberalism: the militarization of criminal-justice institutions and the privatization of these institutions. "State-centric policing" captures the militarization of public law enforcement, which has thickened the "thin blue line," widened the civilian/police divide, and strengthened public law enforcement's monopoly on police work through specialized weaponry and training. In contrast, "shared policing" captures the privatization (and, after 2008, defunding) of public law enforcement. This second understanding of policing presumes that police work is not monopolized by the state but rather available for purchase by the market and is, as such, "shared" (or "responsibilized"; see O'Malley 1992) across certain segments of society. I suggest that public law-enforcement personnel who favor gun control likely embrace some variant of "state-centric policing," while those in public law enforcement who favor gun rights likely embrace a variant of "shared policing." By situating these models of policing in particular moments of neoliberal transformation of police work, I argue that the significance of guns in relation to police work is complex, if not contradictory, in the contemporary American context and requires far greater attention from scholars than it has garnered thus far.

## What We Know about Police Attitudes on Gun Policies—Very Little

The goal of this chapter is to provide a sociological framework for understanding public law-enforcement attitudes on gun policies as embedded in neoliberal trends shaping police work. Given the efforts of both gun-control and gun-rights advocates to gain the support of public law enforcement in public debates about firearms, it is surprising that researchers have all but ignored police attitudes about gun policies. We actually know very little about how police think about gun laws.

Only two studies, both led by Amy Thompson at the University of Toledo, have examined police attitudes on gun policies in detail. The results, though conflicting, support the anecdotal evidence discussed in the introduction that police hold deeply divergent opinions about guns and their role in society. The first study by Thompson, Price, Dake, and Tatchell (2006) surveyed 600 police chiefs in cities with populations greater than 25,000. Their results suggest that police support gun control: 63 percent agreed that "the government should do everything it can to keep handguns out of the hands of criminals, even if it means making it more difficult for law-abiding citizens to purchase handguns" (2006, 308), and of fourteen gun-control measures, respondents supported eleven in the majority. Interestingly, age, perhaps as an indication of socialization into police culture (Barker 1999; Hunt 1985), was associated with attitudes toward gun control. In the second study, Thompson and colleagues (2011) conducted the first national study on the gun-policy attitudes of sheriffs, based on a sample of 650 sheriffs. They found that only four of the fourteen gun-control measures were supported in the majority. Additionally, more than half reported that they were members of the NRA; only a quarter of police chiefs reported being NRA members in Thompson et al. (2006). In addition, most sheriffs reported that they were unwilling to participate in any activities in support of gun control. In line with scholarship suggesting that sheriffs' offices and police departments are fundamentally different kinds of policing organizations (Falcone and Wells 1995), Thompson and colleagues explain the divergence between sheriffs and police chiefs by noting that (1) sheriffs are more likely to be located in rural areas than police chiefs; (2) sheriffs are less likely to be college graduates; (3) sheriffs are elected, whereas police chiefs are appointed, making the former more responsive to electoral processes that may be heavily influenced by the NRA; (4) sheriffs themselves are more likely to be members of the NRA; and (5) sheriffs are more likely to see guns as recreational rather than criminal, given the distribution of firearm violence in urban as opposed to rural areas. Linking these findings to public policy, they conclude that "sheriffs may be less helpful than police chiefs as colleagues for public-health campaigns to reduce firearm trauma" (2011, 715).

These two studies raise a number of questions about how public law-enforcement agents think about guns and—by extension—how guns figure into police work in divergent ways. Yet scholars lack a framework for making sense of this paradoxical divergence in police attitudes toward guns. If the gun is central to police-officer identity, as some scholars have argued (Bayley 1976; Crank 2004), to what extent are divergent attitudes about guns embedded in divergent attitudes about police work and police-civilian relationships, viewed more broadly? How are such attitudes on guns reflective of recent political and socioeconomic transformations in US society, transformations that have simultaneously expanded the punitive arm of the state yet have undermined public law-enforcement monopoly on police work through the proliferation of private policing (Simon 2007, 2010; Stenning 2009)?

Such questions not only have important public policy consequences (as indicated by Thompson et al. 2006; Thompson et al. 2011). They also shed light on how the long-standing tensions between the police role and democratic principles (Bittner 1970; Skolnick 1966) unfold in a neoliberal context where both illegal and legal guns are readily available. Given the dearth of scholarship on public law enforcement and gun politics, the goal of this chapter is to develop a preliminary framework for situating this divergence in police attitudes on guns within the broader American political economy. In this preliminary framework, I suggest that police hold divergent views on guns because they resolve the core contradictions surrounding the role of guns in police work in different ways.

## Guns and Police Work

While there is surprisingly sparse scholarship on officer attitudes toward gun control, there is significant evidence that guns play a central, and contradictory, role in police work. As tools of both villains (criminals) and heroes (cops), guns distinguish police work by endangering officers as well as empowering them. Looking at the ways in which "criminal guns" as opposed to "cop guns" shape police work provides a starting point for making sense of police attitudes toward how police think about guns in the hands of civilians—that is, gun politics.

### Criminal Guns

Police work is unique in that officers face the threat of death as an everyday aspect of their occupation. Police homicides are overwhelmingly committed with firearms (R. Kaminski and Marvell 2002; Kyriacou et al. 2006; Margarita 1979), even though police deaths have dropped markedly since the early 1970s due to enhanced emergency care, the adoption of bulletproof vests, and the introduction of community policing, among other factors (Batton and Wilson 2006; Kyriacou et al. 2006; Quinet, Bordua, and Lassiter 1997). As Quinet, Bordua, and Lassiter (1997, 290) write, "A commonsense argument would suggest that increased access to firearms would have an effect on the rate of felonious line-of-duty deaths of police officers." If this is true, then police themselves should be keenly concerned about gun policies that may affect the ease with which civilians can access firearms.

The presumption that police should support gun-control measures out of concern for their own occupational safety, however, does not bear out in terms of data. The first presumption is that police are, in fact, more likely to face homicide than Americans at large. Criminologists demonstrate that starting in the late 1980s, police have actually experienced lower rates of homicide as compared to other Americans with the same demographic characteristics (Quinet et al. 1997; Southwick 1998). Second, despite the fact that most police homicides are committed with firearms, criminologists have found mixed results with regard to the relationship between gun availability and police homicides: Lester (1984, 1987) finds that gun density (measured by the number of violent crimes committed with a gun) has a positive effect on police homicides; Quinet et al. (1997),[5] R. Kaminski and Marvell (2002), and Southwick (1998) find no effect of gun accessibility on police homicides, with the latter study concluding that it "appears that more guns in the hands of the public do not have an adverse effect on the safety of either the public or the police" (1998, 597).[6] Mustard (2001) finds that states with so-called concealed-carry laws experienced slightly reduced police homicides.

There is thus surprisingly scant evidence linking guns to police fatalities. A great deal of research on police homicides has focused on analyzing the attributes of the victims, perpetrators, and contexts of these crimes (Batton and Wilson 2006; Margarita 1979), with criminologists arguing that there is a clear structural basis for police homicides even if these factors appear to differ from homicides in general (Peterson and Bailey 1988). These studies demonstrate that police homicides are not distributed evenly among police officers, and even if scholars remain at odds in terms of what factors[7] are at play, there seems to be little support for the relationship between gun availability and police homicide.

However, perhaps the link between gun availability and officer safety should be drawn not with respect to police fatalities per se but rather to officer stress: "police officer" regularly ranks as one of the most stressful jobs. As Margarita (1979, 218) writes, "The elusive concept of danger on the job translates perhaps most powerfully to police in psychological and emotional terms, and influences police officers' perceptions of potential pressure situations. Officers may feel that the chances of being attacked are constant, random, and unpredictable." While scholars have disagreed on whether police work is inherently more stressful than other occupations (Webb and Smith 1980), they have identified a series of factors that characterize police work as stressful.[8]

According to Henry (2004, 3), police officers' "death encounters" markedly set police work off from other occupations: "In conjunction with the frequency of their death encounters, the wide range of circumstances and situations in which the death encounters can occur, and a variety of other factors intrinsic to police work, this perceived potential for a highly personalized death encounter sets the police officer's experience of death events apart from 'ordinary' death experiences." As Waters and Ussery (2007, 175) write, "For most officers, the roles and tasks associated with being a law enforcement officer can be debilitating. For each call, there is the potential for a violent confrontation with the ever-present possibility of being killed by an unknown assailant behind the next door." While police agencies differ from military units in significant ways, "it is the Fact Of Death that so closely links the police with their military cousins" (Buerger 2000, 454).

While shooting deaths are relatively rare, they leave a profound impact on the officers involved as well as on the police community more broadly. On the one hand, post-shooting stress trauma (PST) have profound effects on the officers involved (Gersons 1989; Honig and Roland 1998; Loo 1986), resulting in "sleep pattern disturbances, nightmares, hallucinations, flashbacks, distortions, isolation and withdrawal, alcoholism, overeating, promiscuity, and abuse of sick time" (Bettinger 1990, 90). On the other hand, the impact of these incidences reverberates far beyond the immediate officers involved: "Officer-involved shootings such as killing someone in the line of duty, a fellow officer being killed, or being shot at by a suspect have all been identified as stressful encounters in police work" (Abdollahi 2002, 7). Henry (1995, 93) therefore argues that the ever-present risk of death has a profound impact on police subculture:

> The effect of such exposure on individual officers and upon the subculture as a whole can be both functional and deleterious. Themes, images and symbols of death pervade the folklore of the police subculture, and to a lesser extent, the anecdotal and descriptive academic literature of policing. Exposure to death serves a functional and integrative purpose in the socialization of young officers, constituting an important rite of passage.

As a result, police see themselves, on the one hand, as "survivors" (Henry 1995) if not "burned out Samaritans" (Ellison and Genz 1978).

Rather than the causal relationship between gun availability and police deaths, it is this exposure to death, its centrality in police subculture, and the high incidence of firearms-related violence among officer injuries that turns guns—in the hands of criminals—into occupational stressors. This would be in line with Anderson, Litzenberger, and Plecas's (2002) findings that police suffer from "anticipatory" stress as well as Kaminski and Martin's (2000) findings that there are high levels of dissatisfaction about physical-defense and control tactics training among police. As charged symbols of death and injury, guns, particularly those wielded by criminals, embody the threats and stressors associated with police work. This broader impact explains why, for example, the presence of guns as an everyday part of police work has been identified as a stressor in police work (Samaha 2005).

## Cop Guns

While officers face the threat of death as part of their profession, they are also unique in their capacity to use force on behalf of the state. Rojek, Alpert, and Smith (2010, 301) summarize that "police officers are separated from other professionals in that their job provides them with the authority to use force." As Bayley (1976) notes, alongside the badge, the handgun is one of the central symbols of American police authority. The use of legitimate force, symbolized by the cop's gun, shapes how police understand the social utility of their work, how they draw boundaries between themselves and civilians, and how they justify their authority. Put differently, police work is governed by a moral universe distinct from that which governs civilians, a world in which the use of force is rendered socially acceptable rather than reprehensible (Skolnick 1966).

John Crank (2004) details how the gun is central to the unique social utility of police, their raison d'etre. He argues that "in the culture of policing, guns transform police work into a heroic occupation, providing both a bottom line and an unquestionable righteousness that pervades all police-citizen encounters.... with guns, police are not just good guys, but good guys with stopping power, a distinction that celebrates the use of all necessary force to resolve any dispute, however violent" (Crank 2004, 127). Accordingly, "guns embody the most thrilling aspects of police work," and "with a gun, a police officer can be as righteously good as a bad guy can be dastardly bad" (2004, 133, 132). Viewed alongside accounts of violence against the police, Crank's account suggests that the significance of the gun is a double-edged sword: in the hands of criminals, the gun represents violence, death, threat, and (anticipatory) stress, but in the hands of law enforcement, it represents heroism, justice, and even enjoyment.

Legitimate force therefore distinguishes police from criminals and civilians. First, the officer's legal gun comes to be defined in relation to the presumed illegal gun of the criminal: "violence in the form of the club and the gun is for the police a means of persuasion. Violence from the criminal, the drunk, the quarrelling family, and the rioter arises in the course of police duty ... the armed criminal who has demonstrated a casual regard for the lives of others and a general hatred of the policeman forces the use of violence by the police in the pursuit of duty" (Westley 1953, 35). Moreover, Hunt (1985) and Waegel (1984) found that officers use justificatory accounts to explain their use of force against criminals. These accounts allow officers to "preserve the self-image of police as agents of the conventional order" (Hunt 1985, 339) by explaining their use of force by referring to the "moral reprehension" of certain kinds of criminals: "cop haters who have gained notoriety as persistent police antagonizers; cop killers or any person who has attempted seriously to harm a police officer; sexual deviants ... ; child abusers; and junkies and other 'scum' who inhabit the street" (Hunt 1985, 332; see also Waegel 1984).

On the one hand, these attitudes reflect broader "tough on crime" public sentiment that cuts across the line between police and civilians: As Waegel (1984, 148) notes, "Police need only listen to sentiments frequently expressed within the wider culture to find support for their beliefs concerning rightful or deserved punishments. Public figures who call for the castration of rapists or the use of penal colonies or other repressive responses to crime may contribute to a moral climate favoring informal sanctions by police."

On the other hand, legitimate force, and the moral quandaries that come with it, distinguishes police from civilians. As Waegel (1984, 149) goes on, "police see themselves as unavoidably caught between two wrongs: it's wrong that criminals don't get what they deserve, and it's wrong to take justice into one's own hands. The dilemma is addressed by a subcultural injunction: sometimes a cop has to break the law to enforce the law." Klockars (1980) refers to this as the "Dirty Harry problem." The disconnect between "following the rules" and "getting the job done" represents a core predicament of police work, and it becomes most salient surrounding the use of force: A nationally representative survey of 900 police officers found that a significant minority of police officers believe that "police are not permitted to use as much force as is often necessary in making arrests" (31.1 percent agree or strongly agree) and that "it is sometimes acceptable to use more force than is legally allowable to control someone who physically assaults an officer" (24.5 percent agree or strongly agree) (Weisburd, Greenspan, and Hamilton 2000). This predicament is exacerbated by perceptions among public law enforcement that the public is distrustful, uncooperative, and hostile toward police and that police officers lack institutional support beyond law-enforcement agencies themselves (Worden 1989). Further thickening the line between police and civilians, police may use force, or displays of force, intentionally in order to maintain authority during interactions with civilians, especially amid perceptions of threat. Scholars have repeatedly demonstrated that police interact with civilians in ways that maintain and enhance police authority (Alpert and Dunham 2004; Cooper 2009; Sykes and Clark 1975). Alpert and Dunham (2004) argue that through an "authority maintenance ritual," police apply coercion in proportion to the extent to which a civilian undermines the officer's authority. How do officers evaluate whether a civilian has undermined their authority? Rojek et al. (2010) suggest that the presence of a gun is key:

> The officer states that she or he only used force when multiple verbal instructions were ineffective. This account clearly attempts to connect the officer's maintenance of authority by means of a legal and reasonable response to the suspect's aggressive combative behavior.... *The most commonly identified threat was the actual or possible possession of a weapon, particularly a firearm....* Our research uncovered situations where officers justified their actions to maintain their authority. Officer respondents consistently sought to explain escalating combative behavior as based on a threat to themselves and/or the safety of the public and simultaneously transformed their perception of suspects. (2010, 312, 322; emphasis added)

The use of force to maintain authority is therefore both instrumental and symbolic: Westley (1953, 39) argues that "policemen use the resource of violence to persuade their audience (the public) to respect their occupational status... [which suggests] that the monopoly of violence delegated to the police, by the state, to enforce the ends of the state has been appropriated by the police as a personal resource to be used for personal and group ends."

## Criminal Guns, Cop Guns ... and Civilian Guns

Existing literature suggests that there are deep contradictions regarding the role of guns in police work; they are both a source of empowerment and endangerment, of courage and criminality, and perhaps of pride and prejudice. But even if guns can take on multiple roles, these studies still presume a neat dichotomy between illegal guns carried by non-police criminals and law-abiding guns carried by police. These studies do not consider that guns in the hands of civilians could be legally sanctioned, and they do not challenge the presumption—as per Rojek et al. (2010) cited above—that the presence of a gun in civilian hands necessarily is combative, questionable, or criminal.

Yet the proliferation of concealed-carry laws, which allow Americans to obtain a concealed-carry license on a "shall-issue" basis, upsets this neat dichotomy between cop and criminal guns. With more than 8 million Americans legally licensed to carry a concealed gun, how do police understand civilian guns: more like the guns carried by criminals, or more like the guns carried by cops? What contexts lead police to view civilian guns in one way versus the other?

These are the questions that must be asked to make sense of Thompson's findings. The answers, I suggest here, are embedded in different moments of American neoliberalism. Neoliberalism is a political system in which social institutions, including the state, are subordinated to the market, and social problems are imagined as best addressed through market means. On the one hand, this means that neoliberalism is associated with the privatization of social welfare; the transformation of remaining social programs into hand-maidens of corporate interests; and the increasing infiltration of the market into public domains through private-public partnerships (for example, on how this process operates with regard to the Department of Homeland Security, see Monahan 2010). This paradigm recasts consumption as a civic virtue (à la George Bush's proposed solution to the War on Terror—"shopping"), and it also stipulates that individuals, through private acts of consumption, will take responsibility for problems that in other historical periods and contexts have been addressed by the state (this is the process that O'Malley (1992) labels "responsibilization"). As I argue elsewhere, the proliferation of gun carrying for the purposes of protection is an example of the devolution of state responsibility onto citizens: gun carriers are motivated by perceptions of police powerlessness and believe that it is their own responsibility to protect themselves rather than rely on the inefficacious state (Carlson 2012). On the other hand, however, neoliberalism entails the subordination of the state not only through privatization and responsibilization but also through an expansion of the punitive arm of the state. Loic Wacquant in particular has unpacked how neoliberalism has led to the growth in the criminal-justice system as a mechanism for managing social marginality as a replacement for the dismantled social-welfare system.

Neoliberalism has reshaped how policing is achieved in two ways. First, regarding the expansion in, and militarization of, the criminal-justice arm of the state, US police departments exhibited a 25 percent increase in sworn officers from 1992 to 2008 (COPS 2011; Reaves 2012), and as will be detailed below, some police departments themselves have started to resemble military units in terms of their tactics, training, and weaponry. Second, neoliberalism has entailed a turn to the market, meaning that collective needs are increasingly addressed through non-state, privatized mechanisms. Expansions in private policing are thus also correlated with neoliberalism, meaning that public law enforcement may find itself sharing the responsibility of policing with non-state entities. Though they seem contradictory, these two dynamics coexist and, in some contexts, may exacerbate one another through what Garland (2002) calls the "culture of control": While concerns about crime and criminality, on the one hand, provide the state with an ever-broader public mandate to use ever-more punitive methods to combat crime, these same concerns may undermine public confidence in the state insofar as the problem can be easily perceived to outstrip the capacities of the state. This lack of confidence in turn encourages the public to turn to the market for criminal justice in the form of home alarm systems, SUVs, and guns (Simon 2007). Thus, there are two distinct, if inter-related, logics of policing at work under neoliberalism: "state-centric policing" as opposed to "shared policing." I hypothesize that these two logics suggest two distinct predispositions toward gun policies, resolving the contradictions surrounding guns in police work in divergent ways. I suggest that this basic distinction is relevant for understanding police attitudes toward guns, as it reveals divergent orientations regarding who should or should not have access to the means of policing.

## State–Centric Policing

Over the last decades, scholars and civil-rights organizations have raised con-cerns about what has been called the "militarization of policing in America." For example, the ACLU has documented an expansion in combat-grade weapons and equipment among American public law enforcement,[9] while a variety of public-safety concerns—ranging from crime to border control to protests—have justified the development and use of new policing practices and protocols that have blurred the lines between military and public law enforcement (Kraska 2007). In addition to resembling the military, some public law enforcement has started to think like the military: Kraska (2007, 502) has documented "a growing tendency by the police and other segments of the criminal justice system to rely on the military/war model for formulating crime/drug/terrorism control ratio-nale and operations." In other words, the metaphorical "War on Crime" that police have been fighting since the 1970s has, in fact, started to look more and more like an actual war, with police themselves looking more like soldiers. These developments have been exacerbated by the increasing emphasis on "home-land security" within police departments (Monahan 2010; Stewart and Morris 2009). Situated in their broader socioeconomic contexts, these developments are not entirely surprising: on the one hand, police are simply carrying out the mandate of "tough on crime" politics that has characterized American policies toward crime; while on the other hand, the expansion in policing capabilities is squarely in line with punitive expansions in other criminal-justice institutions and far from "peculiar" (Kraska and Cubellis 1997).

Examples of crime-fighting as combat play out not only in the streets of America but also on crime dramas like *Law & Order* and local and national news coverage of crime and law enforcement. In these dramas (whether real or fictitious), the cop becomes a particular kind of protagonist: brave, courageous, and at times heroic, risking his or her life on behalf of the greater social good. The militarization of police strengthens the boundaries between police and civilians: With police monopolizing this most "dangerous" of police work, police ("the good guys") become pitted against certain civilians ("the bad guys"), deepening the "us against them" sentiment that often characterizes police work. A boundary is drawn around who should participate in police work and how: While civilians might serve as the "eyes" and "ears" of public law enforcement, ultimately the core of police work—SWAT teams, police shootings, and other instances of state-sanctioned violence—are reserved for highly trained specialists; that is, the police.

There is an important caveat here, however: While there has been a shift toward militarization among public law enforcement, this shift is neither evenly distributed across police agencies nor are its consequences equally manifest in police-civilian interactions. First, the most austere manifestations of this state-centric version of policing tend to be concentrated in poor, minority areas characterized by high crime levels. In these urban areas, civilians are more easily cast into the role of criminal (for example, police shootings of civilians are higher in such areas). Indeed, urban police departments tend to be larger, and thus, by the sheer nature of their organizational structure, they are able to adapt a more militaristic police model. That said, Kraska and Cubellis (1997) find that small police departments have also begun to introduce military-style weapons, training, and/or specialized units into their agencies. In addition, certain groups of civilians (particularly young men of color) are more likely to be treated with suspicion and harassment by police both within and beyond these urban hot spots (Harris 1999; Meehan and Ponder 2002). This means that different civilians may have very different experiences with the same police department.

What does this tell us about police attitudes toward guns? I suggest that these developments tend to promote a state-centric logic of policing in which the state is the privileged policing agent, with special access to both weapons and expertise: under this logic of policing, police monopoly on military equipment and the expertise to use it (weapons, strategies, and training) is key to drawing the line between civilians and law enforcement, particularly in areas imagined as high-crime and dangerous. In other words, police monopolize the core of police work—the exercise of legitimate violence. For police embracing a more state-centric logic of policing, the widespread availability of guns is fundamentally problematic and can only render police work more dangerous, more stressful, and less effective. Criminals having access to guns endangers police and ramps up the possibility of facing violence during the course of police work, whereas the payoff from civilians having guns seems negligible, if not irrelevant, to police's capacity to carry out police work. Loosened restrictions on guns create new opportunities for violence, which endangers police as they attempt to fight force with force and establish themselves as state-authorized wielders of violence in contrast to criminals. According to a state-centric logic of policing, this aggravates the problem of crime and disorder rather than solving it, not least because it shrinks the distance between civilians and police officers, endangering both.

*Shared Policing*

Clearly, not all police unanimously endorse this military model of policing, and moreover, historically, public law enforcement has not monopolized policing in America (Bayley and Shearing 1996). Urban public law-enforcement agencies were founded only in the mid-to-late 1800s in the US, and only decades thereafter did the gun become indelibly associated with police work. While the share of public versus private policing has waxed and waned, over the past forty years, not only has public law enforcement become more militarized, but there has also been a vast expansion in private policing mechanisms: The proliferation of so-called "cops for hire" (sometimes including current or former sworn law-enforcement personnel who moonlight on the side) and private companies like ADT Security Systems that act as liaisons between citizens and public law enforcement; the booming markets in security commodities like home alarms, cell phones, and firearms; and the legal empowerment of landlords, property owners, and other private entities to enact policing power through innovations like citation issuance (Desmond and Valdez 2013). Companies like Target not only have policing capacities that rival that of public law enforcement—including a certified crime lab, vast surveillance, and even interrogation rooms in stores where arrestees are held until public law enforcement arrives. Collectively, these developments—in which non-police actors are taking on policing duties—are known as "third-party policing" (Desmond and Valdez 2013). We might also view the 8 million-plus Americans who have licenses to carry concealed guns (according to the Bureau of Justice Statistics) as an extension of this "privatization" of policing insofar as individual citizens are compelled to "act like the police" under the assumption that public law enforcement cannot, or will not, be there to protect individual Americans (Carlson 2012).

Police departments with a history and culture of seeing themselves as sharing, rather than monopolizing, police responsibilities will probably be less likely to view guns in the hands of civilians as threatening police work. They may—in the case of some—even view civilian guns as contributing to police work. In which kinds of contexts are police likely to view guns as such?

First, rural areas, which have never transitioned from the long-standing tradition of private policing, have often relied much more than urban areas on informal social controls and intimate sharing of policing duties. Weisheit, Wells, and Falcone (1994) argue that the style of policing in rural areas fundamentally differs from urban areas. They find that rural public law-enforcement officers are accountable not only to their police organization but also to the community at large; they tend to know civilians personally and work with them at a personal level; and they emphasize solving general, rather than crime-specific, problems (1994, 551). Despite the availability of guns in such areas, police officers in rural areas appear less militaristic and less eager to monopolize police work, which confirms the findings of Thompson et al. (2011). But this dynamic is not exclusive to rural areas. For example, the sheriff of Maricopa County, the largest-population county in Arizona, has regularly supported citizen posses becoming involved in policing; in this case, it is therefore not simply the rural/urban divide but cultures of policing that matter (the latter of which often, but not always map, onto the rural/urban divide). The Phoenix Police Department's website, for example, not only highlights the department's civilian volunteer corps but also advertises the availability of off-duty cops "for hire."

Second, and by extension, as police departments experience sudden personnel cuts and defunding, they may increasingly see themselves as dependent on community resources, and this dynamic affects both rural and urban police departments. In contrast to the decades-long expansion in the punitive capacities of the state, state capacities to police and punish have contracted since 2008. According to the US Department of Justice, 10,000 to 15,000 officers have been laid off due to budget cuts since 2008, and according to a survey of police chiefs taken in 2011, "94 percent of respondents agreed that they were seeing 'a new reality in American policing developing'" due to significant reductions in the budgets and personnel since 2008 in police agencies across the United States (COPS 2011, 3). To address these reductions, some police departments are recognizing the need to share policing duties with civilians by "shifting some of the duties typically reserved for sworn staff to civilian employees as a means of cost savings" (known as "civilianization") as well as the increased use of volunteers (COPS 2011). In this context, guns in the hands of civilians may appear less as a liability for police and more as a beneficial extension of policing duties. This would help explain, for example, Milwaukee county sheriff David Clarke's statement that civilians should buy firearms and undergo firearms training because "we're partners now." Under a logic of shared policing, the contradictory role of guns in police work is therefore resolved not by hardening the line between police and non-police (as in the case of state-centric policing) but by dissolving it.

## Conclusion

A showdown has been unfolding in Wisconsin, a historically blue state, and it is not between Tea Party governor Scott Walker and the unions. It is between the Milwaukee county sheriff David Clarke and Milwaukee police chief Edward Flynn. While they oversee virtually the same jurisdiction, their views on gun politics could not be more different: While Flynn testified in front of Congress in early 2013 in support of an assault-weapons ban, Clarke has been advising Milwaukee residents to take up arms. Clarke has called Flynn "arrogant" and a "mouthpiece" for pro-gun-control groups, while Flynn has dismissed Clarke as simply "trying to raise funds for his next campaign."[10] The feud is indicative of the divides among public law enforcement over the issue of gun politics.

Very little research has attempted to document this division or its origins. My goal in this chapter has been to provide some suggestions for how we might make sense of these divergences. Ultimately, the question of how police think about guns may have less to do with how guns endanger police and more with how public law-enforcement officials think about police work, which is itself shaped by department-specific variables such as the violent crime rate, intra-department police culture, and the department's history of civilian-police relations. Because police work in the United States is not only fragmented at the local level but also embedded in contradictory processes of neoliberalism, police officers themselves may hold vastly different views on gun policies—not unlike the vastly different views of Americans more generally.

Public law-enforcement officials differ from the average American in that their working lives are characterized by unique exposure to violent force, wielded both against and by police. Their relationship to violence is embedded—both symbolically and materially—in the contradictory roles that guns play in police work. Dissecting how police think about gun politics has the potential to shed important insights on the relationship between public law enforcement, neoliberalism, and democracy. Unfortunately, the research on how police think about gun politics and how different kinds of gun policies affect police work is surprisingly sparse. This is even more shocking given the important public-policy implications of police support for, or resistance to, various gun-control policies. Future research could fruitfully examine, for example, how officer characteristics (including rank within police agencies, training, and so forth) affect attitudes toward gun policies; how police attitudes on gun policies intersect with "new" policing problems of immigration and homeland security (Beckett and Murakawa 2012); how the National Rifle Association's police-training programs shape, or not, police attitudes on guns;[11] the relationship between firearms companies and public law-enforcement agencies;[12] and the ways in which differences in police attitudes toward guns are patterned by the broader political economy in which police departments are situated.

Americans have long owned guns. But only recently, with the expansion of concealed carry and "stand your ground" laws, have Americans turned in such great numbers to guns as everyday tools for personal protection under the assumption that the police cannot, or will not, be there to save them in the event of a crime (Carlson 2012). As Americans turn to guns to supplement and, perhaps, supplant the police, scholars must also understand how police themselves make sense of, and respond to, laws that determine the ability of civilians to own, carry, and use firearms and how these laws, in turn, shape the work that police themselves do.

## Notes

1. See www.policechiefmagazine.org/magazine/index.cfm?fuseaction =displayandarticle_id=384.

2. See www.nationalmemo.com/biden-outgunned-police-support-assault -weapons-ban.

3. See www.news-sentinel.com/apps/pbcs.dll/article?AID=/20090511/NEWS /905110328 .

4. See www.calsheriffs.org/images/FederalCSSALetterreFirearms012413.pdf .

5. They explain this by noting the high incidence by which police are killed with their own guns.

6. Southwick (1998) finds that handgun sales along with the stock of handguns, rifles, and shotguns have a negative effect on police homicide. He notes that "apparently, more guns in civilian hands makes police relatively safer," but he considers existing criminological knowledge on the relationship between police homicides and homicides

in general in order to conclude that most likely, there is no meaningful effect in either direction.

7. Though findings are highly inconsistent across studies, scholars have found a number of factors increase police homicides, including: economic deprivation and poverty (Batton and Wilson 2006; Kaminski 2008); rates of violent crime (Batton and Wilson 2006; Lester 1984, 1987); black-white inequalities in resources (Jacobs and Carmichael 2002; Kent 2010); racial segregation (Jacobs and Carmichael 2002; Kaminski and Stucky 2009; Kent 2010); divorce rates (Jacobs and Carmichael 2002; Kaminski and Stucky 2009); officer killings of civilians (Kent 2010); and the size of the black population (Kaminski 2008; Kent 2010). Interestingly, some studies have found that the presence of a black mayor (Jacobs and Carmichael 2002; Kent 2010) or black city-council representation (Kaminski and Stucky 2009) reduces police homicides, leading Jacobs and Carmichael (2002) to suggest that police homicides may represent "inarticulate protest" galvanized by racial inequalities in material resources and political representation.

8. These factors include officer predispositions (Waters and Ussery 2007), the hierarchical organization of police agencies (Brandt 1993; Violanti and Aron 1993), sense of lack of control over work (Brandt 1993), the intensive emotional labor involved in police work (Martin 1999), police culture that discourages seeking assistance (Waters and Ussery 2007), dangers associated with certain kinds of calls for public assistance (Waters and Ussery 2007) and a "working environment characterized by uncertainty, danger, and coercive authority" (Paoline III, Myers, and Worden 2000, 576), among other factors.

9. See www.aclu.org/militarization.

10. See www.foxnews.com/politics/2013/03/06/milwaukee-sheriff-blasts-rude-testimony-pro-gun-control-police-chief.

11. For example, there are more than 11,000 NRA-certified public law-enforcement firearms trainers, but we know very little about how this arm of the NRA intersects with its more explicitly political arm.

12. On the one hand, firearms companies may well facilitate the militarization of public law-enforcement agencies by supplying them with new weaponry and expanded firepower. This strategy, for example, played a significant role in the rise of Glock (Barrett 2013). On the other hand, firearms companies have responded to police support for gun control by refusing to sell to public law enforcement. For example, when the state of California banned civilian ownership of one of its firearms in 2008, Barrett Firearms Manufacturer suspended sales to California public law enforcement.

# Chapter 10

# "There Is a GunMAN on Campus"

## Including Identity in Mass Shooting Discourse

### Michael Kimmel and Cliff Leek

BEN AGGER'S 2008 BOOK, *"THERE IS A GUNMAN ON CAMPUS": TRAGEDY AND Terror at Virginia Tech* (Agger and Luke 2008), to which one of the present authors contributed an essay, drew its title from the Emergency Alert warning broadcast throughout various social media at Virginia Tech on the morning of April 16, 2007, when Seung-Hui Cho began his murderous rampage. Most of the essays in that book—indeed, virtually all the public commentary since—emphasized only part of the term "gunman"—the gun. We believe that focusing on the guns is, of course, essential, but we also believe it is not a sufficient explanation. After all, even though Virginia has the largest number of single-sex colleges for females in the United States, it is difficult to imagine an emergency broadcast warning at, say, Mary Baldwin College, warning of a "gunwoman" on campus.

We believe that an essential part of the discussion is contained in the second part of the noun, the "man" part. That is, we argue that an essential part of the discussion of all rampage school shootings is gender. This gender framing is crucial even as, following the tragic mass murder at Sandy Hook Elementary School in Connecticut, the nation engaged in a short-lived, but earnest conversation for the first time in a generation about lethal gun violence. In the aftermath of Sandy Hook, President Obama issued twenty-three executive actions and three presidential memoranda to address gun violence in the United States, all of which were summarized in a report issued by the White House, "Now Is the Time: The President's Plan to Protect Our Children and Our Communities by Reducing Gun Violence" (Obama 2013). In addition, four states enacted sweeping gun-control legislation since the massacre at Sandy Hook (Connecticut, Colorado, New York, and Maryland). However, all national legislation failed, and the moment passed.

Despite popular support (McGinty, Webster, et al. 2013), such a failure was predictable. After all, the proposed federal background-check legislation was fervently opposed by the National Rifle Association (NRA), which donated over a million dollars to political candidates in 2012 and nearly $22 million to candidates and political action committees since 1990 (OpenSecrets 2013). The NRA's alternative to gun control—arming teachers and administrators in schools—would be risible were it not also so dangerously misguided. Indeed, it would not be shocking if, by the time this book is published, we read of a school in which someone reports that there is a gunman, and some well-meaning teacher or administrator shoots an innocent and unarmed person. In fact, a study of shootings at hospitals found that in one out of five shootings, the gun used was taken from an armed guard (Kelen, Catlett, et al. 2012). Most evidence suggests that armed civilians may do more harm than good in the face of an active shooting (Follman 2012).

The oft-repeated NRA slogan—"guns don't kill people, people kill people"—resonates with many Americans because it seems self-evidently true. However, we intend to complicate that aphorism. "Guns don't kill people, people kill people" is, of course, true. It just doesn't go far enough. We will argue that, in considering mass shootings, a few additional statements bring us closer to the truth:

*Guns don't kill people; men and boys kill people*—gender is a major explanatory variable.

*Guns don't kill people, young men and boys kill people*—age is also a primary predictive variable.

*Guns don't kill people, young white men and boys kill people*—race is also a major factor in rampage school shootings.

*Guns don't kill people, young white men and boys with serious psychological problems kill people*—yes, of course, mental illness is also a precipitating factor. Moreover, since we assume that mass murder is irrational, we often assume that mass murderers suffer from some form of mental illness.

*Guns don't kill people, young white men and boys with serious psychological problems <u>and a firm belief in traditional ideas of masculinity</u> kill people*—a belief that masculinity is demonstrated through the capacity for violence also separates those who use lethal violence from those who do not.

And finally, eventually, we will be able to address the guns issue:

*Guns don't kill people, but young white men and boys, often with serious psychological problems, and a firm belief in traditional notions of masculinity, <u>and who have easy access to guns</u> kill people.*

Parrying a monocausal explanation for a complex social problem is always easier than a multipronged approach to a complex problem with multiple causes. Access to guns is a central predictive variable, but several other variables must also be present. In a political climate in which comprehensive gun-control legislation is a near impossibility, addressing these other variables may be our best hope of eventually slowing the steadily climbing rate of mass shootings.

We will explore each of these variables a bit further in trying to understand Adam Lanza's act of mass murder at Sandy Hook Elementary School in 2012.

## Media

Let's first dismiss those explanations that rely on the violent media culture of first-person-shooter video games, aggressive violent rap, and metal musical genres that glorify violence as a motivating factor. Of course, our violent media culture of apocalyptic action movies and glorified graphic violence has to have *some* cognitive impact. Even though the overwhelming majority of game players and media consumers will never commit a violent act in their lives, most research indicates that media images have some effect on our behavior. Had they no effect, the entire advertising industry would collapse!

Indeed, a 2001 review of the literature (Anderson and Bushman 2001) and a 2010 meta-analytic study (Anderson, Shibuya, et al. 2010) both indicate that consumption of violent video games increases aggressive thoughts and feelings and decreases pro-social behavior. The direct effect of media on behavior shrinks to virtual insignificance in the face of other factors, however. This is made clear by the fact that such a violent media culture is evenly spread across the country, yet rampage school shootings are more a regional than a "national" phenomenon. That is, they tend to cluster in rural and suburban areas rather than in urban ones and are also more likely to occur in traditionally Republican-leaning states (Kimmel and Mahler 2003).

What's more, while rampage shootings have been increasing in frequency, overall violent crime has been in steep decline for the past two decades, just at the moment that the violence, mayhem, and gore in these video games has skyrocketed. With the exception of minor increases in violent crime in 2006 and 2012, the overall violent-crime rate in the United States has declined consistently since 1996 (United States Department of Justice 2013; Williams 2013). While we wouldn't necessarily promote a catharsis model of saturation—by which participation in violent media culture actually provides a siphon for aggressive feelings and therefore decreases the likelihood of actually acting violently—neither would we suggest that increased violence in fantasy life leads inevitably to an increase in violence in real life.

## Mental/Psychological Health

We, as a society, stigmatize individuals with mental illness as full of violent potential to the extent that nearly 75 percent of the US public perceives individuals with mental illnesses to be dangerous (Link, Phelan, et al. 1999); that perception of danger is a major source of discrimination against people experiencing mental illness (Corrigan, Markowitz, et al. 2003; Corrigan, Watson, et al. 2004). Even as research indicates that mental illness and developmental disability is linked to the perpetration of violence only when moderated by a context of social stratification (Hiday 1995), our inclination is too often to vilify the illness or disability rather than examining that context.

Let's grant that, from what little we know, Adam Lanza had Asperger's syndrome, a developmental disability. He may have also suffered from bipolar disorder. Pop psychologists will never have the opportunity to properly diagnose him or many other mass shooters, but that won't stop them from trying (Langman 2009). Just as surely, the overwhelming majority of people with mental illnesses or developmental disabilities do not hurt other people. The majority of violence is actually performed by people who would most likely not receive a mental or psychological diagnosis. Just as we recommend avoiding focusing on guns or violent media as monocausal explanations of mass shootings, so too do we recommend avoiding vilifying individuals with mental illnesses or developmental disabilities as a means to prevent this catastrophic violence.

# Gender

One of the bigger surprises in the coverage of Sandy Hook was that gender became increasingly visible. The utter maleness of these mass murders is no longer being ignored, but it also still may not be getting the attention it deserves. According to data collected by Mayors Against Illegal Guns, of the forty-three mass shootings (four or more people murdered) committed in the United States between January 2009 and January 2013, 100 percent of the perpetrators were male (Mayors Against Illegal Guns 2013). According to *Mother Jones*'s collection of data on mass shootings (over four killed, single shooter, public space) there were sixty-two perpetrators of mass shootings in the United States between January 1982 and January 2013; sixty-one of those perpetrators were men (Follman, Aronsen, et al. 2012).

Just as surely, however, most biological males do not embark on such terrible rampages. There is nothing hardwired in men that leads us to commit mass murder, and no amount of testosterone juicing would lead us all to pick up guns and start shooting, seemingly randomly, at children in an elementary school. The research on testosterone is clear that testosterone facilitates aggression but does not cause it, and that the targets of that enhanced propensity toward aggression must already be perceived as legitimate (Sapolsky and Bonetta 1997). Thus, for example, were we to get massive doses of testosterone, it is unlikely that we would hit our university's provost or the football team's middle linebacker. However, the larger context of the domestic-violence epidemic in United States reveals that many men already see women as legitimate targets of violence, so it is no coincidence that mass shootings and domestic violence are deeply linked. An investigation by Mayors Against Illegal Guns found that in at least 45 percent of rampage shootings, the male perpetrator also killed a current or former intimate partner (when it was white men doing the shooting, they killed an intimate partner 76 percent of the time), while in eight of the thirty-two cases in which the shooter killed an intimate partner, he also had a prior domestic-violence charge (Mayors Against Illegal Guns 2013).

Of course, maleness alone doesn't cause aggression, but adherence to traditional ideas of masculinity may well enable it (Kimmel and Mahler 2003; Gallagher and Parrott 2011; Poteat, Kimmel, et al. 2011). Such ideas as "real men don't get mad, they get even" and the entire code of masculinity as elaborated on countless Gender Role Conformity Scales (Mahalik, Locke, et al. 2003; Cohn and Zeichner 2006; Reidy, Sloan, et al. 2009) are the sorts of ideas that propose rampage violence as a reasonable and rational solution to one's problems. Not only do traditional notions of masculinity prevent men from seeking counseling or other forms of help they need (Berger, Levant, et al. 2005; O'Brien, Hunt, et al. 2005), help which may prevent these mass shootings, but violence is also inculcated as a more masculine alternative than help-seeking.

Violence is also seen as redemptive and restorative. It is seen as a way to retaliate against nearly any perceived slight. Righteous retaliation is a deeply held, almost sacred, tenet of masculinity: if you are aggrieved, you are entitled to retribution (Mullins, Wright, et al. 2004). If you feel humiliated or victimized, violence may be perceived as a rational method to restore the status quo, along with one's masculinity.

So it also stands to reason that younger men and boys will be more likely to become rampage school shooters. This is not simply because they are the ones who attend school, while older men tend to be in workplaces where their humiliations may be experienced differently and their reasonable potential targets for their aggression might be more individual. These are not, after all, crimes of opportunity, but crimes methodically planned over a long period of time. Younger men, experiencing what is frequently called the "gender intensi-fication" years of late adolescence, are more likely to cling tenaciously to those toxic notions of masculinity (Galambos, Almeida, et al. 1990).

In the gender intensification years, young men and women face growing pressure to conform to established gender roles. For young men, the norms they are expected to conform to are too often pro-violence and anti-help-seeking. The gender intensification years are also linked to the emergence of a number of mental-health issues, such as depression and anxiety, as a result of many young men's unwillingness or difficulty in conforming to traditional gender norms (Priess, Lindberg, et al. 2009). There are many positive notions of masculinity as well (Kiselica 2011), and our interventions ought to pit those positive ideals against those toxic elements to enable boys and younger men to navigate their way more healthily and less violently (Katz 1995; Hong 2000).

## Race

Finally, and perhaps most controversially, mass murder is largely a *white* thing. Just as serial killers tend to be white (Tithecott 1997), so, too, are virtually all rampage shooters. While men of all races have perpetrated mass shootings in the United States, those perpetrating shootings at elementary and high schools are disproportionately white (90 percent white men). In addition, the perpe-tration of mass shootings by young men is also a disproportionately white phenomenon (80 percent of mass shooters aged twenty or under are white) (Follman, Aronsen, et al. 2012).

Since the 1999 rampage at Columbine High School in Littleton, Colorado, most of the perpetrators of mass killings have also ended the rampage by taking their own lives. This phenomenon represents a new phase of rampage killings: One's goal is not simply retaliation, but instead glory, martyrdom, to be remembered. What can only be described as "suicide by mass murder" has emerged as a corollary to the earlier "suicide by cop" as a phenomenon of those whose real goal is, at least in part, to kill themselves—and to take out as many of "them" as possible on the way. This seems to be nearly an entirely white-male thing.

In urban settings, when young men of color experience that same sense of aggrieved entitlement—that perception of victimhood despite everything men expect for themselves—they may react violently, and even with lethal violence. In these cases, the victims of their violence are usually those whom the shooter believes have wronged him, plus the unintended and accidental victims caught in the line of fire. These encounters rarely end with his suicide.

White-male mass shooters, on the other hand, have a somewhat more grandiose purpose: they want to destroy the entire world in some cataclysmic, video-game, action-movie-inspired apocalypse. If I'm going to die, then so is everybody else, they seem to say. One must feel a sense of aggrieved entitlement to pick up a gun and go on a rampage, that is true. That sense of aggrieved entitlement must also be grandiose, however, if you are going to "make them all pay." This may be mental illness speaking, but it is mental illness speaking with a voice that has a race, a gender, and access to guns.

Even as we challenge ourselves to see the racial difference in perpetrators, we must not ignore the way that our response to this kind of violence is also shaped by race. When we hear of a rampage shooting by a white man, we immediately claim that it is a result of individual pathology; that is, mental illness. The problem is "him," not "us." In contrast, when we hear of a rampage or gang murders in the inner city, we assume that it is the result of a "social pathology"—something about the culture of poverty, the legacy of racism, or some intrinsic characteristics of "them" or "those people." This difference in treatment allows us to avoid talking about what whiteness might have to do with the violence, while always talking about what blackness or brownness has to do with it.

## Guns

The discussion now brings us to guns. Surely, guns played *some* role in this. Access to guns is certainly not a phenomenon that is limited to white men, so guns alone also should not be pursued as a singular cause. Although guns by themselves are not the cause of the rampage, they can help explain its horrific scale and its terrible scope.

In the United States today there are an estimated 310 million privately owned guns despite the ongoing occurrence of mass shootings (Krouse 2012), but consider two of our closest allies as a counterpoint. In 1996, in Dunblane, Scotland, a single gunman killed sixteen children and one adult in an affluent suburb before taking his own life. That same year, a gunman killed thirty-five people and wounded twenty-three more in a Tasmanian resort town; it was Australia's worst mass shooting ever. Both countries immediately passed tough gun-control legislation; Scotland has made it effectively illegal to own a handgun in the United Kingdom. There hasn't been another school shooting since then in Britain, while in Australia, homicides by firearms have declined by about 60 percent over the past fifteen years.

Legislation attempting to limit access to guns is no silver bullet. For various reasons, gun control has had mixed results in the United States. Scholars have pointed to the lack of enforcement as a reason for the failure of gun-control legislation here (Cook and Ludwig 2013). In fact, a recent study regarding the prevention of gun violence found that, if fully enforced, some provisions of the existing 1993 Brady Handgun Violence Prevention Act can reduce gun-violence offense rates among individuals with serious mental illnesses who do not have prior criminal records (Swanson, Robertson, et al. 2013).

After mass shootings like the one at Sandy Hook, the gun-control debate dominates media coverage to the exclusion of other factors. Even in academia, most of the other contributing factors are all but absent from the discussion. One of the first major books on gun violence in America to be published post–Sandy Hook, *Reducing Gun Violence in America: Informing Policy with Evidence and Analysis*, focuses almost solely on gun control as though limiting access to guns would not only solve all of the gun-violence problems but also as if limiting access to guns is the *only* thing that can be done (Webster and Vernick 2013). In the absence—and arguably even in the presence—of comprehensive, enforced, gun-control legislation, it is crucial to look to other factors associated with the perpetration of this senseless violence.

## Conclusion

In the debate regarding the prevention of mass shootings, pundits most often place the blame at one of two poles, either individual mental illness or group social pathology. Arguments for individual mental illness label the perpetrators as monsters or deranged psychopaths who are clearly exceptions to our overall peaceful culture. Meanwhile, arguments that blame a group's social pathology strive to place perpetrators into specific categories or subcultures that exempt the vast majority of society from "their" problems. In both cases, though—individual mental illness or social pathology—we make sure that it is not "our" story, but "their" story. Thus we miss the other variables in this equation: How the shooter is, indeed, one of us, shaped in the same culture, fed the same diet of images and ideas about the legitimacy of white men's righteous rage, and given access to the same guns, subject to the same poorly diagnosed and undertreated mental illnesses, regardless of their cause.

Just as those innocent victims at Sandy Hook are "one of us," so, too, is Adam Lanza. We, the authors, speak inside that frame; we, too, are white and male, and have drunk from the same glass of aggrieved entitlement. Unless we address all the elements of the equation in his horrific act, including race and gender, our nation will continue to produce Adam Lanzas, Dylan Klebolds, James Holmeses, and Jared Loughners, arm them with a small arsenal, and then inspire them to explode.

# Chapter 11

# *Men Who Kill*

### Ben Agger

OVER 400,000 PEOPLE DIE IN THE UNITED STATES PER YEAR FROM SMOKING-related causes, such as lung cancer. An estimated 100,000 die in the United States per year from obesity-related issues, while about 80,000 die from excessive use of alcohol. Approximately 30,000 people die annually in the United States in automobile crashes, about half of which involve alcohol. About 30,000 die from gun violence, about two-thirds of which are suicides. According to the CDC, about a million Americans are HIV-positive. The country lost between 6,000 and 7,000 troops in the conflicts in Iraq and Afghanistan.

In this chapter, I consider our heated national conversation about guns and gun violence, which became even more heated after the December 2012 Newtown, Connecticut, elementary school rampage shooting. It is notable that we are talking about gun violence but not as heatedly about lung cancer, food and exercise, alcohol abuse, automobile safety, or HIV as these phenomena relate to mortality and individual risk. I argue that gun control begins and ends at home, but that gun control, on the aggregate level, basically misses the mark in a society in which private gun ownership is constitutionally protected. I also identify the "elephant in the room," which is the issue of men who kill. Before the Boston Marathon bombing suspects had been identified in April 2013, no one suspected that the bombers were women. This didn't occur to anyone because it is men who kill. Approximately 90 percent of US gun homicides are committed by males.

I work toward a paradigm of gun violence that does not rely heavily on gun-control measures but rather emphasizes gender, class, and risk as relevant factors. I also consider a militarized culture as a backdrop against which male fantasy plays out. The discussion of risk derives from a view of gun violence as a public health issue (see Hemenway 2006). Risk cuts both ways: It may be risky to own a gun and risky not to own one, depending on the context. A woman afraid of being assaulted decides to carry a handgun. She might repel assailants with the gun, but on the other hand, it might accidentally discharge, or her romantic partner may use it against her in a domestic conflict. One thing we know is that, when a gun is owned in a household, the probabilities increase both of a woman being killed (via domestic violence) and of suicide, which accounts for a majority of gun deaths in the United States. It is also not clear that arming oneself is effectively defensive. Both the district attorney and assistant DA in Kaufman County, Texas, were armed, but were nonetheless murdered in early 2013 possibly by an accused husband and wife aggrieved about his firing as justice of the peace.

In my gender/class/risk paradigm, I am largely ignoring the issue of the right to bear arms, and which arms, as I am a sociologist interested in social issues and policy. Most reasonable people would agree that the United States is an armed society (about 300 million guns in circulation, with estimates of the percentage of households that own guns ranging from a third to a half). Most reasonable people would also agree that the Second Amendment gives people the right to protect their castles and to hunt, and most would agree that the Second Amendment was intended to be self-limiting. In my neighborhood, I never see anyone walking around with a bazooka, and I doubt that anyone is searching for fissionable material so they can build a nuke in their basement. Whether so-called assault rifles are protected is an ongoing debate that demonstrates that such matters are debatable. From my perspective, that debate is largely fruitless because I am interested in the underlying correlates of public and private violence, including gender and class. In this collection, Kimmel and Leek also suggest a multivariate understanding of the causes and correlates of rampage shootings, examining the implosive admixture of race, class, and gender that leads young white men to act out a sense of what the authors call aggrieved entitlement.

I neither demonize nor mythologize guns. One can kill with handguns, knives, poison, or one's fists. My Volvo-driving friends may never have known a gun owner (or knew that they knew one), and I often think that zealous defenders of the right to bear arms really believe that the federal government is poised to invade Texas with the First Cav, only to be repelled by a ragtag militia armed with Bushmasters. Liberals believe that guns shoot people, while certain conservatives believe that people shoot guns. In the interest of full disclosure, I tend to agree with the NRA on this point, but I also do not own a gun, nor have I ever shot one. As I will explain, I tend to think that we inhabit a "gun culture" in which certain males live out fantasies of being a Navy SEAL, just as other men imagine themselves playing professional sports. Again, in the interest of full disclosure, I imagine myself winning the Olympic marathon, which perhaps reflects the fact that I grew up in Eugene, Oregon. Fullest disclosure: I think that neither the Volvo drivers nor the NRA members are correct. Borrowing from postmodernism, I think that people are positioned to be shooters by forces largely out of their control. The legal proceedings against George Zimmerman, who was accused and acquitted of killing Trayvon Martin, demonstrate this well: Zimmerman was impelled to shoot by a variety of circumstances involving race, gender, age, clothing, and the fact that he, Zimmerman, had a gun. Vigilantism is a subject position, as postmodernists term it. Of course, "largely" does not mean "entirely." There is an electric moment when the shooter can defy his or her positioning and decide not to shoot. This electric moment is, perhaps, the boundary between the postmodern and the modern, a discussion we will never hear in the halls of Congress as gun control is debated. As we have known for thousands of years, there is no going back on violence, a topic of Merleau-Ponty's (1969) intriguing book, *Humanism and Terror*.

It is also relevant that I am a dual citizen of both the United States, where I grew up and live now, and Canada, where I lived, studied, and taught between 1969 and 1981. Canada is important because it provides a counterpoint to American gun culture; its very existence helps us test some important hypotheses. Canadians own guns, but these are primarily long guns, to be used in hunting, not handguns. Canada has no equivalent of the Second Amendment—the right to bear arms. A majority of Canadians do not think that people should have a legal right to own guns. In 2010, 11,078 Americans were killed in gun homicides, whereas in the same year only 171 Canadians died due to gun homicide. (Suicide is another question, which I also take up later.) Controlling for different population sizes, if the gun-homicide rate in Canada were equal to the US rate, 1,185 people would have been killed in Canada. There is a much lower gun-murder rate in Canada, about a seventh of the US rate. Canadians watch the same violent movies and play the same violent video games as their US counterparts, and, as I said, Canadians hunt. Clearly, we can learn from the Canadian attitude toward guns and gun ownership, even as we attend to certain fundamental differences between the two countries. It is also worth noting that the gun-homicide rate is actually dropping in both countries, perhaps suggesting that the calculation of individual-level risk of gun ownership is having an effect on the gun-homicide rate.

This book came about in the wake of 2012 rampage killings in the United States, first in July in a Denver suburb and then just before Christmas in a Connecticut town called Newtown. In both instances, young males used heavy firepower to kill twelve to twenty people in short-lived shooting sprees. Presumably, they didn't know their victims, in a darkened theater and first-grade classrooms. The Colorado shooter is under indictment and faces the death penalty. The Connecticut shooter, like most rampage killers, committed suicide before the police could apprehend him. We were interested in the shootings themselves, but also in the media spectacles surrounding them, a topic taken up by Jaclyn Schildkraut and Glenn Muschert.

My coeditor, Tim Luke, and I had already edited a book on the Virginia Tech shootings, where Tim teaches political science. *There Is a Gunman on Campus* (Agger and Luke 2008) was our first foray into rampage shootings and school shootings. Neither one of us is trained in criminology, but we both do applied critical theory, which uses a certain theoretical lens to focus attention and analysis on important social problems. We derive from the Frankfurt School of critical theory, which includes thinkers such as Adorno and Marcuse, and, like them, we view ourselves as social scientists who examine the empirical world, albeit not from the ground level but from 40,000 feet, as we fly over the polar ice caps and obtain a big-picture view of the real world.

This is not to say that flying at lofty theoretical heights is the only valid intellectual approach. Such approaches lose in ground-level detail what they gain in panoramic perspective. Equally important is life on the ground, to be addressed by careful empiricists for whom details are more important than the big sweep or the big picture. Flying high and studying life on the ground are both valid forms of empiricism; indeed, they enrich each other. Understanding the lives of James Holmes and Adam Lanza—their upbringing, schooling, mental-health problems, and access to weapons—is crucially important, supplementing and being supplemented by the big-picture view of gun violence afforded by applied critical theory. Mark Worrell, in his chapter, calls for precisely this sort of multilevel analysis as he traces social structure downward into the damaged psyches of young men who kill. Also deriving from the Frankfurt School, Worrell argues against both psychologism and sociologism.

It is especially important to ground gun-homicide and gun-control insights in a global context, as Matt Qvortrup tries to do in his chapter of this book. It is similarly important to think theoretically about different approaches to gun violence, gun control, and gun risk. My own big-picture contribution to this discussion builds to some extent on the work of Katherine Newman (Newman, Fox, Harding, Mehta, and Roth 2004) and David Hemenway. Newman helps profile rampage shooters, while Hemenway focuses gun discussions on concepts of risk.

A certain master narrative of public and school shooters has emerged in our instantaneous media culture that took on new life after the shootings at Columbine High School, also in a suburb of Denver, in 1999. This master narrative insidiously affects our views of all shootings and of gun violence generally. Certain aspects of this master narrative are wrong on the evidence, as authors such as Dave Cullen (2009) have pointed out, with shooters portrayed as video gamers with guns who have been bullied. After examining the four recent mass shootings carefully—Columbine, Virginia Tech, Aurora, and Newtown—I propose a different common profile of rampage shooters:

- They are young males.
- They dislike school.
- They are depressed.
- They are suicidal.
- They have access to, and knowledge of, guns.

There is little evidence that they have been bullied or are compulsive gamers, even though these are often identified as risk factors for rampage killers. The "bullied-gamers-with-guns" master narrative was composed almost immediately after Columbine, when it was reported in the media that Eric Harris and Dylan Klebold belonged to the so-called "Trenchcoat Mafia," a group composed of other marginal kids who were bullied by jocks wearing white hats. Cullen, in his study of Columbine, finds that Harris and Klebold were neither members of this informal mafia of Goths, nor were they bullied. Indeed, they may have done some bullying of their own.

Most gun homicides are not rampage-style or school-related mass shootings. They involve crime, especially crimes involving drugs. One of the reasons that gun control on the aggregate level in the United States does not effectively work to reduce the rate of gun violence is that we construct a mistaken causal model. This is somewhat the same point made by the NRA, but, as we will soon see, I am blending the NRA's analysis with that of Karl Marx, who stresses the connection between crime and poverty. The gun-control paradigm mistakenly conflates two sorts of gun owners: What the NRA's Wayne LaPierre recently called the "good guys" and "bad guys." By good guys he means law-abiding gun owners who use the Second Amendment to legitimize their ownership of guns as a protective means, or those who hunt or who just enjoy gun connoisseurship.

By bad guys LaPierre means criminal gun owners who commit crimes using guns. The gun-control paradigm, as I am calling it, often fails to make this distinction, leading us to "control" the guns of law-abiding citizens, like most of my neighbors in suburban Texas.

When the perceived crime rate increases, people feel risk and arm themselves defensively. Reducing access to guns among defensive armers, however, will have little impact on the rate of gun homicide, most of which is committed by career criminals or the mentally ill. This prompts the question about why people embark on criminal careers for which they need to be armed. Here is where I combine the NRA and Karl Marx. These people embark on such careers because they are impoverished and feel that they have few economic options, especially when they may have dropped out of high school in a bad economy. They make the fateful choice to join a gang and/or embark on a criminal career. Once arrested, they are incarcerated and their recidivism is enhanced; they learn to be better criminals.

And so instead of controlling the guns of "good guys," we should focus on career alternatives for "bad guys," who make the self-defeating and destructive choice to become career criminals. A few modest suggestions include encouraging kids to complete high school, strengthening the family, and, above all, providing well-paying jobs for people who lack a college degree. I am convinced that many college-bound young people in the United States are in college merely to earn a career-related credential and not for the love of learning. Where a high school diploma used to be enough to secure gainful employment, now the entry-level credential is a college degree, if not a master's degree. LaPierre seems to neglect the possibility that bad guys could become good guys, a view that will be ridiculed by law-and-order advocates familiar with the failure of prisons to rehabilitate and reform. I'm not calling for new, bigger, or better prisons; the prison-industrial complex is part of the problem. I am calling instead for economic restructuring that addresses the origin of crime in poverty, which is eradicable. Socialism (and feminism, as I will explain below) is the best form of gun control, a formulation that will offend the many who believe that political liberty comes at the end of a barrel of a legally owned handgun or rifle.

In short, the NRA is correct that people—criminals—shoot guns, not the other way around. Marx helps us to understand that capitalism causes crime, and that armed criminals commit most of the gun homicides, to which good guys react by purchasing more guns in order to protect their castles. Postmodernism helps us understand that shooters occupy subject positions, into which they are thrust. I am not advocating greater expenditures on a prison-industrial complex, because prisons only serve as petri dishes of criminal recidivism. I am urging a rethinking of imprisonment, high school and college, the family, and our labor market in order to provide alternative careers for would-be criminals. Of course, none of this involves abridging or broadening Second Amendment rights. Guns aren't the problem; poverty is.

The renewed discussion of gun violence was provoked by mass death presented as media spectacle. Since Columbine in 1999, rampage shootings have come to dominate gun-control discourse, both in public policy and in the media. Most of the prominent rampage shootings have involved legal guns or illegally transferred, though legally purchased ("straw"), guns. There is little evidence that exposure to media violence causes violence. It has become a liberal shibboleth that we need "less" media violence, an eradication of school bullying, and stricter gun laws in order to prevent the next Newtown. A rigorous look at rampage killings—including Columbine, Virginia Tech, Aurora, and Newtown—suggests, however, that rampage killers are young men who are unhappy in school, depressed, suicidal, and somewhat familiar with weapons. The shooters were not necessarily bullied, nor were they inspired by video games like *Mortal Kombat* or *Grand Theft Auto*. Suicidality looms large because, as I have already noted, household gun ownership tends to result in suicides, as was seen in Newtown, Virginia Tech, and Columbine.

In a media culture, rampage shootings reproduce themselves as troubled young men seek their few moments of notoriety. In retrospect, Adam Lanza's mother was taking a significant risk by exposing her sons to guns and by allowing guns in the household. Gun control wouldn't have prevented this school shooting, however. It is reasonable to call for mental-health measures, but such diagnostic clarity is often clearer in retrospect and not before the fact. Lots of depressed and suicidal kids don't kill themselves and others. They may turn to alcohol, drugs, and promiscuous sexuality; they may drop out of school. There are many ways to unravel.

Perhaps the problem we should be talking about is violence writ large, not just gun violence. The United States seems always to be embroiled in war, which bears a huge human cost. Poverty and hunger involve violence. Intimate-partner violence is still found in some relationships. Prison is violent, and it breeds additional violence. Male aggression seems to underlie much of the violence I am talking about, a statement that risks biologism or sociobiologism. But women rarely kill and almost never engage in rampage killings. Moreover, they tend not to use guns when they commit suicide.

Yet men, globally, are usually the decision makers. I ask my students to perform a thought experiment: If all the world's countries were headed by female leaders, would there be less war? Most answer affirmatively, but there is cautious debate about the reasons for this. Is it nature or nurture? I think it may be both, suggesting that the boundary between the natural and social may be blurry. If biological destiny isn't involved, it is difficult indeed to explain why angry women don't shoot up schools and theaters, especially at a historical moment when women are liberated to attend college, run corporations, and join the military (albeit not yet in combat roles).

I began with a list of social problems, including lung cancer, alcohol-related behavior, and persistent HIV, that are more mortal than gun homicide. Perhaps I should add being male to the list. This is not to decide in favor of nature and against nurture; clearly, boys can be brought up to be caring and compassionate men. Gender is a continuum, not a dichotomous variable. I have not been persuaded even by tragedies such as Newtown that we need aggregate-level gun control, instead of the kind of "gun-control-based-on-risk-assessment" that begins at home. I am not convinced that violent video games and other media play any role in gun violence. I am of course against bullying, but am not persuaded that the rampage shooters were singled out as targets of bullying. Neither am I motivated by the aftermath of Newtown and Aurora to redouble my commitment to the Second Amendment, which has always struck me as ambiguous. Did Madison in 1791 intend for private citizens to protect their farms using firearms? Or did he really want to arm a militia that could resist external tyranny or perhaps quell a slave revolt? The very fact that we don't know—that the Bill of Rights requires contemporary interpretation—suggests that defense of, or opposition to, the Second Amendment cannot take place on grounds of literalism but only with careful and considered argumentation. In his contribution to this volume, James Welch explores what he calls "the ethos of the gun" as he teases out the centrality of gun ownership to our conceptions of liberty.

I conclude that so-called gun control begins at home: Everyone must decide for themselves what sort of risks they run by having guns in the house. For many, benefits may outweigh the risks. For the Lanza family, the risks were grave indeed. On the societal level, there is little evidence that universal background checks or registries will move the needle on the gun-homicide rate. I am not even convinced that banning assault rifles and limiting the size of magazines will bring that rate down, although there are other arguments for those bans and limitations. Among those arguments is symbolism: Civilized societies do not allow citizens to own and use weapons of war. But, then again, many US states have the death penalty, which makes us unusual by comparison to European nations, which have abandoned state-sanctioned death as uncivilized.

My friendly neighbor protects himself with a handgun. He imagines Obama's socialist hordes swooping down to rob him of his 401(k) and his armory of guns. Laughingly, I reassure him that Obama has bigger fish to fry. Truly, my neighbor is not part of the gun-violence problem, unless a tragic accident occurs in his household. He is a good guy, but not a good guy who is likely to deter an armed intruder. By owning a gun, he feels less at risk in a chaotic world in which violence seems to be random. He is like many Texans, who view gun ownership as part of their birthright. My neighborhood is not more dangerous because of him, but neither is it safer, in my view. I have lived in Texas since 1994, and I have never seen evidence that I inhabit an armed state. Indeed, Texans seem much more polite and less prone to interpersonal conflict than do residents of New York, where I used to live. There is less road rage here in Texas, and everyone knows that cars are lethal weapons when men drive under the influence of alcohol or anger.

I think our national conversation should not be about gun control but rather about the institutionalized violence of war and prisons, the incidence of HIV, the risk of sedentary lifestyles, fast food and factory meat, alcohol dependence and binge drinking, a shallow media culture, schools that fall short, and a credential economy that requires college, which often involves heavy indebtedness. We should also debate suicide, and thus mental health and anomie, especially whereas the suicide rate by gun is twice as high as the rate of gun homicides. In socioeconomic terms, I wish we would discuss criminal careers as the last resorts they are, and recognize that gun violence responds to deep economic inequalities that are passed across generations. Above all, we should be discussing why men kill.

Rampage killings attract attention, and understandably so. Innocents are murdered, senselessly, often by semiautomatic weapons. Similarly, the recent Boston Marathon bombings left three people dead and nearly 200 injured, some of whom lost limbs and had their lives forever changed. They were doing nothing more than watching a marathon on a public holiday. The first-graders killed in Newtown had their whole lives in front of them. It is true that human history has been a tableau of suffering, inhumanity, injustice, and violence. Gun-violence debates today often seen amnesiac, implying that citizens acquired weapons of mass destruction only with the origin of the first assault rifles in 1943, in the German army (*Sturmgewehr*), or somewhat earlier, with the Gatling gun in the United States (c. 1862). This view neglects the history of mass killing in warfare, first with lances, swords, and crossbows, and then, beginning in the fourteenth century, with gunpowder and muskets. Our moral revulsion at rampage killings loses touch with the prehistory and evolution of killing technologies, primarily used in wars of conquest.

In the US context, debates about the limitations of the Second Amendment were already raging a full decade before the Nazi's introduction of the assault rifle (see Dizard 1999). The rise of organized crime during Prohibition (as a response to Prohibition) saw the demonization of machine guns and short-barreled shotguns. In 1934, a year after Prohibition was repealed, the National Firearms Act limited the use of various "gangland" weapons such as the Thompson .45 caliber submachine gun, known as the "Tommy" gun. This chronology reveals continuity in the evolution of weapons and the legislative backlash in the form of gun control, with the German assault rifle entering the scene a decade after the National Firearms Act in the United States. Globalization kicks in with the 1950 prototype Uzi submachine gun (and, later, smaller machine-pistol variants), produced by the Israelis for use by the Israel Defense Forces beginning in 1954. The Uzi was massively popular among armies and police all the way into the 1980s, demonstrating that criminals and agents of social control match force with force. There is nothing new under the weapons sun, only incremental steps in automated killing that span the millennia, from the lance and spear to the Glock and AR-15. Winkler (2011) offers a panoramic overview of American gun-control efforts and debates and Spitzer (2011) tracks gun-control politics.

Glocks are interesting here (see Barrett 2012). They are semiautomatic pistols first developed for use by the Austrian Army in 1982. Fully 65 percent of US law-enforcement agencies are now said to have adopted the Glock, which also remains a weapon of choice for individual gun owners. It has a polymer (plastic) frame, making it light and easy to carry. Current gun-control debates in the United States revolve around the question of magazine size for semi-automatic handguns, an issue that came to the fore after the 2011 shooting of Arizona congresswoman Gabrielle Giffords by Jared Lee Loughner. Reportedly, Loughner employed a .9 mm Glock handgun with a thirty-three-round magazine. The constitutional debate over "appropriate" magazine size would have perplexed Madison, for whom the "bad guys" were the occupying British army and not today's street criminals. Today, that distant postcolonial war has been transposed into street fighting between police and criminals, and among citizens themselves, as public life has become dangerous in part because the right to join a repelling militia has been transposed into "stand your ground" laws. I truly do not believe that Madison wanted to arm George Zimmerman, who deputized himself to do avenging work.

The call for post-Newtown gun control needs to be heard as a millennial call for disarmament and perpetual peace. Instead, the bid to end gun violence is reduced to federal policy, which usually amounts to a Band-Aid solution or to nothing (given both the influence of gun manufacturers on the NRA and the NRA's apparent influence over members of Congress, on both sides of the aisle). Policy makes a difference, as we have seen amply during the twentieth century, which could well be viewed as a century of civil-rights gains, of minorities and women primarily, and—lately—of gays and lesbians. There is little evidence, however, that policy of the gun-control sort will put a dent in male rage expressed in shootings and bombings.

There are two common threads in millennial violence: economic inequality (breeding and bred by conquest and domination) and the male gender. Perhaps it is still too soon to judge whether women in policing and in the military, liberated by the Civil Rights Act of 1964 and Title IX in 1972, will catch up to men's will to power. Perhaps we will begin to see women involved in more shootings and rampage killings. The first few months of 2013 have seen the daily media spectacle of the Jodi Arias case, involving a twenty-seven-year old woman who savagely killed her ex-boyfriend with a combination of knives and a handgun, which was probably legally owned by her grandparents. Arias, in her rage, acted against gender type, just as she fulfilled aspects of her gender role by clinging desperately to a boyfriend who used her only for sex. Whether her possible death penalty will ever be carried out probably depends on the appeals process in the state of Arizona and on shifting gender sentiment about the execution of women. One might make a feminist argument that, by committing murderous mayhem, Arias should be treated like a man, who would probably receive the death penalty for butchering an ex. My own view is that the death penalty is state-sanctioned violence that has no place in a civilized society, but I also notice that gender relationships today are often marked by rage sparked by rejection, insecurity, and need. Violence is brought forth in the crucible of rage when weapons are relatively easy to obtain. Keep in mind, however, that Arias did her killing mainly with a knife, with which she stabbed her victim twenty-nine times. The gunshot was probably delivered after her victim was already dead.

The Arias trial, which combined violence and sex, was covered closely by the HLN network. Some of its anchors, and many in the general public, called for her head, astonished that a woman could behave murderously like a man. For months on end, Arias was described with words like "satanic" and "monstrous." Male death at the hands of a spurned woman made for riveting reality television, and the blanket coverage incited mobs who made threats against the experts who testified on Arias's behalf, on character witnesses supporting her, and on her female cocounsel.

Of interest, then, is why and how we prioritize certain kinds of death over others. There is a moral demography of death which allows us to assign extra weight to the Newtown victims but deny any weight to the police shooting of the Tsarnaev brother, who built and planted the Boston Marathon bombs. No one mourned for bin Laden, brought down at long last by Navy SEALs, who were deployed by a Democratic president widely viewed as a friend of gun control and an enemy of the NRA. Indeed, that same president reacted with such revulsion to the pre-Christmas killings in Newtown that he began his second administration with a vow to enact certain piecemeal gun-control reforms, in the name of the dead children, presumably. Again we see that moral demography of death. Interestingly, although young people were killed in the July 2012 theater shooting in a Denver suburb, a shooting in which an assault rifle was apparently used, that killing spree sparked no such national conversation. Those deaths, during the midnight Batman-movie premiere, counted for more than the bin Laden and Tsarnaev deaths but less than the death of the Connecticut first-graders. Who, other than immediate family, grieves for the five people killed in a New York City automobile accident only two days after the July 20 Colorado theater killings? Or for the 1,034 people killed in the Dhaka, Bangladesh, textile-factory collapse on April 24, 2013? These textile workers were probably working in a sweatshop supplying westerners with clothing. A full 98 percent of Americans purchase clothes manufactured outside of the United States, suggesting that the roots of violence and death are structural.

Earlier, I talked about my experiences in Canada, where I lived and attended college and graduate school and launched my academic teaching career. I love Canada: It is multicultural, tolerant, nonimperial. Canada has no sense of "manifest destiny," as did the United States. As Margaret Atwood and others have written, Canada derives its identity in part from being "not-American." Canada, unlike the United States, was not born of revolutionary violence. Canada was on the side of the mother country, England, during our Revolutionary War. The United States sought postcolonial status, and thus we sent our armed militias, people's armies, into battle against British regular forces. In the Second Amendment, Madison legitimized the right to join a people's army in order to overthrow a despot. There is some irony in the fact that the Boston Marathon bombing occurred on Patriots' Day, which commemorates the revolutionary severing of the United States from England. Patriots' Day is meant to be peaceful in Boston, with a marathon and a Red Sox game. The possibly jihadist bombing on that peaceful day, however, recalls our revolutionary past.

Canada could be said to be lucky because it did not spring from revolutionary soil and thus does not have to cope with the implications of the Second Amendment, which broaden the right to arm a militia into the right of individual gun ownership, a broadening that Madison may not have supported were he alive today. On the other hand, only as recently as 1982 did Canadians begin to enjoy their version of our other crucial amendment, the First, which grants us freedom of speech and free assembly. Before 1982, the right to free speech in Canada was merely a federal statute there. While the United States venerates life, liberty, and the pursuit of happiness, Canadians value peace, order, and good government. Canada chose not to resist England; thus, it never needed a people's army to expel occupying forces from Massachusetts and the other colonies.

For those of us who are baby boomers, who grew up during the 1960s, guns were present on the nightly news, as body counts were reported daily during the decade-long war in Vietnam. The guerrilla war of attrition that the United States waged in Vietnam centered both on gun violence and the destruction dropped from the air. The M16 rifle entered the American psyche, as did napalm and B-52 carpet bombing. Helicopters would drop ground troops, armed with M16s, into a landing zone and then evacuate the wounded to field hospitals. This was a no-win situation from the beginning. The white and black New Left began in pacifism, but ended up in a revolutionary counterposition, with the Weather Underground and the Black Panthers. We could not stop the war, or the Klan, and so Students for a Democratic Society and the Student Nonviolent Coordinating Committee turned toward violence, albeit of a limited kind. Weatherman went underground after the Manhattan townhouse explosion in 1970, and the Panthers never came close to implementing their founding ten-point program. In an ironic twist, gun control of a contemporary variety started in 1967 in California, under Ronald Reagan's governorship, as the Milford Act was designed to prevent the Panthers from brandishing their shotguns in public.

The right's issue then has become the left's issue now. Everyone hates hatred and the violence that can flow from it. However, if gun-control Band-Aids, such as background checks and restrictions on gun shows, do not lower the aggregate rate of gun homicides, we need to reframe the issue of guns. I began by mentioning a risk-based paradigm as a way of conceptualizing gun control. This paradigm suggests that gun control begins and basically ends at home, at least in a country with the equivalent of a Second Amendment. People, rationally, would think through the costs and benefits of gun ownership in terms of risk and risk avoidance. Two real-world examples come to mind.

When we lived in Buffalo, New York, a serial rapist preyed on women living alone near a downtown college campus. Some of these women armed themselves in order to reduce their risk of victimization. The risk of being raped exceeded the risk of shooting oneself accidentally or being shot by a cohabiting intimate. By contrast, Adam Lanza's mother miscalculated her risk, afforded her troubled son access to guns, and provided him with knowledge of gun use and exposure to gun culture. She is reported to have been a person preparing for the collapse of government and the onset of anarchy, in which case it might be rational to have an armory of weapons. She also knew, however, that her son was troubled, if not necessarily in ways that would have clearly predisposed him to violence.

The vast majority of legally owned guns in the United States are never or rarely shot. Their purpose is defensive, much like a fire extinguisher. It is estimated that 39 percent of US households contain guns, with an average of four guns per household. Predictably, these households tend to be found in the Midwest and South and not in bicoastal urban areas. To some extent, gun ownership tracks the red-state/blue-state divide, which is political, cultural, and religious. Rural people are more likely to be gun owners than urban people, with men more likely to own guns than women. In this volume, Robert Young explores defensive arming and argues that certain gun owners are motivated less by fear than by a desire to punish, a case he supports by examining the connection between gun ownership and support of capital punishment.

Progressives have a difficult time with all this because, since gun ownership was protected in the 1790s, handguns and shotguns abound. It is a very short step from the fact of the proliferation of legally owned guns to the conclusion that a reduction in arms would bring significant reduction in the rate of gun homicide. Matt Qvortrup marshals data to suggest that this isn't so. He also finds that banning assault rifles, in his global sample, tends to reduce the rate of gun homicides, an inconvenient fact for those who want assault rifles to be protected under the Second Amendment.

I think that bicoastal liberals might have an easier time with gun violence and gun control if they conceptualized gun control as an individual-level household decision based on risk. Many progressives believe that people are rational and can weigh evidence effectively. Indeed, there is evidence of this, as the vast majority of Americans have reacted to the occurrences in Newtown and Aurora with a willingness to see the government curtail assault rifles and large magazines and institute universal background checks. However, background checks, as of this writing, were defeated in the Senate; most Republican senators and even a few Democratic ones voted against it, fearing difficult fights for reelection and perhaps worrying that they would lose the financial backing of the gun lobby.

I have identified war as a significant source of institutionalized violence. I regret culture wars as well. Pacifist liberals and gun-owning conservatives

seem to inhabit different universes and cannot talk to each other construc-
tively. Perhaps I have lived in Texas too long (canceling out my time spent in
Canada), but it seemed to me, after Aurora in July 2012, that a theater patron
carrying a legal concealed handgun might have stopped James Holmes, the
rampaging shooter. This is not to abandon the risk paradigm of gun ownership, but to notice that a single strategy does not hold all the answers. I do not
want "everyone" carrying guns in public, but I would certainly trust off-duty
police officers and military personnel on leave to protect me and my family in
a dimly-lit theater. Many gun opponents find this stance outrageous because
they contend that innocent people could be shot by errant bullets, but it is true
that Holmes was doing plenty of shooting of his own. Indeed, one could classify
prudent and legal concealed carrying under the risk paradigm if it is adequately
demonstrated that the gun owner possesses the skill and experience to repel
public shooters. I am not certain that a weekend course in gun ownership, use,
and maintenance is adequate, but I do not know how much training is actually
required to fend off a shooter in a crowded theater.

Some commonsense approaches to risk assessment that might guide prospec-
tive gun owners as they decide whether to house guns or not suggest themselves:

- One's level of familiarity with firearms.
- One's criminal environment and, in effect, the costs of being unarmed.
- Whether one has children in the home, especially teenage boys.
- The quality of one's adult intimate relationship and in particular, the
  adults' ability to engage in peaceful conflict resolution.
- Whether the household adults drink alcohol and/or use drugs.

Stepping back as a way of summing up might lead one to conclude that we
are having the wrong national conversation. "Gun violence" should be replaced
as the dependent variable with the issue of violence in a larger context, including
bombing, shooting, beating, war, and rampage sprees. Who kills, we ask? With
what does killing correlate? I would replace the independent variable "guns"
with the variable "gender," because I think gender explains much of the vari-
ance in the dependent variable "violence." I know that gun issues are central
these days, but, again, a look at the history of killing technologies suggests that
men have always found ways to kill and conquer, all the way from spears and
lances to the Gatling gun and assault rifles. So the enormous energy expended
to bring about piecemeal gun-control reforms and abolish violent video games
might be better devoted to a serious conversation about what we can do to make
men less lethal. This does not decide in favor of (or against) biologism, which

blames all of this on testosterone or its absence. The dichotomous Victorian construction of gender, split between the nurturing feminine and aggressive masculine, certainly factors in, making the nature/nurture dispute impossible to resolve in its own terms. The vast majority of men do not kill or conquer, even if we may have impulses not shared by most women. The fact remains, however, that killers tend to be men, whether the men are armed with knives, homemade bombs, or handguns.

Doug Kellner, in his *Guys and Guns Amok* (2008), discusses the connection between masculinity and firearms. I would broaden this to include all acts of violence, as I recommended in the previous paragraph. I performed another thought experiment with my students, inviting them to rewrite the Second Amendment to allow only women to bear arms. This would be "men control," not "gun control." There was laughter, as the young men and women grappled with the implications of such a statute. Any such exercise, like the one described earlier about female heads of state, is uncomfortable because gendered self-knowledge gives people access to their private, perhaps deeply suppressed desires. Maybe violent video games and media, like organized sports, bleed off men's aggressive but repressed desires, in effect suggesting that warlike video games and media turn most young men into pacifists.

So my new favorite independent variable—gender—implies that men, too, are victims of the tyranny of gender. The whole second-wave women's movement (with the right to vote being the first wave) critiques gender tyranny that disallowed women from playing roles in public life and even from playing sports. Every feminist knows, however, that men have gender troubles as well, even as males have had disproportionate power and wealth. Chodorow (1978) in *Reproduction of Mothering* notes that young men pay a price for being denied opportunities to nurture. Newman, in her wide-ranging discussion of rampage shooters, addresses the way in which some young men who embark on rampages may have developed problematic masculinity, that is, gender identities that are not perfectly consistent with rugged individualism. Murphy (2012), writing immediately after Newtown, argues for a narrative of mass shootings that focuses on men.

In the aftermaths of Columbine, Virginia Tech, Aurora, and Newtown, it may cut against the grain to portray the young male shooters as having been victims of gender, when, in fact, they killed so many innocents. The relationship between gender and violence is not perfect, is not one-to-one. However, the fact remains that women don't kill in these ways; they never have and probably never will. Something is going on that needs explanation and redress. As of this writing, I would place much greater emphasis on gender identity as it damages both men and women than I would on gun-control measures that, for the most part, simply remove weapons from the hands and homes of good guys but leave intact larger structures of gender and class that condition violence.

Finally, gender interacts with another variable, which is not peculiar to the United States but is found in many premodern and millennial societies, notably the propensity of people, mainly of my gender, to go to war. Call this "militarization," reflecting, in our case, the fact that the United States emerged from revolutionary violence, as Tim Luke eloquently discusses in the opening chapter of this book. We derive the Second Amendment directly from this revolutionary tradition. Our nation always seems to be at war, often in distant countries, suggesting that Melman's (1974) notion of a permanent war economy is appropriate here. However, the economics of conquest and imperialism are not the only issues. Also at issue—the idea of gender again—is the propensity of men to go to war and to celebrate war and military violence as patriotic. The 1960s, of course, pivoted on civil rights and on massive opposition to the Vietnam War. Today, as the country has shifted further to the right, we see an idolatry and iconography of military veterans and active troops, which I am reading as a celebration of the supposedly legitimate violence of warfare.

It is no accident in this context that the gun-rights lobby borrows the military-assault rifle as its do-or-die issue. Men make war with M16s and AK-47s, while defenders of the Second Amendment want to, in the language of Weatherman, "bring the war home," this time defending not a Bolshevik version of Marxism but the homestead and the homeland. It is a fact that men make war. American men make their share of war, albeit defended as legitimate nation-building that derives from our manifest destiny to rid the world of tyranny. The militariza-tion of America is bound up with both our revolutionary past (which gives us the Second Amendment) and with a notion and practice of masculinity that glorifies violence under the guise of war. On my reading, terror is not peculiar to religious extremism but is simply the unpredictable eruption of violence in everyday life, all the way from Klan lynching to suicide bombers in Jerusalem to the use of napalm in Vietnam. Adam Lanza was a terrorist, but so were the perpetrators of the My Lai massacre and the shooters at Kent State and Jackson State. This country was founded on the original violence against Native Ameri-cans, which cleared the way for western conquest. In all cases, terror, including war, is a male project. Bombing for peace is war.

Assault rifles entered the collective unconscious of men beginning with the Vietnam War, when M16s were seen on television and film. The problem with the good/bad guy motif is that there is actually a third group of gun owners, between criminals and defensive armers. This third group includes men living out military fantasies by buying arms and perhaps using them on the gun range. For me, the key issue here is men's fantasies, which reflect deep-seated desires for potency and power. So the good/bad guy distinction needs to be reformulated in a triple distinction among "Defensive Armers," "Shooters," and, in the middle, "Fantasizers." There is a thin boundary between Shooters and Fantasizers, a line that is pierced when men in crisis are depressed, possibly suicidal, and caught up in an avenging military or police fantasy life. How else to understand George Zimmerman's lethal pursuit of Trayvon Martin? Firearms and fear mix with testosterone and territoriality. This is not to suggest that camo-clad, gun-toting men necessarily become killers. The vast majority don't, disqualifying a reductionism based on militarized fantasies. Moreover, to reference my earlier point about postmodern subject positions, men are not to be blamed for having heroic special-forces fantasies. The militarization of American life encompasses many, including women, who pledge allegiance, honor soldiers, and support our many international interventions. It is not an accident that Holmes, Lanza, and the Columbine shooters wore military paraphernalia on killing day. One might productively study the motivations of people who carry concealed handguns, perhaps suspecting that they combine defensive arming with various levels of avenging fantasies. Jennifer Carlson, in this volume, explores the shift of policing to citizens protected by "stand your ground" laws, a framing that perfectly fits Zimmerman's intentionality.

Freud felt that fantasies can be constructive, diverting people from their unhappiness and allowing them to achieve imaginary fulfillment. I went to buy a fishing reel recently. At the gun and fishing counter, I noticed that a number of assault rifles for sale had camouflage coloring. This is a military configuration, permitting guerrilla disguise. Yet the people purchasing them aren't going to use them in combat, presumably. The camo disguise allows gun owners to fantasize about being soldiers without going into combat, much as my participation in road races allows me to imagine myself winning Olympic gold. Gun-control enthusiasts often assume that guns in themselves are problematic, when, in fact, gun ownership may have a fantasy-serving component that precludes and prevents entry into combat. Fantasizers are often connoisseurs, acquiring guns for fantasy-serving fun. Reality is messy; Adam Lanza's mother reportedly armed herself defensively, but also enjoyed taking her sons to the shooting range. She bet wrong, and died for it, because her estimate of risk was incorrect, given her younger son's instability.

The conversation I seek would be about gender, the relationship between poverty and crime (and the phenomenon of defensive arming), and American militarization. Men who make war kill. As early as 1795, Kant (2006) understood that "perpetual peace" rests on the abolition of standing armies. I am especially concerned with the sensibilities of men who kill, those who fail to divert their anger. Freud (2005) well understood that civilization rests on basic repression of our impulses; Marcuse (1955) added that we experience "surplus" repression as capitalism diverts people not only from libidinal adventurism but from their own liberation. When basic repression breaks down, men who have the means to do so may go berserk, if they don't join the military or become alcoholics. As of this writing, President Obama has not extricated the United States from Afghanistan and we are poised to intervene militarily in Syria even as he deplores the Senate's reluctance to move on a universal registry for gun owners. Obama, like most centrist Democrats today, seems to support the death penalty, another example of state-sanctioned killing, albeit sanitized in some states as lethal injection. Today, 65 percent of Americans support the death penalty, which makes us the only global democracy other than India to put murderers to death. State-sanctioned killing, whether on the battlefield or the prison death chamber, expresses exactly the atavism that seems to underlie the desire to own and use guns on people who have been "othered" as nonhuman. Atavism is especially harmful to women and children, who find themselves in harm's way. Yes, we need to debate mental illness, assault rifles, and large magazines. But we also need to talk about the hearts of men.

# References

Abrams, P., and R. L. Levy (Producers), and W. Becker (Director). 2002. *National Lampoon's Van Wilder* [Motion picture]. United States: Lions Gate Films.

Addington, L. A. 2013. "Surveillance and Security Approaches Across Public School Levels." In *Responding to School Violence: Confronting the Columbine Effect*, edited by G. W. Muschert, S. Henry, N. L. Bracy, and A. A. Peguero. Boulder, CO: Lynne Rienner.

Abdollahi, M. Katherine. 2002. "Understanding Police Stress Research." *Journal of Forensic Psychology Practice* 2 (2): 1–24.

Agamben, Giorgio. 1998. *Homo Sacer: Sovereign Power and Bare Life*. Stanford: Stanford University Press.

Agger, Ben. 2007. "Cho, Not Che? Positioning Blacksburg in the Political." *Fast Capitalism* 3(1). Accessed April 27, 2013. www.uta.edu/huma/agger/fastcapitalism/3_1/agger.html.

Agger, Ben, and Timothy W. Luke. 2008. *There Is a Gunman on Campus: Tragedy and Terror at Virginia Tech*. Lanham, MD: Rowman & Littlefield.

Alpers, Philip, and Marcus Wilson. 2013. *Guns in the United Kingdom: Facts, Figures and Firearm Law. Sydney School of Public Health, University of Sydney*, GunPolicy .org February 13. Accessed February 14, 2013. www.gunpolicy.org/firearms/region /united-kingdom/

———. 2012. *Global Impact of Gun Violence. Sydney School of Public Health, University of Sydney*. GunPolicy.org December 17. Accessed May 9, 2013. www.gunpolicy .org/firearms/region.

Alpert, G., and R. Dunham. 2004. *Understanding Police Use of Force*. New York: Cambridge University Press.

Amnesty International. 2013. "Abolitionist and Retentionist Countries." Accessed May 31, 2013. www.amnesty.org/en/death-penalty/abolitionist-and-retentionist-countries.

Anderson, C. A., et al. 2010. "Violent Video Game Effects on Aggression, Empathy, and Prosocial Behavior in Eastern and Western Countries: A Meta-Analytic Review." *Psychological Bulletin* 136 (2): 151.

Anderson, C. A., and B. J. Bushman. 2001. "Effects of Violent Video Games on Aggressive Behavior, Aggressive Cognition, Aggressive Affect, Physiological Arousal, and Prosocial Behavior: A Meta-Analytic Review of the Scientific Literature." *Psychological Science* 12 (5): 353–359.

Anderson, Gregory, Robin Litzenberger, and Darryl Plecas. 2002. "Physical Evidence of Police Officer Stress." *Policing: An International Journal of Police Strategies* 25 (2): 399–420.

Andresen, Martin A. 2007. "Homicide and Medical Science: Is There a Relationship?" *Canadian Journal of Criminology and Criminal Justice* 49 (2): 185–204.

Associated Press. 2013. "Newtown Victim's Daughter Confronts Sen. Ayotte over Gun Control Bill Vote." *Fox News*. May 1. www.foxnews.com/politics/2013 /05/01/newtown-victim-daughter-confronts-sen-ayotte-over-gun-control-bill -vote.

Averill, J. 1979. "Anger." In *Nebraska Symposium on Motivation 1978*, edited by Richard D. Dienstbier. Lincoln, NE: University of Nebraska Press.

Ayres, I., and J. J. Donohue III. 2002. *Shooting Down the More Guns, Less Crime Hypothesis* (No. w9336). National Bureau of Economic Research.

Balko, Radley. 2013. *Rise of the Warrior Cop: The Militarization of America's Police Force.* New York: Public Affairs.

———. 2006. *Overkill: The Rise of Paramilitary Police Raids in America.* Washington, DC: Cato Institute.

Bandura, Albert. 1973. *Aggression: A Social Learning Analysis.* New York: Prentice-Hall.

Bankston, William B., and Carol Y. Thompson. 1989. "Carrying Firearms for Protection: A Causal Model." *Sociological Inquiry* 59: 75–87.

Barker, Joan C. 1999. *Danger, Duty, and Disillusion: The Worldview of Los Angeles Police Officers.* Prospect Heights, IL: Waveland Press, Inc.

Barrett, Paul M. 2013. *Glock: The Rise of America's Gun.* New York: Random House.

Batton, Candice, and Steve Wilson. 2006. "Police Murders: An Examination of Historical Trends in the Killing of Law Enforcement Officers in the United States, 1947 to 1998." *Homicide Studies* 10: 79–97.

Bayley, David H. 1976. *Forces of Order.* Berkeley, CA: University of California Press.

Bayley, David H., and Clifford D. Shearing. 1996. "The Future of Policing." *Law & Society Review* 30 (3): 585–606.

BBC. 2013. "US Gun Debate: Guns in Numbers." January 16. www.bbc.co.uk/news /world-us-canada-20759139.

Beckett, Katherine, and Naomi Murakawa. 2012. "Mapping the Shadow Carceral State: Toward an Institutionally Capacious Approach to Punishment." *Theoretical Criminology* 16 (2): 221–244.

Bem, Daryl J. 1972. "Self-Perception Theory." In *Advances in Experimental Social Psychology*. Vol. 6, edited by Leonard Berkowitz. New York: Academic Press.

———. 1970. *Beliefs, Attitudes and Human Affairs.* Belmont, CA: Brooks/Cole.

Berger, J. M., et al. 2005. "Impact of Gender Role Conflict, Traditional Masculinity Ideology, Alexithymia, and Age on Men's Attitudes Toward Psychological Help Seeking." *Psychology of Men & Masculinity* 6 (1): 73.

Berkowitz, Leonard. 1965. *Aggression*. Boston, MA: McGraw-Hill.

Bernard, T. 1999. "Juvenile Crime and the Transformation of Juvenile Justice: Is There a Juvenile Crime Wave?" *Justice Quarterly* 16 (2): 337–356.

Berry, Rex. 2013. "Should We Sacrifice Children for the Sake of Guns?" *Tulsa World*, March 7. Accessed April 29, 2013: www.tulsaworld.com/article.aspx/Should _we_sacrifice_children_for_the_sake_of_guns/20130307_65_a17_cutlin134297.

Bettinger, K. J. 1990. "After the Gun Goes Off." *State Peace Officers Journal* (Summer): 90–93.

Bilton, N. 2013. "Smart Guns Can't Kill in the Wrong Hands." *New York Times*. January 7. http://bits.blogs.nytimes.com/2013/01/06/disruptions-smart-gun -technology-could-prevent-massacres-like-newtown/.

Bittner, Egon. 1970. *The Functions of Police in Modern Society*. Washington, DC: National Institute of Mental Health.

Blabbermouth.net. 2010. "Marilyn Manson Signs with Cooking Vinyl Records." November 10. Accessed April 27, 2013. www.blabbermouth.net/news.aspx?mode =Article&newsitemID=149002.

Bonnie, R. J., J. S. Reinhard, P. Hamilton, and E. L. McGarvey. 2009. "Mental Health System Transformation after the Virginia Tech Tragedy." *Health Affairs* 28 (3): 793–804.

Bordua, David J., and Alan J. Lezotte. 1979. "Patterns of Legal Firearms Ownership: A Cultural and Situational Analysis of Illinois Counties." *Law and Policy Quarterly* 1: 147–175.

Bowling, Benjamin. 1999. "The Rise and Fall of New York Murder: Zero Tolerance or Crack's Decline?" *British Journal of Criminology* 39 (4): 531–554.

BoxOffice.com. n.d. *Natural Born Killers*. Accessed April 27, 2013. www.boxoffice.com /statistics/movies/natural-born-killers-1994.

Brady Campaign Press Release. 2011. "One Million Mental Health Records Now in Brady Background Check System." *BradyCampaign.org*. January 7. http://bradycampaign .org/media/press/view/1336.

Brandt, David E. 1993. "Social Distress and the Police." *Journal of Social Distress and the Homeless* 2 (4): 305–313.

Broder, J. M. 1999. "Washington Memo; Searching for Answers after School Violence." *New York Times*. May 10. www.nytimes.com/1999/05/10/us/washington -memo-searching-for-answers-after-school-violence.html?pagewanted=all &src=pm.

Brooks, D. 2007. "The Mortality Line." *New York Times*. April 19. http://select.nytimes .com/2007/04/19/opinion/19brooks.html?hp.

Brooke, J. 1999. "Terror in Littleton: The Gun Debate; Shootings Firm Up Gun Control Cause, at Least for Present." *New York Times*. April 23. www.nytimes

.com/1999/04/23/us/terror-littleton-gun-debate-shootings-firm-up-gun-control-cause-least-for.html.

Bruni, F. 1999. "Senate Narrowly Rejects Plan to Restrict Gun-Show Sales." *New York Times.* May 13. www.nytimes.com/1999/05/13/us/senate-narrowly-rejects-plan-to-restrict-gun-show-sales.html.

Buerger, Michael E. 2000. "Reenvisioning Police, Reinvigorating Policing: A Reponse to Thomas Cowper." *Police Quarterly* 3: 451–464.

Bureau of Justice Statistics. 2001. *Homicide Trends in the United States, 1980–2008.* Accessed May 27, 2013. www.bjs.gov/content/pub/pdf/htus8008.pdf.

Burns, R., and C. Crawford. 1999. "School Shootings, the Media, and Public Fear: Ingredients for a Moral Panic." *Crime, Law & Social Change* 32: 147–168.

Buss, Arnold H. 1980. *Self-Consciousness and Social Anxiety.* San Francisco, CA: W. H. Freeman and Company.

Carlson, Jennifer. 2012. "'I don't dial 911!' American Guns and the Problem of Policing." *British Journal of Criminology* 52 (6): 1113–1132.

Carr, D. 2013. "Guns, Maps and Data That Disturb." *New York Times.* January 13. www.nytimes.com/2013/01/14/business/media/guns-maps-and-disturbing-data.html?_r=0.

Centers for Disease Control and Prevention. 2013. Accessed May 27, 2013. www.cdc.gov/violenceprevention/suicide/statistics/mechanism01.html.

———. 2010. www.cdc.gov/reproductivehealth/Data_Stats.

Cerulo, K. A. 1998. *Deciphering Violence: The Cognitive Structure of Right and Wrong.* New York: Routledge.

Chapman, S., Philip Alpers, K. Agho, and M. Jones. 2006. "Australia's 1996 Gun Law Reforms: Faster Falls in Firearm Deaths, Firearm Suicides, and a Decade without Mass Shootings." *Injury Prevention* 12 (6): 365–372.

Chodorow, Nancy. 1978. *The Reproduction of Mothering.* Berkeley, CA: University of California Press.

Chyi, H., and M. McCombs. 2004. "Media Salience and the Process of Framing: Coverage of the Columbine School Shootings." *Journalism and Mass Communication Quarterly* 81 (1): 22–35.

Clotfelter, Charles, T. 1981. "Crime Disorders and the Demand for Handguns," *Law and Policy* 3 (4): 425–441.

Cohn, A., and A. Zeichner. 2006. "Effects of Masculine Identity and Gender Role Stress on Aggression in Men." *Psychology of Men & Masculinity* 7 (4): 179.

Conklin, John. 2003. *Why Crime Rates Fell.* New York: Allyn and Bacon.

Cook, P. J., and J. Ludwig. 2013. "The Limited Impact of the Brady Act." *Reducing Gun Violence in America: Informing Policy with Evidence and Analysis*, 21.

———. 2006. "Aiming for Evidence-Based Gun Policy." *Journal of Policy Analysis and Management* 25 (3): 691–735.

Cooley, Charles Horton. 1902. *Human Nature and the Social Order.* New York: Scribner's.

Cooper, Frank. 2009. "'Who's the Man?' Masculinities Studies, Terry Stops, and Police Training." *Columbia Journal of Gender and Law* 18: 671–742.

COPS. 2011. "The Impact of the Economic Downturn on American Police Agencies." Washington, DC: US Department of Justice.

Cornell, Saul. 2006. *A Well Regulated Militia: The Founding Fathers and the Origins of Gun Control in America*. Oxford: Oxford University Press.

Cornford, F. M. 2004 [1912]. *From Religion to Philosophy*. Mineola, NY: Dover.

Corrigan, P. W., et al. 2004. "Implications of Educating the Public on Mental Illness, Violence, and Stigma." *Psychiatric Services* 55 (5): 577–580.

Corrigan, P., et al. 2003. "An Attribution Model of Public Discrimination towards Persons with Mental Illness." *Journal of Health and Social Behavior* 44 (2): 162–179.

Crank, John P. 2004. *Understanding Police Culture*. New York: Anderson Publishing Co.

Criminal Justice Act. 1988. S.39.

Cullen, Dave. 2009. *Columbine*. New York: Twelve, Hachette Book Group.

Dauvergne, Mia. 2012. *Adult Correctional Statistics in Canada, 2010–2011*. Ottawa: Statistics Canada.

DeFronzo, James. 1979. "Fear of Crime and Handgun Ownership." *Criminology.* 17: 331–339.

Desmond, Matthew, and Nicol Valdez. 2013. "Unpolicing the Urban Poor: Consequences of Third-Party Policing for Inner-City Women." *American Sociological Review* 78 (1): 117–141.

Dizard, Jan E., Robert Muth, and Stephen P. Andrews (eds.). 1999. *Guns in America: A Reader*. New York: NYU Press.

Donohue, E., V. Schiraldi, and J. Ziedenberg. 1998. *School House Hype: School Shootings and the Real Risks Kids Face in America*. Washington, DC: Justice Policy Institute. www.justicepolicy.org/uploads/justicepolicy/documents /98-07_rep_schoolhousehype_jj.pdf.

Donohue, John, and Steven Levitt. 2001. "The Impact of Legalized Abortion on Crime." *The Quarterly Journal of Economics* CXVI (2): 379–420.

Doom. n.d. In *Wikipedia*. Accessed April 27, 2013. https://en.wikipedia.org/wiki/Doom _%28video_game%29.

Douthat, R. 2013. "Media Balance and Bias." *New York Times.* April 13. www.nytimes .com/2013/04/14/opinion/sunday/douthat-media-balance-and-bias.html.

Dowd, M. 1999. "Liberties; Hunker in the Bunker." *New York Times.* April 25. www .nytimes.com/1999/04/25/opinion/liberties-hunker-in-the-bunker.html.

Durkheim, Emile. 1995 [1912]. *The Elementary Forms of Religious Life*. Translated by Karen Fields. New York: The Free Press.

———. 1973. "Individualism and the Intellectuals." In *Emile Durkheim: On Morality and Society*, edited by Robert N. Bellah. Chicago and London: The University of Chicago Press, 43–57.

———. 1961. *Moral Education*. Translated by Everett K. Wilson and Herman Schnurer. Mineola, NY: Dover.

————. 1951 [1897]. *Suicide*. New York: The Free Press.

Dwyer, J., and E. S. Rueb. 2012. "In a Town of Traditions, Grief Engulfs Holiday Joy." *New York Times*. December 16. www.nytimes.com/2012/12/16/nyregion/for-newtown-horror-halts-a-season-of-celebration.html.

Ellison, K. W., and J. L. Genz. 1978. "Police Officer as Burned-Out Samaritan." *FBI Law Enforcement Bulletin* 47 (3): 1–7.

Elsass, H. J., and J. Schildkraut. 2013. *Breaking News of Social Problems: Examining Media Effects and Panic over School Shootings*. Unpublished manuscript.

Emerson, Ralph Waldo. 1957a. "Nature." In *Selections*, edited by Stephen Whicher. Boston, MA: Houghton Mifflin.

————. 1957b. "American Scholar." In *Selections*, edited by Stephen Whicher. Boston, MA: Houghton Mifflin.

————. 1957c. "Self-Reliance." In *Selections*, edited by Stephen Whicher. Boston, MA: Houghton Mifflin.

Fagan, J., F. Zimring, and J. Kim. 1998. "Declining Homicide in New York City." *Journal of Criminal Law and Criminology* 88 (4): 1277–1334.

Falcone, D., and L. Wells. 1995. "The County Sheriff as Distinctive Policing Modality." *American Journal of Police* 15 (3/4): 123–149.

Farago, Ladislas. 2005 [1964]. *Patton: Ordeal and Triumph*. New York: Obolensky [Westholme].

FBI. 2011. *Crime in the United States 2011*. Accessed May 27, 2013. www.fbi.gov/about-us/cjis/ucr/crime-in-the-u.s/2011/crime-in-the-u.s.-2011/tables/table-1.

Ferraro, Kenneth F. 1995. *Fear of Crime*. Albany, NY: State University of New York Press.

Fernandez, Ephrem. 2008. "The Angry Personality: A Representation on Six Dimensions of Anger Expression." In *The SAGE Handbook of Personality Theory and Assessment: Volume 2—Personality Measurement and Testing*, edited by Gregory J. Boyle, Gerald Matthews, and Donald H. Saklofske. Thousand Oaks, CA: Sage Publications.

Fields, Gary. 2011. "Rampage Gun's Reputation Built on Style, Ease of Use." *Wall Street Journal*. January 12, A5. http://online.wsj.com/article/SB10001424052748704515904576076261511207484.html

Fischer, David Hackett. 1989. *Albion's Seed*. New York: Oxford University Press.

Follman, Mark. 2013. "New Research Confirms Gun Rampages are Rising—and Armed Civilians Don't Stop Them." *Mother Jones*, April 11. Accessed May 15, 2013: www.motherjones.com/politics/2013/04/mass-shootings-rampages-rising-data.

————. 2012. "Do Armed Civilians Stop Mass Shooters? Actually, No." *Mother Jones*. http://www.motherjones.com/politics/2012/12/armed-civilians-do-not-stop-mass-shootings.

Follman, M., et al. 2012. "A Guide to Mass Shootings in America." *Mother Jones*. Accessed July 8, 2013. www.motherjones.com/politics/2012/07/mass-shootings-map.

Fort Worth Star-Telegram. 2013. "Fort Worth Police Kill Armed Resident." Accessed May 30, 2013. www.star-telegram.com/2013/05/29/4891451/fort-worth-police-kill-armed-resident.html.

Foucault, Michel. 2013. *Lectures on the Will to Know: Lectures at the Collége de France, 1970–1971 and Oedipal Knowledge.* New York: Palgrave.

———. 2010. *The Birth of Biopolitics: Lectures at the Collége de France, 1978–1979.* New York: Palgrave.

———. 2007. *The Politics of Truth.* New York: Semiotext(e).

———. 2007. *Security, Territory, Population: Lectures at the Collége de France, 1977–1978.* New York: Palgrave.

———. 1991. *The Foucault Effect: Studies in Governmentality with Two Lectures by and an Interview with Michel Foucault,* edited by Graham Burchell, Colin Gordon, and Peter Miller. Chicago: University of Chicago Press.

———. 1988. *Technologies of the Self: A Seminar with Michel Foucault,* edited by Luther H. Martin, Huck Gutman, and Patrick H. Hutton. Amherst, MA: University of Massachusetts Press.

———. 1979. *Discipline and Punish: The Birth of the Prison.* New York: Vintage.

*Frontline.* 2013. "Raising Adam Lanza." Accessed May 13, 2013. www.pbs.org/wgbh/pages/frontline/raising-adam-lanza.

Freud, Sigmund. 2005. *Civilization and Its Discontents.* New York: Norton.

Frymer, B. 2009. "The Media Spectacle of Columbine: Alienated Youth as an Object of Fear." *American Behavioral Scientist,* 52 (10): 1387–1404.

Galambos, N. L., et al. 1990. "Masculinity, Femininity, and Sex Role Attitudes in Early Adolescence: Exploring Gender Intensification." *Child Development* 61 (6): 1905–1914.

Gallagher, K. E., and D. J. Parrott. 2011. "What Accounts for Men's Hostile Attitudes toward Women? The Influence of Hegemonic Male Role Norms and Masculine Gender Role Stress." *Violence against Women* 17 (5): 568–583.

Garland, David. 2002. *The Culture of Control: Crime and Social Order in Contemporary Society.* Chicago: University of Chicago Press.

Garofoli, J. 2007. "New-Media Culture Challenges Limits of Journalism Ethics." April 20. http://articles.sfgate.com/2007-04-20/news/17242016_1_new-media-traditional-media-traditional-news-sources/3.

Geertz, C. 1973. *The Interpretation of Cultures.* New York: Basic Books.

Gerbner, George, Larry Gross, Michael Morgan, Nancy Signorielli, and James Shanahan. 2008. "Growing Up with Television: Cultivation Processes." In *Perspectives on Media Effects,* edited by Jennings Bryant and Dolf Zillman. Hilldale, NJ: Lawrence Erlbaum Associates, 43–68.

Gersons, Berthold P. R. 1989. "Patterns of PTSD among Police Officers Following Shooting Incidents: A Two-Dimensional Model and Treatment Implications." *Journal of Traumatic Stress* 2 (3): 247–257.

Gilligan, James. 1997. *Violence.* New York: Vintage Books.

Giroux, Henry. 2013. "Neoliberalism's War against Teachers in Dark Times: Rethinking the Sandy Hook Elementary School Killings." In *America's Education Deficit and the War on Youth.* New York: Monthly Review Press, 159–182.

Glaberson, W. 2012. "Nation's Pain Is Renewed, and Difficult Questions Are Asked Once More." *New York Times*. December 14. www.nytimes.com/2012/12/15/nyregion/sandy-hook-shooting-forces-re-examination-of-tough-questions.html?_r=0.

Glassner, Barry. 1999. *The Culture of Fear: Why Americans Are Afraid of the Wrong Things*. New York: Basic Books.

Glynos, Jason. 2001. "The grip of ideology: a Lacanian approach to the theory of ideology," *Journal of Political Ideologies*, 6 (2): 191-214.

Goodman, Melvin A. 2013. *National Insecurity: The Cost of American Militarism*. San Francisco, CA: City Lights Publishers.

Graber, D. A. 1980. *Crime News and the Public*. Chicago, IL: University of Chicago Press.

Graham, Stephen. 2011. *Cities under Siege: The New Military Urbanism*. London: Verso.

Griffiths, Elizabeth, and George Tita. 2009. "Homicide In and Around Public Housing: Is Public Housing a Hotbed, a Magnet, or a Generator of Violence for the Surrounding Community?" *Social Problems* 56 (3): 474–493.

Hagan, John. 1984. *The Disreputable Pleasures: Crime and Deviance in Canada*, 2nd ed. Toronto: McGraw-Hill Ryerson.

Hagan, John, and Jeffrey Leon. 1977. "Philosophy and Sociology of Crime Control." *Sociological Inquiry* 47: 181–208.

Halbwachs, Maurice. 1978 [1930]. *The Causes of Suicide*. Translated by Harold Goldblatt. London: Routledge and Kegan Paul.

Hale, Matthew. 1736. *Historia Placitorum Coronae*, Vol. 1. London.

Hamilton, W. L. 1999. "How Suburban Design Is Failing Teen-Agers." *New York Times*. May 6. www.nytimes.com/1999/05/06/garden/how-suburban-design-is-failing-teen-agers.html?pagewanted=all&src=pm.

Harmon, A. 2012. "Fearing a Stigma for People with Autism." *New York Times*. December 18. www.nytimes.com/2012/12/18/health/fearing-a-stigma-for-people-with-autism.html.

Harrendorf, S., M. Heiskanen, and S. Malby. 2010. *International Statistics on Crime and Justice*. Vienna: UNODC.

Harris, Anthony R., Stephen H. Thomas, Gene A. Fisher, and David J. Hirsch. 2002. "Murder and Medicine: The Lethality of Criminal Assault 1960–1999." *Homicide Studies* 6: 128–166.

Harris, David A. 1999. "The Stories, the Statistics, and the Law: Why 'Driving While Black' Matters." *Minnesota Law Review* 94: 265–326.

Harrison, Jane Ellen. 1966. *Epilegomena to the Study of Greek Religion* and *Themis* (Reprint ed.). New York: University Books.

Hedges, Christopher. 2002. *War Is the Force That Gives Us Meaning*. New York: New Press.

Hemenway, David. 2006. *Private Guns, Public Health*. Ann Arbor, MI: University of Michigan Press.

Hendrix, G. 2007. "Violent Disagreement: What Seung-Hui Cho Got Wrong about *Oldboy.*" *Slate.* April 20. www.slate.com/id/2164753/.

Henry, S. 2009. "School Violence beyond Columbine: A Complex Problem in Need of an Interdisciplinary Analysis." *American Behavioral Scientist* 52 (9): 1246–1265.

———. 2000. "What Is School Violence? An Integrated Definition." *Annals of the American Academy of Political and Social Science* 567: 16–29.

Henry, Vincent. 2004. *Death Work: Police, Trauma, and the Psychology of Survival.* New York: Oxford University Press.

———. 1995. "The Police Officer as Survivor: Death Confrontations and the Police Subculture." *Behavioral Sciences & the Law* 13 (1): 93–112.

Hepburn, L., M. Miller, D. Azrael, and D. Hemenway. 2007. "The US Gun Stock: Results from the 2004 National Firearms Survey." *Injury Prevention* 13 (1): 15–19.

Herbert, B. 1999. "In America; Addicted to Violence." *New York Times.* April 22. www .nytimes.com/1999/04/22/opinion/in-america-addicted-to-violence.html.

Hiday, V. A. 1995. "The Social Context of Mental Illness and Violence." *Journal of Health and Social Behavior* (36): 122–137.

Hipp, John R., and Adam Boessen. 2013. "Egohoods as Waves Washing Across the City: A New Measure of 'Neighborhoods.'" *Criminology* 51 (2): 287–327.

Honig, Audrey L., and Jocelyn E. Roland. 1998. "Shots Fired; Officer Involved." *Police Chief.*

Hong, L. 2000. "Toward a Transformed Approach to Prevention: Breaking the Link between Masculinity and Violence." *Journal of American College Health* 48 (6): 269–279.

Hulchanski, David. 2007. *The Three Cities within Toronto: Income Polarization Among Toronto's Neighbourhoods, 1970–2005.* Toronto: Cities Centre.

Hunt, Jennifer. 1985. "Police Accounts of Normal Force." *Journal of Contemporary Ethnography* 13 (4): 315–341.

Inwood, Michael. 1992. *A Hegel Dictionary.* Oxford: Blackwell.

Izard, Carroll E. 1991. *The Psychology of Emotions.* New York: Plenum Press.

Jacobs, David, and Jason T. Carmichael. 2002. "Subordination and Violence against State Control Agents: Testing Political Explanations for Lethal Assaults Against the Police." *Social Forces* 80 (4): 1223–1251.

Jefferson County Sheriff's Office. 1999. *Columbine Documents.* Golden, CO: Jefferson County Sheriff's Office Records Unit. www.schoolshooters.info/PL/Original _Documents_files/JCSO%2025,923%20-%2026,859.pdf.

Jewkes, Y. E. 2004. *Media & Crime: Key Approaches to Criminology.* Los Angeles, CA: Sage Publications.

Kagan, Robert. 2012. *The World America Made.* New York: Knopf.

Kain, E. 2012. "'Black Ops 2' Tops 11M Units Sold in First Week, No Signs of Call of Duty Fatigue Yet. " *Forbes.* November 24. Accessed April 27, 2013. www.forbes .com/sites/erikkain/2012/11/24/black-ops-2-tops-11m-units-sold-in-first-week -no-signs-of-call-of-duty-fatigue-yet.

Kaminski, Robert J. 2008. "Assessing County-Level Structural Covariates of Police Homicides." *Homicide Studies* 12 (4): 350–380.

Kaminski, Robert J., and Thomas D. Stucky. 2009. "Reassessing Political Explanations for Murders of Police." *Homicide Studies* 13 (3): 3–20.

Kaminski, Robert, and Jeffrey Martin. 2000. "An Analysis of Police Officer Satisfaction with Defense and Control Tactics." *Policing: An International Journal of Police Strategies* 23 (2): 132–153.

Kaminski, Robert, and Thomas Marvell. 2002. "A Comparison of Changes in Police and General Homicides: 1930–1998." *Criminology* 40 (1): 171–190.

Kant, Immanuel. 2006 [1795]. *Toward Perpetual Peace and other Writings on Politics, Peace and History*. New Haven, CT: Yale University Press.

Katz, Jackson. 2006. *The Macho Paradox*. Naperville, IL: Sourcebooks.

Katz, J. 1995. "Reconstructing Masculinity in the Locker Room: The Mentors in Violence Prevention Project." *Harvard Educational Review* 65 (2): 163–175.

Kelen, G. D., et al. 2012. "Hospital-Based Shootings in the United States: 2000 to 2011." *Annals of Emergency Medicine* 60 (6): 790–798.e791.

Kellner, Douglas. 2013. "Media Spectacle and Domestic Terrorism: The Case of the *Batman/Joker* Cinema Massacre." *Review of Education/Pedagogy/Cultural Studies* 35 (1): 1–21.

———. 2012. "The Dark Side of the Spectacle: Terror in Norway and the UK Riots." *Cultural Politics* 8 (1, March): 1–43.

———. 2008a. *Guys and Guns Amok: Domestic Terrorism and School Shootings from the Oklahoma City Bombing to the Virginia Tech Massacre*. Boulder, CO: Paradigm Publishers.

———. 2008b. "Media Spectacle and the 'Massacre at Virginia Tech.'" In *There Is a Gunman on Campus*, edited by Ben Agger and Timothy W. Luke. Lanham, MD: Rowan & Littlefield, 29–54.

———. 2006. "Toward a Critical Theory of Education." In *Critical Theory and Critical Pedagogy Today. Toward a New Critical Language in Education*, edited by Ilan Gur-Ze'ev. University of Haifa: Studies in Education: 49–69.

———. 2004. "Technological Transformation, Multiple Literacies, and the Re-visioning of Education." *E-Learning* 1 (1): 9–37.

———. 2003. *Media Spectacle*. London: Routledge.

Kellner, Douglas, and Jeff Share. 2007. "Critical Media Literacy, Democracy, and the Reconstruction of Education." *Media Literacy: A Reader*, edited by Donald Macedo and Shirley R. Steinberg. New York: Peter Lang, 3–23.

Kennedy, Leslie, David Forde, and Robert Silverman. 1989. "Understanding Homicide Trends: Issues in Disaggregation for National and Cross-National Comparisons." *Canadian Journal of Sociology* 14 (4): 479–486.

Kent, Stephanie L. 2010. "Killings of Police in US Cities since 1980: An Examination of Environmental and Political Explanations." *Homicide Studies* 14 (1): 3–23.

Killias, M. 1993a. "Gun Ownership, Suicide and Homicide: An International Perspective." *Journal of Criminology* 12 (4): 186–188.

————. 1993b. "International Correlations between Gun Ownership and Rates of Homicide and Suicide." *CMAJ: Canadian Medical Association Journal* 148 (10): 1722.

Kimmel, Michael. 2008. *Guyland. The Perilous World Where Boys Become Men. Understanding the Critical Years Between 16 and 26.* New York: HarperCollins.

Kimmel, M. S., and M. Mahler. 2003. "Adolescent Masculinity, Homophobia, and Violence. Random School Shootings, 1982–2001." *American Behavioral Scientist* 46 (10): 1439–1458.

Kiselica, M. 2011. "Promoting Positive Masculinity while Addressing Gender Role Conflict: A Balanced Theoretical Approach to Clinical Work with Boys and Men." *An International Psychology of Men: Theoretical Advances, Case Studies, and Clinical Interventions*: 127–156.

Kleck, Gary. 1979. "Capital Punishment, Gun Ownership, and Homicide." *American Journal of Sociology* 84: 882–910.

Klockars, Carl B. 1980. "The Dirty Harry Problem." *ANNALS of the American Academy of Political and Social Science* 452: 33–47.

Korte, Gregory. 2013. "Outrage Inflates NRA, Leader Says." *USA Today.* May 6, 1A.

Kraska, Peter B. 2007. "Militarization and Policing—Its Relevance to 21st Century Police." *Policing* 1 (4): 501–513.

Kraska, Peter, and Louis Cubellis. 1997. "Militarizing Mayberry and Beyond: Making Sense of American Paramilitary Policing." *Justice Quarterly* 14 (4): 607–629.

Krevoy, B., S. Stabler, C. B. Wessler, B. Farrelly, and G. Olson (Producers), and P. Farrelly and B. Farrelly (Directors). 1994. *Dumb and Dumber* [Motion picture]. United States: New Line Cinema.

Krouse, W. J. 2012. *Gun Control Legislation.* DIANE Publishing.

Kubrin, Charis, and Ronald Weitzer. 2003. "Retaliatory Homicide: Concentrated Disadvantage and Neighborhood Culture." *Social Problems* 50 (2): 531–554.

Kurtz, H. 2012. "In Between Mass Shootings, the Media Have Been MIA on Guns." *Daily Beast.* December 17. www.thedailybeast.com/articles/2012/12/17/in-between-mass-shootings-the-media-has-been-mia-on-guns.html.

Kyriacou, D. N., E. H. Monkkonen, C. Peek-Asa, R. E. Lucke, S. Labbett, K. S. Pearlman, and H. R. Hutson. 2006. "Police Deaths in New York and London during the Twentieth Century." *Injury Prevention* 12: 219–224.

Land, Kenneth C., Patricia L. McCall, and Lawrence E. Cohen. 1990. "Structural Covariates of Homicide Rates: Are There Invariances across Time and Social Space?" *American Journal of Sociology* 95: 922–963.

Langman, P. 2009. "Rampage School Shooters: A Typology." *Aggression and Violent Behavior* 14 (1): 79–86.

LaPierre, Wayne. 2012. *NRA Press Conference.* December 21. http://home.nra.org/pdf/Transcript_PDF.pdf.

Larkin, Ralph W. 2011. "Masculinity, School Shooters, and the Control of Violence." In *Control of Violence*, edited by W. Heitmeyer et al. New York: Springer Science+Business Media, 315–344.

————. 2007. *Comprehending Columbine.* Philadelphia: Temple University Press.

Lerner, Jennifer S., and Dacher Keltner. 2001. "Fear, Anger, and Risk." *Journal of Personality and Social Psychology* 81 (1): 146–159.

Lester, David. 1987. "The Police as Victims: The Role of Guns in the Murder of Police." *Psychological Reports* 60: 366.

————. 1984. "The Murder of Police Officers in American Cities." *Criminal Justice and Behavior* 11 (1): 101–113.

Lenton, Rhonda. 1989. "Homicide in Canada and the USA: A Critique of the Hagan Thesis." *Canadian Journal of Sociology* 14 (2): 163–178.

Lewin, T. 1999. "Terror in Littleton: The Teenage Culture; Arizona High School Provides Glimpse inside Cliques' Divisive Webs." *New York Times.* May 2. www.nytimes.com/1999/05/02/us/terror-littleton-teen-age-culture-arizona-high-school-provides-glimpse-inside.html?pagewanted=all&src=pm.

Lichtblau, E. 2013. "Makers of Violent Video Games Marshal Support to Fend Off Regulation." *New York Times.* January 12. Accessed April 27, 2013. www.nytimes.com/2013/01/12/us/politics/makers-of-violent-video-games-marshal-support-to-fend-off-regulation.html?_r=0.

Lichtblau, E., and M. Rich. 2012. "N.R.A. Envisions 'a Good Guy with a Gun' in Every School." *New York Times.* December 22. www.nytimes.com/2012/12/22/us/nra-calls-for-armed-guards-at-schools.html.

Lijphart, Arend. 2012. *Patterns of Democracy: Government Forms and Performance in Thirty-Six Countries.* New Haven, CT: Yale University Press.

Link, B. G., et al. 1999. "Public Conceptions of Mental Illness: Labels, Causes, Dangerousness, and Social Distance." *American Journal of Public Health* 89 (9): 1328–1333.

Linz, J. J. 1994. "Presidential or Parliamentary Government: Does It Make a Difference?" In *The Failure of Presidential Democracy. Comparative Perspectives,* edited by J. J. Linz and A. Valenzuela. Baltimore: Johns Hopkins University Press, 1–94.

Lipset, Seymour. 1972. *Agrarian Socialism: The Cooperative Commonwealth Federation in Saskatchewan, a Study in Political Sociology.* Berkeley, CA: University of California Press.

Lizotte, Alan J., David J. Bordua, and Carolyn S. White. 1981. "Firearms Ownership for Sport and Protection: Two Not So Divergent Models." *American Sociological Review* 46: 499–503.

Loftin, Colin. 1979. *Detroit Area Study, 1979: A Study of Metropolitan Issues.* ICPSR09801-V1. [machine-readable data file]. Ann Arbor, MI: Interuniversity Consortium for Political and Social Research [distributor].

Loo, Robert. 1986. "Post-Shooting Stress Reactions among Police Officers." *Behavioral Medicine* 12 (1): 27–31.

Lott, J. R. 2010. *More Guns, Less Crime: Understanding Crime and Gun Control Laws.* Chicago: University of Chicago Press.

Luckenbill, David F. 1977. "Criminal Homicide as a Situated Transaction." *Social Problems* 25 (2): 176–186.

Ludwig, J. 1998. "Concealed-Gun-Carrying Laws and Violent Crime: Evidence from State Panel Data." *International Review of Law and Economics* 18 (3): 239–254.

Luke, Timothy W. 2008. "April 16, 2007 at Virginia Tech—To Multiple Recipients: 'A Gunman is Loose on Campus … '" *There Is a Gunman on Campus: Tragedy and Terror at Virginia Tech*, eds. Ben Agger and Timothy W. Luke. Lanham, MD: Rowman & Littlefield. 1–28.

Luo, M. 2007. "Privacy Laws Slow Effort to Widen Gun-Buyer Data." *New York Times.* May 2. http://query.nytimes.com/gst/fullpage.html?res=9803E1DE103EF931A35 756C0A9619C8B63.

MacIntyre, A. 1972. "Is a Science of Comparative Politics Possible?" In *Philosophy, Politics and Society*, edited by Peter Laslett, Walter G. Runciman, and Quentin Skinner. Oxford: Oxford University Press.

Maguire, B., G. A. Weatherby, and R. A. Mathers. 2002. "Network News Coverage of School Shootings." *Social Science Journal* 39 (3): 465–470.

Mahalik, J. R., et al. 2003. "Development of the Conformity to Masculine Norms Inventory." *Psychology of Men & Masculinity* 4 (1): 3.

Manson, M. 1999. "Columbine: Whose Fault Is It?" *Rolling Stone.* June 24. www .rollingstone.com/culture/news/columbine-whose-fault-is-it-19990624.

Marcuse, Herbert. 2006. *Art and Liberation. Collected Papers of Herbert Marcuse*, Vol. 4, edited by Douglas Kellner. London and New York: Routledge.

———. 2001. *Toward a Critical Theory of Society. Collected Papers of Herbert Marcuse*, Vol. 2, edited by Douglas Kellner. London and New York: Routledge.

———. 1955. *Eros and Civilization: A Philosophical Inquiry into Freud.* New York: Vintage.

Margarita, Mona. 1979. "Police as Victims of Violence." *Justice System Journal* 5: 218–233.

Martin, Susan Ehrlich. 1999. "Police Force or Police Service? Gender and Emotional Labor." *ANNALS of the American Academy of Political and Social Science* 561 (1): 111–126.

Marx, Karl. 1976. *Capital*, Vol. 1. Translated by Ben Fowkes. New York: Penguin.

Marx, Karl, and Friedrich Engels. 1972. *The Marx-Engels Reader*, edited by Robert C. Tucker. New York: W. W. Norton.

Mason, P. 2006. "Lies, Distortion and What Doesn't Work: Monitoring Prison Stories in the British Media." *Crime, Media, Culture* 2 (3): 251–267.

Mayors Against Illegal Guns. 2013. *Analysis of Recent Mass Shootings, Mayors Against Illegal Guns.*

Mayr, A., and D. Machin. 2012. *The Language of Crime and Deviance: An Introduction to Critical Linguistic Analysis in Media and Popular Culture.* London: Continuum.

McCarthy, Cormac. 2010. *The Sunset Limited.* New York: Vintage.

McDowall, David, and Colin Loftin. 1982. "Collective Security and Demand for Legal Handguns." *American Journal of Sociology* 46: 499–503.

McGinty, E. E., et al. 2013. "Public Opinion on Proposals to Strengthen US Gun Laws." *Reducing Gun Violence in America: Informing Policy with Evidence and Analysis*: 239.

McPhedran, S., and J. Baker. 2008. "Australian Firearms Legislation and Unintentional Firearm Deaths: A Theoretical Explanation for the Absence of Decline Following the 1996 Gun Laws." *Public Health* 122: 297–299.

Meehan, Albert J., and Michael C. Ponder. 2002. "Race & Place: The Ecology of Racial Profiling African American Drivers." *Justice Quarterly* 19 (3): 399–430.

Melman, Seymour. 1974. *The Permanent War Economy: American Capitalism in Decline.* New York: Simon & Schuster.

Merleau-Ponty, Maurice. 1969. *Humanism and Terror.* Boston, MA: Beacon.

Mill, John Stuart. 1888. *A System of Logic.* New York: Harper & Row.

Monahan, Torin. 2010. *Surveillance in the Time of Insecurity.* Brunswick, NJ: Rutgers University Press.

Moore, Solomon. 2009. "Number of Life Terms Hits Record." *New York Times.* July 22.

Moss, M., and R. Rivera. 2012. "In Town at Ease with Its Firearms, Tightening Gun Rules Was Resisted." *New York Times.* December 16. www.nytimes.com/2012/12/17/nyregion/in-newtown-conn-a-stiff-resistance-to-gun-restrictions.html?pagewanted=all&_r=0.

Mullins, C. W., et al. 2004. "Gender, Streetlife and Criminal Retaliation*." *Criminology* 42 (4): 911–940.

Murphy, Meghan. 2012. "But What About the Men? On Masculinity and Mass Shootings." December 18. *Feminist Current.* Reposted at http://rabble.ca/blogs/bloggers/feminist-current/2012/12/what-about-men-masculinity-and-mass-shootings.

Muschert, G. W. 2010. "School Shootings." In *Transnational Criminology Manual,* Vol. 2, edited by Martine Herzog-Evans. Nijmegen, Netherlands: Wolf Legal Publishing, 73–89

———. 2007a. "Research in School Shootings." *Sociology Compass* 1 (1): 60–80.

———. 2007b. "The Columbine Victims and the Myth of the Juvenile Superpredator." *Youth Violence and Juvenile Justice* 5 (4): 351–366.

Muschert, G. W., and D. Carr. 2006. "Media Salience and Frame Changing across Events: Coverage of Nine School Shootings, 1997–2001." *Journalism and Mass Communication Quarterly* 83 (4): 747–766.

Muschert, G. W., S. Henry, N. L. Bracy, and A. A. Peguero (eds.). 2014. *Responding to School Violence: Confronting the Columbine Effect.* Boulder, CO: Lynne Rienner.

Muschert, G. W., and L. Janssen. 2012. "Deciphering Rampage: Assigning Blame to Youth Offenders in News Coverage of School Shootings." In *School Shootings: Mediatized Violence in a Global Age,* edited by G. W. Muschert and J. Sumiala. Bingley, UK: Emerald Publishing, 181–200.

Muschert, G. W., and M. Ragnedda. 2010. "Media and Violence Control: The framing of School Shootings." In *The Control of Violence in Modern Society: Multidisciplinary Perspectives, From School Shootings to Ethnic Violence,* edited by W. Heitmeyer, H. G. Haupt, S. Malthaner, and A. Kirschner. New York: Springer Publishing, 345–361.

Mustard, David B. 2001. "The Impact of Gun Laws on Police Deaths." *Journal of Law and Economics* (October): 635–657.

National Institute of Justice. 1997. "Homicide in Eight US Cities: Trends, Context and Policy Implications." *US Department of Justice.*

*National Post.* 2001. "Study Claims that Abortion Cuts Crime." May 17, A1.

Newman, K. S. 2006. "School Shootings Are a Serious Problem." In *School Shootings*, edited by S. Hunnicutt. Farmington Hills, MI: Greenhaven Press, 10–17.

Newman, Katherine, Cybelle Fox, David J. Harding, Jul Mehta, and Wendy Roth. 2004. *Rampage: The Social Roots of School Shootings.* New York: Basic Books.

NRA.com. n.d. "NRA History: About Us." http://home.nra.org/history/document /about.

Obama, Barack. 2013. *Now Is the Time: The President's Plan to Protect Our Children and Our Communities by Reducing Gun Violence.* Washington, DC: White House.

O'Brien, Miles. 2013. "Sins of the Sons." *PBS Newshour*, February 20. Accessed April 29, 2013: www.pbs.org/newshour/updates/science/jan-june13/miles_blog_02-19.html.

O'Brien, R., et al. 2005. "'It's Caveman Stuff, But That Is to a Certain Extent How Guys Still Operate': Men's Accounts of Masculinity and Help Seeking." *Social Science & Medicine* 61 (3): 503–516.

O'Grady, William, Patrick F. Parnaby, and Justin Schikschneit. 2010. "Guns, Gangs, and the Underclass: A Constructionist Analysis of Gun Violence in a Toronto High School." *Canadian Journal of Criminology and Criminal Justice* 55 (1): 55–77.

O'Grady, Bill, Stephen Gaetz, and Kristy Buccieri. 2013. "Tickets ... and More Tickets: A Case Study of the Enforcement of the Ontario Safe Streets Act." *Canadian Public Policy.*

O'Malley, Pat. 1992. "Risk, Power and Crime Prevention." *Economy and Society* 21 (3): 252–275.

OpenSecrets. 2013. "OpenSecrets.org." Accessed July 2, 2013. www.opensecrets.org /orgs/summary.php?id=D000000082.

Ouimet, Marc. 2002. "Explaining the American and Canadian Crime 'Drop' in the 1990s." *Canadian Journal of Criminology* (January): 33–50.

Paine, Thomas. 1993. *American Crisis I.* In *The Life and Major Writings of Thomas Paine*, edited by Foner, Philip. New York: Citadel Press.

———. 1993. *American Crisis II.* In *The Life and Major Writings of Thomas Paine*, edited by Foner, Philip. New York: Citadel Press.

———. 1993. *American Crisis III.* In *The Life and Major Writings of Thomas Paine*, edited by Foner, Philip. New York: Citadel Press.

Paoline, Eugene A., III, Stephanie M. Myers, and Robert E. Worden. 2000. "Police Culture, Individualism, and Community Policing: Evidence from Two Police Departments." *Justice Quarterly* 17 (3): 575–605.

Perreault, Samuel. 2012. "Homicide in Canada, 2011." *Juristat.* Ottawa: Statistics Canada.

Persson, Torsten, and Guido Tabellini. 2003. *The Economic Effects of Constitutions.* Cambridge, MA: MIT Press.

Peterson, Ruth D., and William C. Bailey. 1988. "Structural Influences on the Killing of Police: A Comparison with General Homicides." *Justice Quarterly* 5 (2), 207–233.

Pew Research Center for the People and the Press. 2012. "Election, Tragedies Dominate Top Stories of 2012." December 20. www.people-press.org/2012/12/20 /election-tragedies-dominate-top-stories-of-2012.

———. 2007. "Widespread Interest in Virginia Tech Shootings, but Public Paid Closer Attention to Columbine." April 25. http://people-press.org/report/322 /widespread-interest-in-virginia-tech-shootings.

———. 1999. "Columbine Shooting Biggest News Draw of 1999." December 28. http:// people-press.org/report/48/columbine-shooting-biggest-news-draw-of-1999.

Pew Research Center's Project for Excellence in Journalism. 2006. "Cable TV Audience: 2006 Annual Report, Fox News vs. CNN." March 13. www.journalism.org /node/507.

Pinker, Steven. 2011. *The Better Angels of Our Nature: Why Violence Has Declined.* New York: Viking.

Plassmann, F., and J. Whitley. 2003. "Confirming 'More Guns, Less Crime.'" *Stanford Law Review*: 1313–1369.

Porter, John. 1979. *The Measure of Canadian Society: Education, Equality and Opportunity.* Toronto: Gage.

Poteat, V. P., et al. 2011. "The Moderating Effects of Support for Violence Beliefs on Masculine Norms, Aggression, and Homophobic Behavior during Adolescence." *Journal of Research on Adolescence* 21 (2): 434–447.

Priess, H. A., et al. 2009. "Adolescent Gender-Role Identity and Mental Health: Gender Intensification Revisited." *Child Development* 80 (5): 1531–1544.

Quinet, Kenna Davis, David J. Bordua, and Wright Lassiter III. 1997. "Line of Duty Police Deaths: A Paradoxical Trend in Felonious Homicides in the United States." *Policing and Society* 6 (4): 283–296.

Quinn, K. 2010. "Man Boards Plane at IAH with Loaded Gun in Carry-On." *ABC 13 News.* December 17. http://abclocal.go.com/ktrk/story?section=news/local&id =7848683.

Qvortrup, Matt. 2011. "Terrorism and Political Science." *The British Journal of Politics & International Relations.* Vol. 14 (4): 503–517.

Ragin, C. C. 1995. "The Distinctiveness of Comparative Social Science." In *Comparing Nations and Cultures: Readings in a Cross-Disciplinary Perspective* Englewood Cliffs, NJ: Pearson.

Reaves, Brian A. 2012. "Hiring and Retention of State and Local Law Enforcement Officers, 2008–Statistical Tables: US Department of Justice."

Reidy, D. E., et al. 2009. "Gender Role Conformity and Aggression: Influence of Perpetrator and Victim Conformity on Direct Physical Aggression in Women." *Personality and Individual Differences* 46 (2): 231–235.

"Remarks from NRA Press Conference on Sandy Hook School Shooting, Defended on Dec. 21, 2012 (transcript)." 2012. *Washington Post.* December 21. www

.washingtonpost.com/politics/remarks-from-the-nra-press-conference-on-sandy
-hook-school-delivered-on-dec-21-2012-transcript/2012/12/21/bd1841fe-4b88
-11e2-a6a6-aabac85e8_story_2.html.

Roberts, J. 2009. "Gun Used in Rampage Traced to Va. Shops." *CBS News.* February
11. www.cbsnews.com/2100-500690_162-2695059.html.

Robinson, M. B. 2011. *Media Coverage of Crime and Criminal Justice.* Durham, NC:
Carolina Academic Press.

Rojek, Jeff, Geoffrey P. Alpert, and Hayden P. Smith. 2010. "Examining Officer and
Citizen Accounts of Police Use-of-Force Incidents." *Crime & Delinquency* 58 (2):
301–327.

Rosenthal, A. 2012. "The N.R.A. Crawls from Its Hidey Hole." *New York Times.*
December 21. www.nytimes.com/2012/12/22/opinion/the-nra-crawls-from-its
-hidey-hole.html.

Rudin, S., L. Lawrence, T. Caplan, A. Schroeder, and B. M. Berg (Producers), and
A. Heckerling (Director). 1995. *Clueless* [Motion picture]. United States: Para-
mount Pictures.

Samaha, Joel. 2005. *Criminal Justice.* Independence, KY: Cengage Learning.

Sampson, Robert. 2013. "2012 Presidential Address to the American Society of Criminology, The Place of Context: A Theory and Strategy for Criminology's Hard
Problems." *Criminology* 51 (1): 1–31.

———. 2012. *The Great American City: Chicago and the Enduring Neighbourhood Effect.*
Chicago: University of Chicago Press.

Sampson, Robert J., Jeffrey D. Morenoff, and Thomas Gannon-Rowley. 2002. "Assessing
'Neighborhood Effects': Social Processes and New Directions in Research." *Annual
Review of Sociology* 28: 443–478.

Sanchez, R. 1998. "Educators Pursue Solutions to Violence Crisis; As Deadly Sprees
Increase, Schools Struggle for Ways to Deal with Student Anger." *Washington Post.*
May 23. http://pqasb.pqarchiver.com/washingtonpost/.

Sapolsky, R. M., and L. P. Bonetta. 1997. *The Trouble with Testosterone, and Other Essays
on the Biology of the Human Predicament.* New York: Scribner's.

Savidge, M., D. Kagan, C. Lin, J. Chen, T. Clark, B. Shaw, W. Blitzer, and P. Thomas.
1999. "Gunmen Rampage through Colorado High School." *CNN Breaking News.*
April 20. Atlanta, GA: CNN.

Schachter, Stanley, and Jerome Singer. 1962. "Cognitive, Social, and Psychological
Determinants of Emotional State." *Psychological Review* 69: 379–399.

Scheff, Thomas M., and Suzanne M. Retzinger. 1997. "Shame, Anger and the Social
Bond: A Theory of Sexual Offenders and Treatment." *Electronic Journal of Sociology* ISSN: 1198 3655.

Schildkraut, J. 2012a. "Media and Massacre: A Comparative Analysis of the Reporting
of the 2007 Virginia Tech Shootings." *Fast Capitalism* 9 (1). www.uta.edu/huma
/agger/fastcapitalism/9_1/schildkraut9_1.html.

———. 2012b. "The Remote Is Controlled by the Monster: Issues of Mediatized Violence and School Shootings." In *School Shootings: Mediatized Violence in a Global Age*, edited by G. W. Muschert and J. Sumiala. Bingley, UK: Emerald Publishing Group, 235–258.

Schildkraut, J., H. J. Elsass, and M. C. Stafford. 2013. "Could It Happen Here? Moral Panics, School Shootings, and Fear of Crime among College Students." Unpublished manuscript.

Schildkraut, J., and T. C. Hernandez. 2013. "Laws That Bit the Bullet: A Review of Legislative Responses to School Shootings." Unpublished manuscript.

Schildkraut, J., and G. W. Muschert. 2013. "Media Salience and the Framing of Mass Murder in Schools: A Comparison of the Columbine and Sandy Hook Massacres." *Homicide Studies*, 18 (1). 2014 forthcoming.

Schmitt, Carl. 2006. *Political Theology: Four Chapters on the Concept of Sovereignty.* Chicago: University of Chicago Press.

Seelye, K. Q. 1999. "Campaigns Find All Talk Turns to Littleton." *New York Times.* May 20. www.nytimes.com/1999/05/20/us/campaigns-find-all-talk-turns-to-littleton .html.

Seelye, K. Q., and D. Brooke. 1999. "Terror in Littleton: The Gun Lobby; Protest Greets N.R.A. Meeting in Denver." *New York Times.* May 2. Accessed April 26, 2013. www .nytimes.com/1999/05/02/us/terror-in-littleton-the-gun-lobby-protest-greets-nra -meeting-in-denver.html.

Seidman, Charles E. 1980. "The Urban Arms Race: A Quantitative Analysis of Private Arming." *Unpublished PhD diss.* New Haven, CT: Yale University.

Sellars, John. 2006. *Stoicism.* Berkeley, CA: University of California Press.

Simmel, Georg. 1955. *Conflict and the Web of Group-Affiliations.* New York: The Free Press.

Simon, Jonathan. 2010. "Consuming Obsessions: Housing, Homicide, and Mass Incarceration since 1950." *University of Chicago Legal Forum* 165: 141–180.

———. 2007. *Governing through Crime: How the War on Crime Transformed American Democracy and Created a Culture of Fear.* New York: Oxford University Press.

Sklansky, David Alan. 2011. "The Persistent Pull of Police Professionalism." *New Perspectives in Policing.* Washington, DC: US Department of Justice.

Skogan, Wesley G., and Michael G. Maxfield. 1981. *Coping with Crime.* Beverly Hills, CA: Sage Publications.

Skolnick, Jerome. 1966. *Justice Without Trial: Law Enforcement in Democratic Society.* New York: Wiley.

Smith, Tom W., Peter V. Marsden, Michael Hout and Jibum Kim. 2013. *General Social Surveys, 1972–2012* [machine-readable data file]. Chicago: National Opinion Research Center [producer]. The Roper Center for Public Opinion Research [distributor]. Storrs, CT: University of Connecticut.

Solms, Mark, and Oliver Turnbull. 2002. *The Brain and the Inner World*. New York: Other Press.

Soraghan, M. 2000. "Colorado after Columbine: The Gun Debate." *State Legislatures* 26 (6): 14–21.

Southwick, Lawrence. 1998. "An Economic Analysis of Murder and Accident Risks for Police in the United States." *Applied Economics* 30: 593–605.

Spencer, J. W. 2005. "It's Not as Simple as It Seems: Ambiguous Culpability and Ambivalent Affect in Media Representations of Violent Youth." *Symbolic Interaction* 28 (1): 47–65.

Spencer, J. W., and G. W. Muschert. 2009. "The Contested Meaning of the Crosses at Columbine." *American Behavioral Scientist* 52 (10): 1371–1386.

Spitzer, Robert J. 2011. *The Politics of Gun Control*, 5th ed. Boulder, CO: Paradigm Publishers.

Springhall, J. 1999. "Violent Media, Guns, and Moral Panics: The Columbine High School Massacre, 20 April 1999." *Paedagogica Historica* 35 (3): 621–641.

Sprott, Jane, and Carla Cesaroni. 2002. "Similarities in Homicide Trends in the United States and Canada: Guns, Crack, or Simple Demographics?" *Homicide Studies* 6 (4): 348–359.

Stenning, Philip. 2009. "Governance and Accountability in a Plural Policing Environment—the Story So Far." *Policing & Society* 3(1): 22–33.

Stewart, Daniel M, and Robert G. Morris. 2009. "A New Era of Policing? An Examination of Texas Police Chiefs' Perceptions of Homeland Security." *Criminal Justice Policy Review* 20 (3): 290–309.

Stinchcombe, Arthur L., Rebecca Adams, Carol Heimer, Kim Scheppele, Tom W. Smith, and D. Garth Taylor. 1980. *Crime and Punishment: Changing Attitudes in America*. San Francisco, CA: Jossey-Bass.

Stolberg, S. G. 1999. "The Nation: By the Numbers; Science Looks at Littleton, and Shrugs." *New York Times*. May 9. www.nytimes.com/1999/05/09/weekinreview/the-nation-by-the-numbers-science-looks-at-littleton-and-shrugs.html.

Surette, R. 1992. *Media, Crime, and Criminal Justice*. Pacific Grove, CA: Brooks/Cole Publishing Company.

Swanson, J., et al. 2013. "Preventing Gun Violence Involving People with Serious Mental Illness." *Reducing Gun Violence in America: Informing Policy with Evidence and Analysis*: 33.

Sykes, R, and J. Clark. 1975. "A Theory of Deference Exchange in Police-Civilian Encounters." *American Journal of Sociology* 81: 584–600.

Taagepera, Rein, and Matt Qvortrup. 2012. "Who Gets What, When, How—Through Which Electoral System?" *European Political Science* 11: 244–258.

Tavernise, Sabrina. 2013. "Share of Homes with Guns Shows 4-Decade Decline." *New York Times*, March 9. Accessed May 1, 2013. www.nytimes.com/2013/03/10/us/rate-of-gun-ownership-is-down-survey-shows.html.

Teune, Henry, and Adam Przeworski. 1970. *The Logic of Comparative Social Inquiry*. New York: John Wiley & Sons.

Thomas, William I., and Dorothy Thomas. 1929. *The Child in America*, 2nd ed. New York: Alfred Knopf.

Thompson, Amy, James H. Price, Jagdish Khubchandani, and Jamie Dowling. 2011. "Sheriffs Perceptions of Firearm Control Policies." *Journal of Community Health* 36: 715–720.

Thompson, Amy, James H. Price, Joseph A. Dake, and Thomas Tatchell. 2006. "Police Chiefs' Perceptions of the Regulation of Firearms." *American Journal of Preventative Medicine* 30 (4): 305–312.

Thompson, Carol Y., William B. Bankston, and Roberta St. Pierre. 1991. "Single Female-Headed Households, Handgun Possession, and Fear of Rape," *Sociological Spectrum* 11 (3): 231–244.

TheWebStats.com. 2011. MSNBC.com. www.thewebstats.com/msnbc.com.

Thoreau, Henry David. 1937. "Civil Disobedience." In *Walden and Other Writings*, edited by Brooks Atkinson. New York: The Modern Library.

Tithecott, R. 1997. *Of Men and Monsters: Jeffrey Dahmer and the Construction of the Serial Killer*. University of Wisconsin Press.

United Nations Office on Drugs and Crime. 2011. *2011 Global Study on Homicide*. Vienna: UNODC.

United States Department of Justice. 2013. "Crime in the United States." Accessed July 17, 2013.

Verhovek, S. H. 1999. "Terror in Littleton: The Overview; 15 Bodies Are Removed from School in Colorado." *New York Times*. April 22. www.nytimes.com/1999/04/22/us/terror-in-littleton-the-overview-15-bodies-are-removed-from-school-in-colorado.html?pagewanted=all&src=pm.

Violanti, John M., and Fred Aron. 1993. "Sources of Police Stressors, Job Attitudes, and Psychological Distress." *Psychological Reports* 72: 899–904.

Virginia Tech Review Panel. 2007. *Mass Shootings at Virginia Tech April 16, 2007: Report of the Review Panel*. Arlington: Governor's Office of the Commonwealth of Virginia. www.governor.virginia.gov/TempContent/techpanelreport.cfm.

Wacquant, Loic. 2009. *Prisons of Poverty*. Minneapolis, MN: University of Minnesota Press.

———. 2001. "The Penalization of Poverty and the Rise of Neoliberalism." *European Journal on Criminal Policy and Research* 9 (4): 401–412.

———. 1999. "How Penal Common Sense Comes to Europeans: Notes on the Transatlantic Diffusion of the Neoliberal Doxa." *European Societies* 1 (3): 319–352.

Waegel, William B. 1984. "How Police Justify the Use of Deadly Force." *Social Problems* 32 (2): 144–155.

Walker, Jesse. 2012. "Are Mass Shootings Becoming More Common in the United States?" *Reason*, December, 17. Accessed May 15, 2013. http://reason.com/blog/2012/12/17/are-mass-shootings-becoming-more-common.

Walker, W. (Producer). 1999. *Larry King Live* [Television Broadcast]. May 6. Atlanta, GA: Cable News Network and Turner Broadcasting System, Inc. Transcript retrieved from www.cnn.com/ALLPOLITICS/stories/1999/05/07/gore.lkl.transcript.

Warner, J. L. (Producer), and M. Curtiz (Director). 1942. *Casablanca* [Motion picture]. United States: Warner Bros.

Waters, Judith, and William Ussery. 2007. "Police Stress: History, Contributing Factors, Symptoms, and Interventions." *Policing: An International Journal of Police Strategies & Management* 30 (2): 169–188.

Weaver, R. K., and B. A. Rockman. 1995. *Do Institutions Matter? Government Capabilities in the United States and Abroad.* Brookings: Washington, DC.

Webb, Stephen D., and David L. Smith. 1980. "Police Stress: A Conceptual Overview." *Journal of Criminal Justice* 8: 251–257.

Weber, Max. 1949. *The Methodology of the Social Sciences.* Translated by E. Shils and A. M. Henderson. Glencoe, IL: Free Press.

Webster, D., and J. Vernick (eds.). 2013. *Reducing Gun Violence in America: Informing Policy with Evidence and Analysis.* Baltimore, MD: Johns Hopkins University Press.

Weisburd, D., S. D. Mastrofski, J. J. Willis, and R. Greenspan. 2006. "Changing Everything So That Everything Can Remain the Same: Compstat and American Policing." In *Police Innovation: Contrasting Perspectives*, edited by D. Weisburd and A. A. Braga. Cambridge, MA: Cambridge University Press.

Weisburd, David, Rosann Greenspan, and Edwin E. Hamilton. 2000. "Police Attitudes toward Abuse of Authority: Findings from a National Study." Washington, DC: US National Institute of Justice.

Weisheit, Ralph A., L. Edward Wells, and David N. Falcone. 1994. "Community Policing in Small Town and Rural America." *Crime & Delinquency* 40 (4): 549–567.

Westley, William A. 1953. "Violence and the Police." *American Journal of Sociology* 59 (1): 34–41.

Williams, T. 2013. "Violent Crime in U.S. Rises for First Time Since 2006." *New York Times.*

Williams, J. Sherwood, and John H. McGrath. 1976. "Why People Own Guns." *Journal of Communication* 26: 22–30.

Wills, Garry. 2012. "Our Moloch." *New York Review of Books*, December 15. Accessed April 29, 2013. www.nybooks.com/blogs/nyrblog/2012/dec/15/our-moloch.

Winkler, Adam. 2011. *Gunfight: The Battle over the Right to Bear Arms in America.* New York: W. W. Norton.

Witkin, G. 2012. "On Anniversary of Virginia Tech Shooting, Law to Close Loophole Hasn't Accomplished Much." *iWatchNews.org.* April 16. www.iwatchnews.org/2012/04/16/8660/anniversary-virginia-tech-shooting-law-close-loophole-hasnt-accomplished-much.

Wolin, Sheldon. 2008. *Democracy Incorporated.* Princeton, NJ: Princeton University Press.

Worden, R. 1989. "Situational and Attitudinal Explanations of Police Behavior: A Theoretical Reappraisal and Empirical Assessment." *Law and Society Review* 23 (4).

Worrell, Mark P. 2013. *Terror: Social, Political, and Economic Perspectives.* London and New York: Routledge.

———. 2011. *Why Nations Go to War: A Sociology of Military Conflict*. London and New York: Routledge.

———. 2009. "A Faint Rattling: A Research Note on Marx's Theory of Value." *Critical Sociology* 35 (6): 887–892.

Wright, James D., and Linda Marston. 1975. "The Ownership of the Means of Destruction: Weapons in the United States." *Social Problems* 23: 93–107.

Young, Robert L. 2004. "Guilty until Proven Innocent: Conviction Orientation, Racial Attitudes, and Support for Capital Punishment." *Deviant Behavior* 25 (2): 151–167.

———. 1986. "Gender, Region of Socialization, and Ownership of Protective Firearms." *Rural Sociology* 51: 169–182.

———. 1985. "Perceptions of Crime, Racial Attitudes, and Firearms Ownership." *Social Forces* 64 (2): 473–486.

Young, Robert L., and Carol Y. Thompson. 1995. "Religious Fundamentalism, Punitiveness, and Firearms Ownership." *Journal of Crime and Justice* 18 (2): 81–98.

Zak, Dan. 2013. "The Prophets of Oak Ridge." *Washington Post*. Accessed May 1, 2013. www.washingtonpost.com/sf/style/2013/04/29/the-prophets-of-oak-ridge.

Ziskin, L., and I. Bryce (Producers), and S. Raimi (Director). 2002. Spiderman [Motion picture]. United States: Columbia Pictures.

# Index

# About the Editors and Contributors

**Ben Agger** teaches sociology and humanities at the University of Texas at Arlington, where he also directs the Center for Theory. Working in critical theory and media/cultural studies, he recently published the book *Texting toward Utopia: Kids, Writing, and Resistance*, and he is working on a book entitled *The Age of Opinion*, on the topic of message-board democracy.

**Jennifer Carlson** (PhD 2013, UC Berkeley) is an Assistant Professor in the Department of Sociology at University of Toronto. Her recent publications appear (or are forthcoming) in *British Journal of Criminology*, *Violence Against Women*, and *Feminist Criminology*. Her research focuses on gender, the politics of policing, and gun politics. She is working on a book entitled *Clinging to their Guns? The New Politics of Gun Carry in Everyday Life* (under contract at Oxford University Press).

**Douglas Kellner** is George Kneller Chair in the Philosophy of Education at UCLA and is author of many books on social theory, politics, history, and culture, including works in cultural studies such as *Media Culture* and *Media Spectacle*. His *Guys and Guns Amok: Domestic Terrorism and School Shootings from the Oklahoma City Bombings to the Virginia Tech Massacre* won the 2008 AESA award as the best book on education. In 2010, he published *Cinema Wars: Hollywood Film and Politics in the Bush/Cheney Era*, and in 2012, he published *Media Spectacle and Insurrection, 2011: From the Arab Uprisings to Occupy Everywhere!* His website is found at www.gseis.ucla.edu/faculty/kellner/kellner.html.

**Michael Kimmel** is Distinguished University Professor of Sociology and Gender Studies at Stony Brook University (SUNY) in Stony Brook, New York. His books include *The Gendered Society*, *Manhood in America*, and *Guyland*. His new book, *Angry White Men*, was published in 2013.

**Cliff Leek** is a PhD student in the Department of Sociology at Stony Brook University (SUNY) where he also serves as a program coordinator for the new Center for the Study of Men and Masculinities. He has a BA in US Race and Gender Studies from Willamette University and has worked as a prevention specialist for the Oregon attorney general's Sexual Assault Task Force. His primary research interests are nongovernmental organizations (NGOs), violence prevention, race, and gender, with particular attention to the intersections of whiteness and masculinity.

**Timothy W. Luke** is University Distinguished Professor and Chair in the Department of Political Science in the College of Liberal Arts and Human Sciences at Virginia Polytechnic Institute and State University in Blacksburg, Virginia. He also is program chair for Government and International Affairs for Virginia Tech's School of Public and International Affairs in the College of Architecture and Urban Studies, and he served as the founding director of the interdisciplinary Alliance for Social, Political, Ethical, and Cultural Thought (ASPECT) doctoral program in the both of these colleges at Virginia Tech. His research interests include modern cultural, social, and political theory as well as the workings of contemporary environmental movements, international politics, museum politics, and material culture.

**Glenn W. Muschert** (PhD, University of Colorado at Boulder) is Associate Professor in the Sociology, Criminology, and Social Justice Studies Programs at Miami University in Oxford, Ohio. His scholarly interests lie in the sociological study of crime and social problems, including the mass media discourse of school shootings, moral panics, and surveillance technologies. He has published numerous articles and chapters in the fields of sociology, criminology, and media studies. His recent publications include *School Shootings: Mediatized Violence in a Global Age* (Emerald 2012); *The Digital Divide: The Internet and Social Inequality in International Perspective* (Routledge 2013); and *Responding to School Violence: Confronting the Columbine Effect* (Lynne Rienner 2013).

**Bill O'Grady** is a professor in the Department of Sociology and Anthropology at the University of Guelph, Canada. His research interests are in the areas of crime, marginal youth, and homelessness. He is coeditor of *Youth Homelessness in Canada: Implications for Policy and Practice* (2013) and coauthor of "Tickets

... and More Tickets: a Case Study of the Enforcement of the Ontario Safe Streets Act" in *Canadian Public Policy* (Forthcoming).

**Matt Qvortrup** is a lawyer and a political scientist. Matt Qvortrup earned his doctorate at the University of Oxford, and was the winner of the Oxford University Press Law Prize 2012. Formerly head of the Gun Crime Section in the British Home Office (Department of the Interior), he is currently a Senior Research Fellow at the UK Defence Academy. His most recent publications include *The British Constitution* (2013) and *Direct Democracy* (2013).

**Jaclyn V. Schildkraut** is a doctoral student in the School of Criminal Justice at Texas State University. Her research interests include school shootings, homicide trends, mediatization effects, and crime theories. She has published in *Homicide Studies*, *Fast Capitalism*, the *American Journal of Criminal Justice*, and *Criminal Justice Studies*.

**James Welch IV** is an assistant professor in the Interdisciplinary Studies program at the University of Texas at Arlington. He is also serves on the board of directors of the Association for Interdisciplinary Studies, as vice president of development. His publications focus on the development of interdisciplinary theory and its application to complex contemporary problems, such as sustainability.

**Mark P. Worrell** teaches sociological theory, religion, and politics at SUNY Cortland. His most recent books are *Terror: Social, Political, and Economic Perspectives* (2013) and *Why Nations Go to War: A Sociology of Military Conflict* (2011), both published by Routledge. Worrell is a frequent contributor to the journals *Critical Sociology* and *Fast Capitalism*.

**Robert L. Young** is professor of Sociology at the University of Texas at Arlington. His areas of specialization include symbolic interactionism, social psychology, and, most recently, human-animal studies. His publications, which cover such topics as the social psychology of gun ownership, attitudes toward the death penalty, the dynamics of social interaction, the sociology of language and discourse, and nonhuman animal cognition, appear in a variety of journals, including *Symbolic Interaction*, *Social Psychology Quarterly*, *Social Forces*, *Criminology*, *Deviant Behavior*, and *Society and Animals*.